UNDERSTANDING DIGITAL TECHNOLOGIES AND YOUNG CHILDREN

Understanding Digital Technologies and Young Children explores the possibilities digital technology brings to enhance the learning and developmental needs of young children.

Globally, the role of technology is an increasingly important part of everyday life. In many early childhood education frameworks and curricula around the world, there is an expectation that children are developing skills to become effective communicators and are using digital technology to investigate their ideas and represent their thinking. This means that educators throughout the world are expected to actively enhance children's learning in ways that provide learning experiences with technology that are balanced and purposeful to allow the transformation of traditional authentic learning experiences. Digital technologies can be used to explore, manipulate, discover, play and interact with real and imaginative worlds to allow active meaning-making.

With a wide range of expert contributors, this book provides a comprehensive examination of the current research on technology and young children and the importance of engagement for learning. This approach encourages the reader to rethink the possibilities and potential of digital technologies for learning in the early years, especially in the years before formal schooling when children might be attending early childhood settings.

This will be a valuable reference for anyone looking for an international perspective on digital technology and young children and is particularly aimed at current and future teachers.

Susanne Garvis is a Professor of Child and Youth Studies at the University of Gothenburg, Sweden.

Narelle Lemon is a Senior Lecturer in Curriculum Studies at La Trobe University, Melbourne, Australia.

UNDERSTANDING DIGITAL TECHNOLOGIES AND YOUNG CHILDREN

An international perspective

Edited by Susanne Garvis and Narelle Lemon

Routledge
Taylor & Francis Group

LONDON AND NEW YORK

First published 2016
by Routledge
2 Park Square, Milton Park, Abingdon, Oxon OX14 4RN

and by Routledge
711 Third Avenue, New York, NY 10017

Routledge is an imprint of the Taylor & Francis Group, an informa business

British Library Cataloguing in Publication Data
A catalogue record for this book is available from the British Library

Library of Congress Cataloging in Publication Data
Understanding digital technologies and young children : an international perspective / edited by Susanne Garvis and Narelle Lemon.
pages cm
ISBN 978-1-138-80440-1 (hardback) -- ISBN 978-1-138-80441-8 (pbk.) -- ISBN 978-1-315-75302-7 (e-book)
1. Early childhood education--Computer-assisted instruction. 2. Children--Effect of technological innovations on. 3. Child development. 4. Computers and children. I. Garvis, Susanne, editor.
LB1139.35.C64U63 2015
004.083--dc23
2015005480

ISBN: 978-1-138-80440-1 (hbk)
ISBN: 978-1-138-80441-8 (pbk)
ISBN: 978-1-315-75302-7 (ebk)

Typeset in Bembo
by Saxon Graphics Ltd, Derby

Printed and bound in the United States of America by Publishers Graphics, LLC on sustainably sourced paper.

CONTENTS

EXTRACTS

FIGURES

TABLES

CONTRIBUTORS

Marni J. Binder is an Associate Professor in the School of Early Childhood Studies at Ryerson University, Toronto, Canada. Her current research interests include the arts in the teaching and learning of young children, multiple literacies, multimodalities, children's visual narratives, transformative literacy, as well as spirituality and mindfulness through holistic education.

Cathy Burnett is Professor of Literacy and Education at Sheffield Hallam University, United Kingdom. She has published widely in the field of literacy and new technologies. She is on the editorial boards for *Literacy* and *Journal of Early Childhood Literacy* and is joint research convenor for the United Kingdom Literacy Association.

Sarah Chu is a Ph.D. candidate in Curriculum and Instruction at the University of Wisconsin–Madison with a specialization in Digital Media. Her research is centred on informal learning and play in museums using digital games and exhibits. She is currently a research assistant in the EDGE Lab at Ryerson University.

Susan Danby is Professor of Early Childhood Education at Queensland University of Technology, Australia. She has published widely in social interaction in home and school settings, helpline talk, childhood studies and qualitative methodologies. She is currently an Australian Research Fellow investigating young children's experiences using mobile technologies.

Karen Daniels is Senior Lecturer in Primary and Early Years English at Sheffield Hallam University, United Kingdom. She has published in the field of early language and literacy, with a focus on young children's cultural agency and children's authoring practices in early years education settings.

Christina Davidson is a Senior Lecturer in the Faculty of Education at Charles Sturt University, Australia. Her recent work focuses on young children's accomplishment of their social activity during use of digital technologies at home and at preschool.

Christine Deckers has studied the subjects geography, biology and German to become a teacher at the University of Siegen since 2004, which she completed in 2008 with the first state examination. In 2012, she obtained her doctorate in educational sciences at the University of Siegen, Germany.

Susan Edwards is Associate Professor of Early Childhood Education at Australian Catholic University. Her research is on early childhood curriculum provision with a particular focus on digital technologies and sustainability in the early years.

Martina Endepohls-Ulpe is Academic Director and Senior Lecturer at the University of Koblenz–Landau, Institute for Psychology, Germany. She acquired her postdoctoral lecturer qualification in 2010. Research topics are girls in science and technology, technology education, high ability (gifted children) and gender difference in the educational system, especially the situation of boys.

Susanne Garvis is Professor of Child and Youth Studies at the University of Gothenburg, Sweden. She also holds an adjunct position at Griffith University, Australia. Her research interests include narrative methodology and learning approaches with young children, families and educators.

Lisa M. Given is Associate Dean, Research (Education) and Professor of Information Studies at Charles Sturt University, Australia. A former director of the International Institute for Qualitative Methodology and member of the Australian Research Council's College, Lisa's research explores individuals' information behaviours, web usability, social media use, information literacy and qualitative inquiry.

Michael Henderson is Senior Lecturer of Educational Technologies in the Faculty of Education, Monash University, Australia. Michael's research lies in the use of educational technologies, particularly internet-based technologies. Recent work has included instructional design in e-learning and its implications in terms of cognition, ethics and risks.

Annika Lantz-Andersson is Senior Lecturer in Education at the University of Gothenburg and a member of the Linnaeus Centre for Research on Learning, Interaction and Mediated Communication in Contemporary Society (LinCS) as well as part of the University of Gothenburg strength area of learning research (LETStudio). Annika has a Ph.D. in educational science (2009) and her research focuses on social interaction, the use of digital technologies and what that implies for learning.

Narelle Lemon is Senior Lecturer in Curriculum Studies at La Trobe University, Australia. Her research agenda is focused on engagement and participation in the areas of teacher capacity, building and cultural organisations in galleries, museums and other alternative education settings, arts education, social media for professional development including Twitter and women in academia.

Mona Lundin is Senior Lecturer in Education at the University of Gothenburg and a member of the Linnaeus Centre for Research on Learning, Interaction and Mediated Communication in Contemporary Society (LinCS), as well as part of the University of Gothenburg strength area of learning research (LETStudio). Mona has a Ph.D. in educational science (2009) and her research focuses on communication and learning in professional contexts from a dialogical and microanalytical perspective.

Karen McLean is a Senior Lecturer in the Faculty of Education and Arts at Australian Catholic University. Her research interests are focused on literacy and technologies in the early years, including pedagogical approaches and play-based learning.

Malin Nilsen is a preschool teacher and Lecturer at the Department of Education, Communication and Learning at the University of Gothenburg, Sweden. She has a postgraduate degree (Licentiate) in Child and Youth Studies and her research interest is digital technologies in preschool.

Andrea Nolan is a Professor at Deakin University, Australia, where she leads the early childhood research agenda and is inaugural chair of the Victorian Early Childhood Research Consortium. Andrea's research is on ECEC workforce development, focusing on issues related to professionalism and practice.

Jason Nolan is autistic. He directs the Experiential Design and Gaming Environments (EDGE) Lab and is an Early Childhood Studies Professor at Ryerson University, Canada. His research focuses on user-initated and adaptive design for children with disabilities, multi-sensory and STEM learning environments, autonomy and sensory play.

Elin Eriksen Ødegaard is a Professor at the Centre of Educational Research, Bergen University College, and a Visiting Professor at UiT The Arctic University of Norway, Norway. Her publications include narrative research about children and teachers, cultural formation in kindergarten and how kindergarten as a complex arena shapes conditions for meaning-making and local pedagogical practice.

Geir Olaf Pettersen is a Lecturer of ICT in Learning and Mathematics Education at Department of Education, UiT The Arctic University of Norway. He teaches in kindergarten education and primary teacher education. His research interests are mathematics and ICT in kindergarten and primary school.

Niklas Pramling is Professor of Education at the Linnaeus Centre for Research on Learning, Interaction and Mediated Communication in Contemporary Society (LinCS), a national centre of excellence funded by the Swedish Research Council. His main interest is educational communication, particularly in relation to the arts, metaphor, narrative and technology.

Claudia Quaiser-Pohl is Professor of Developmental Psychology and Psychological Assessment at the University Koblenz-Landau, Germany. Her research topics are spatial cognition, enhancement of cognitive skills in preschool children, family development from a cross-cultural perspective, applied family psychology and the empowerment of women in the STEM field.

Ewa Skantz Åberg is a Ph.D. candidate at the Centre for Education Science and Teacher Research (CUL) at the University of Gothenburg, Sweden. Her ongoing research concerns how digital technologies mediate children's story-making practices. She also has a special interest in children's narrating as a communicative tool.

Helen Skouteris is a Professor in Developmental Psychology from Deakin University, Australia. She is an expert in maternal and child health and wellbeing, has been the recipient of six grant applications since 2010 and has authored over 110 peer-reviewed journal papers.

Reesa Sorin is Associate Professor of Early Childhood Education and Arts Education at James Cook University, Australia. She has taught and researched extensively in Canada and Australia, and has research collaborations in Scotland and Singapore. Her research interests include conceptualisations of childhood; fear and emotional literacy in childhood; arts-based research, teaching and learning for sustainability; and dogs in the learning environment.

Karen Thorpe is a Professor in the School of Psychology at Queensland University of Technology, Australia. She researches the effects of early experiences, in home and education settings, on child learning through large-scale longitudinal studies and observational designs. In 2013 she was named among Australia's 100 Women of Influence for translation of research into public policy.

Monica Volden is Lecturer in Mathematics Education at the Department of Education, UiT The Arctic University of Norway. She teaches kindergarten education and primary teacher education. Her research interests are mathematics in kindergarten and primary school.

Cecilia Wallerstedt is Associate Professor of Education at the University of Gothenburg, Sweden and a member of the Linnaeus Centre for Research on Learning, Interaction and Mediated Communication in Contemporary Society (LinCS). She has a Ph.D. in Arts Education and her research interest is music education and learning.

Nicola Yelland is a Research Professor in the School of Education at Victoria University, Australia. Over the last decade her teaching and research has been related to the use of new technologies in school and community contexts. This has involved projects that have investigated the innovative learning of children, as well as a broader consideration of the ways in which new technologies can impact on the pedagogies that teachers use and the curriculum in schools.

INTRODUCTION

Susanne Garvis and Narelle Lemon

There have been many social, economic and technological changes in the late twentieth century and early twenty-first century across the world, resulting in a change of experiences for childhood. For children in developed countries, most experience a range of digital technologies as part of their everyday lives. Digital technologies include multiple desktop and mobile technologies as well as digital toys (O'Hara, 2011) and internet-enabled technologies that operate as platforms for young children's consumption of digital media and associated popular culture (Gutnick, Robb, Takeuchi & Kotler, 2011).

Research suggests children are avid users of technology in their home environment. Zevenbergen and Logan (2008) argue that preschool-age children are immersed in practices surrounding technology use very early in their lives, such that they quickly demonstrate confidence and competency in using technology prior to commencing school. However, we cannot assume that all children have access to the same technologies within their home environment due to socioeconomic status, gender and geography (Selwyn & Facer, 2009; Vandewater et al., 2007; Willis & Tranter, 2006).

Selwyn (2012) proposes that more in-depth understanding about how technologies are used across social settings is necessary to move educational technology research beyond a focus on how technologies should be used to improve learning (such as literacy or numeracy). He argues that educational technology research should adopt a more critical orientation to thinking about the relationship between technologies, education and the social and cultural experiences (Selwyn, 2012, p. 216). Given there have been rapid advances in the age of digitation and technology (Hobbs, 2010), there is a need for young children to develop "new skills" in reading, navigating and participating in highly digitally mediated environments (Bittman et al., 2011). The role of early childhood education is to support such skills.

According to Yelland (2011), despite 30 years of research, digital technologies with young children are still not fully integrated with pedagogical perspectives on play. Part of the problem exists with curriculum documents separating play as a basis for learning from the use of technologies (Edwards, 2013). For example, in the Early Years Learning Framework for Australia (Department of Education, Employment and Workplace Relations [DEEWR], 2009), play is considered essential for supporting children's learning, while technology is listed as a separate description and skill. This notable difference between play and technology is also evident in early childhood curriculum in Finland, Sweden, New Zealand and the United States (Edwards, 2013).

This book seeks to address a current gulf in the research literature by providing a comprehensive examination of the current international research on digital technology and young children. This approach encourages the reader to rethink the possibilities and potential of digital technologies for learning in the early years, especially with very young children. Each chapter presents research projects from around that world that explore young children working with digital technologies. Countries represented include Australia, Germany, Sweden, Norway, Canada and England.

In the first chapter, Susan Danby and team contribute to understandings of digitally mediated interactions in early childhood classrooms. Through the task of composing an email, we find how the teacher directs the children to what counts procedurally, such as the components of an email and the teacher's moral work in producing a culturally correct form of personal communication. The second chapter builds on the concept of meaning-making and digital technologies. The second chapter by Cathy Burnett and Karen Daniels prompts us to examine how literacy is conceptualised in the early years and specifically highlights the significance of embodiment and materiality to meaning-making using digital technologies.

Narrative and digital technologies appear as a trend across the book. In Chapter 3, Susanne Garvis explores how digital technologies can enhance narrative meaning-making in Australia. Similar concepts are explored in Chapter 7 in the Swedish early childhood context. In Chapter 7 Ewa Skantz Åberg and team explore a pair of six-year-old children taking on the task of collaboratively making a story using a digital-story program named Storybird. The story-making task offers the children opportunities for reasoning and negotiating meaning mediated by the images provided by the software application. In Chapter 5, Narelle Lemon explores the use of digital cameras with young children to explore and create narratives of their learning environments.

The concept of meaning-making also emerges in Chapter 10 by Nicola Yelland. In this chapter she presents findings from an Australian iPad project that explores the potential of the tablets for learning and meaning-making in the early years. Evidence emerges that playful explorations with iPads can provide contents for learning and investigations that are rich in engagement and interest.

Some chapters also provide the opportunity to explore the role of the teacher in digital technologies. In Chapter 9, Martina Endepohls-Ulpe and team report findings from a survey of teachers and teacher assistants in Germany about the provision of and views about digital technologies. Findings highlight the uneven distribution of digital technologies across kindergartens.

Continuing with the role of the teacher, Chapter 4 by Susan Edwards and team suggests that an understanding of young children's thinking about the internet, known as "internet cognition", is a necessary precursor to learning about internet safety and digital literacies. Without such knowledge it is problematic to expect teachers to know how and what to teach in relation to both cyber safety and digital literacies

Some authors have also chosen to explore digital technologies and subject domains. In Sweden, Malin Nilsen and team (Chapter 11) analysed an art activity in a preschool setting in which the participants used an app on a tablet computer to mediate a visual information template. The chapter raises some interesting questions for the reader. For example, is it possible that new technology changes our basic conceptions of an activity, or creates new practices, rather than only being integrated as a tool in what we are already doing?

Chapter 6 from Norway investigates what happens when teacher-researchers invite a group of children to an activity with the aim of providing experiences with mathematics. Geir Olaf Pettersen and team discuss two selected episodes from a series of video observations over time, providing rich descriptions of activities that combine digital artefacts with non-digital.

Different early childhood contexts are also explored. In Chapter 12, Karen McLean and team report on the use of iPads in playgroups for engaging families in young children's learning. In Chapter 8, Marni Binder and team describe an arts-based collaborative research project with four- and five-year-old children in Canada and Australia to generate perceptions and awareness of environments. Children constructed postcards, providing them with opportunities to make meaning of their and others' worlds. The online format encouraged the children to search beyond the postcards to find out more about their own and others' environments and to begin the discourse on issues of sustainability.

The book is intended to draw together research from different countries to provide the reader with a broader understanding of digital technologies and young children from different perspectives. Each chapter explores the possibilities of digital technologies to encourage meaning-making in early childhood settings, while also asking further questions about participation, sustainability, the teacher's role, participation and cultural understanding. Looking across all of the chapters, the book acts as a starting point for further questions, discussions and research about digital technologies and young children. As our understanding grows about the potential of digital technologies and young children, we can continue to shape and reshape policy, practices and beliefs within early childhood education and care.

Susanne Garvis, University of Gothenburg

References

Bittman, M., Rutherford, L., Brown, J., & Unsworth, L. (2011). Digital natives? New and old media and children's outcomes. *Australian Journal of Education, 55*(2), 161–175.

Department of Education Employment and Workplace Relations (DEEWR) for the Council of Australian Government. (2009). *Belonging, Being and Becoming: The Early Years Learning Framework (EYLF) For Australia.* Canberra: DEEWR.

Edwards, S. (2013). Digital play in the early years: a contextual response to the problem of integrating technologies and play-based pedagogies in the early childhood curriculum. *European Early Childhood Education Research Journal, 21*(2), 199–212.

Gutnick, A. L., Robb, M., Takeuchi, L., & Kotler. J. (2011). *Always Connected: The New Digital Media Habits of Young Children.* New York: The Joan Ganz Cooney Center at Sesame Workshop.

Hobbs, R. (2010). *Digital Media and Literacy: A Plan of Action. A White Paper on the Digital and Media Literacy Recommendations of the Knight Commission on the Information Needs of Communities in a Democracy.* Washington DC: The Aspen Institute.

O'Hara, M. (2011). Young children's ICT experiences in the home: some parental perspectives. *Journal of Early Childhood Research, 9*(3), 220–232.

Selwyn, N. (2012). Ten suggestions for improving academic research in education and technology. *Learning, Media and Technology, 37*, 213–219.

Selwyn, N., & Facer, K. (2009). Beyond digital divide: towards an agenda for change. In: E. Ferro, Y. Dwivedi, R. Gil-Garcia, & M. Williams (Eds), *Overcoming Digital Divides: Constructing an Equitable and Competitive Information Society* (pp. 1–20). Hershey, PA: IGI Global.

Vandewater, E., Rideout, V., Wartella, E., Huang, X., Lee, J., & Shim, M. (2007). Digital childhood. *Pediatrics, 119,* 1006–1015.

Willis, S., & Tranter, B. (2006). Beyond the digital divide: internet diffusion and inequality in Australia. *Journal of Sociology, 42,* 43–59.

Yelland, N. (2011). Reconceptualising play and learning in the lives of young children. *Australasian Journal of Early Childhood, 36*(2), 4–12.

Zevenbergen, R., & Logan, H. (2008). Computer use in preschool children: rethinking practice as digital natives come to preschool. *Australian Journal of Early Childhood, 33,* 2–44.

1

COMPOSING AN EMAIL

Social interaction in a preschool classroom

Susan Danby, Christina Davidson, Lisa M. Given and Karen Thorpe

Abstract

This chapter contributes understandings of digitally mediated interactions in early childhood classrooms. Ethnomethodological and conversation analysis approaches are used to analyse a video-recorded episode of children and teacher composing an email in a preschool classroom. In their talk we find how the teacher directs the children to what counts procedurally, such as the components of an email, and the teacher's moral work in producing a culturally correct form of personal communication. Such considerations of situated examples can encourage investigations of digital practices that extend beyond operational skills to broader understandings of digital practices as cultural and situated activities.

Introduction

With young children engaging increasingly in a diverse range of digital contexts in early childhood classrooms, there is growing interest in examining how they acquire, produce and understand digital texts. In Australia, 90 per cent of children aged five to 14 years were engaged with the internet in the preceding 12 months (Australian Bureau of Statistics, 2012), with children younger than five years also users of internet-enabled technology (Danby et al., 2013; Davidson, 2009, 2010; Marsh et al., 2005; Plowman, Stephen & McPake, 2010; Spink, Danby, Mallan & Butler, 2010). As well as in home settings, preschool classrooms also are engaging in digital contexts.

The concept of "digital literacy" has become a commonplace term, used often to refer to various digital forms that mediate social participation and engagement in home, school and community contexts (Sefton-Green, Nixon & Erstad, 2009). New curriculum documents in Australia place emphasis on digital technology in classroom settings, with early childhood policy and curriculum guidelines recommending the introduction of technology in meaningful ways into classrooms, such as using technology to support communication and engagement in the cultural and everyday experiences of home and community, and for information seeking (Department of Education, Employment and Workplace Relations for the Council of Australian Governments, 2009). A government policy position supporting digital literacy, however, poses questions as to how teachers are to meet such expectations (Sefton-Green et al., 2009). While some teachers embrace these guidelines, others are less sure about the value of technology or how to engage with print and digital texts (Thorpe et al., 2015). Further, there is little empirical evidence showing everyday practices with digital technology in early childhood classrooms.

In using digital technologies, there are "new opportunities and challenges for those working in formal and informal educational contexts" (Merchant, 2007, p. 118). Lankshear and Knobel (2003) suggest that questions emerge of how teachers in early childhood classrooms engage in digital literacies, and how teachers and students produce and distribute texts by electronic means. This does not suggest that the "old" ways of doing literacy are no longer important, but there is a new imperative for focusing on material aspects of text production and social communication afforded through digital literacies (Merchant, 2007). While often glossed over, participating in digital practices also means recognizing that there are multiple and complex skills, knowledge and practices, often intertwined, within the cultural and social spaces of the classroom (Cope & Kalantzis, 2009; Sefton-Green et al., 2009). In this chapter, we investigate how a teacher introduces to a class of preschool children the activity of sending an email to a staff member who has recently moved to another town. We focus on how email as a communication activity becomes talked about, and how it is threaded into talk with the children, as they compose the email.

The study

This paper investigates the video-recorded interactions of a teacher and a class of children aged four and five years in a preschool classroom as they collaboratively compose an email to a former staff member. The preschool is located within an urban community in southeast Queensland, Australia. The data corpus is from an Australian Research Council project, *Interacting with knowledge, interacting with people: web searching in early childhood,* which explores how teachers and children in preschool classrooms, and families in home settings, engage in web searching and other digital activities. This chapter investigates an extended video-recorded sequence selected from over 170 hours of video-recorded classroom interaction of teachers and children in nine early childhood centres. The episode shows a whole group-time activity where the teacher introduces to the group of approximately 20 preschool-aged children the idea of sending an email to a teacher who had recently left the centre. The video data were transcribed using Jeffersonian notation (Jefferson, 2004) (see appendix for transcription notation). Children, teachers and place locations have pseudonyms.

Ethnomethodological perspectives are employed, along with conversation analysis, to investigate the everyday, in situ accomplishment of classroom practices with digital technologies (Baker, 1997; Freebody, 2013; Garfinkel, 1967; Sacks, 1992). As Hutchby (2001) points out, studying new forms of practices associated with technology use helps understand participation in everyday social interaction.

Introducing the cultural practices of composing texts to be shared

The analytic focus in this paper is how the teachers and children engage in the cultural practices of composing texts to be shared. These material practices do not happen in a social vacuum, but within social contexts constituted through the embodied actions of members, and spatial and time dimensions of engaging in everyday classroom activities (Fenwick, Edwards & Sawchuk, 2011). The analytic focus is how the teachers and children negotiate the material, social and technical aspects of a teacher and a cohort of children writing an email. Any whole group activity, including writing an email, involves a social organisation that encompasses how the teacher manages the setting for that activity and, in the course of that, how talk is produced and assembled (Macbeth, 2003). Much of what constitutes reading in classroom settings involves talk about reading (Freebody, 2013; Heap, 1991). Topics include the format of the text, the physical layout of the text, and the type of document being read. As members of the classroom culture, children are engaged in talk "concerned with when reading can be said to have been done, also recognizing when others have done it, or are doing it" (Heap, 1991, p. 127). It is through this process that children understand the purpose and meaning of reading.

In the episode we explore in this chapter, the type of document being discussed is personal correspondence in the form of email communication involving digital resources. Email communication plays as important a role as other social forms of interaction, offering the opportunity to communicate quickly, in asynchronous mode, with others at a distance and in different time zones (Waldvogel, 2007). A greeting sets the tenor of what is to come in an email, as its presence (or absence) establishes the connection with the addressee (Waldvogel, 2007). Similarly, a closing also does important work, helping to confirm and establish the relationship for future communications (Waldvogel, 2007). As Heap (1991) points out, through the type of document, "we are able to bring to bear sets of assumptions and practices for recovering from the document its meaning, i.e., the text" (p. 113). In other words, talk involves becoming familiar with the layout of the text as well as its function. Investigating talk in the school context, then, involves a "situated perspective" (Heap, 1991, p. 122) to consider "what reading is" through talk about "what counts as reading" (p. 103). Similarly, talk about composing an email becomes constituted as what counts as sending a form of digital personal communication. In the children's talk about composing and sending an email, the children are members of classroom culture where there are opportunities to learn from others, peers and teacher, about what digital personal communication looks like. Through such experiences, the children can be seen to be operating as competent members of culture, learning about what counts as digital personal communication.

The analysis will establish the procedural and moral work of producing the digital text. That is, in the talk of the children and their teacher we can find what counts procedurally as X, such as what to look at when reading, and the moral work that accomplishes Y, such as the culturally correct way to produce personal communication in the form of an email. In particular, the authority of the teacher can be displayed by drawing the children's attention to the procedural conventions, and also how culturally correct or incorrect versions of texts can be produced for the young learner. Investigating situated examples of these practices can highlight the complex work that children and teachers do as they engage with digital texts.

Analysis

The session begins with the teacher, Miss Sally, sitting beside an electronic whiteboard, and the children sitting on the carpet in front of her. To the side of the whiteboard is a small desk with a desktop computer and keyboard. Henry, one of the children in the class, is invited to come to this desk to type, and the teacher aide (Linda) sits beside him. She and the teacher are able to make direct eye contact, and the teacher can see what Henry is typing. The cohort of children do not see what Henry is typing, although they can see what appears on the whiteboard, as their gaze is focused directly on the teacher in front of them, and on the whiteboard to the right of where they are sitting.

The first excerpt shows the beginning of the email activity. The preschool password has to be typed in. Before this happens, the teacher asks Henry if his "typing fingers" are ready, and directs him to where the teacher aide is sitting at the desk. After the password was entered, and the email program opened, the activity is now at a point where the task of writing the email begins. The teacher's attention is directed to the cohort. She asks a question in line 188, Extract 1.1, that is directly related to writing the email. In this extract, we see the teacher's orientation to progressing the activity.

Extract 1.1 Writing the email

Time segment: 04:55–06:27

Line	Speaker	Speech
188	T:	↑what↓ are we going to say to miss sue.
189		=how ↑do ↓we start.=
190		=how will ↑we↓ start.=
191		=how do we start a letter.
192	C18:	↑eh↓we miss you¿
193	T:	we miss you¿
194		but h–how sh–
195	C19:	=we love you¿
196	T:	we love you,
197	C19:	em em_ (0.7)
198		we got th– we got some eggs.
199		(0.7)
200	T:	I would start with ( )
201	C20:	[(someone get the mail.)]
202	C21:	[they laid.]
203	T:	from protection bay south ( ),
204	C22:	they l:aid.
205	T:	the chickens hav–
206		=↑I↓ would start off with dear miss s:ue.
207		can you¿ (0.7)
208		do you think that's a good idea?
209		dear
210	C23:	[love (0.2)love kindergarten protection bay.
211	T:	[and ↑you↓ watch the letters come up.
212		watch the letters come up as we type.
213	C24:	((inaudible))
214		(0.7)
215	T:	<dear miss sue>.

216		okay.
217		(0.8)
218	T:	who said we miss you.
219		(1.2)
220	T:	anna wants to write we miss you?
221	C24:	and we love you?
222	T:	okay,
223	C25:	and the chickens hatched.
224	C26:	and (.) and the chickens hatched some eggs,
225	C27:	and chickens
226	T:	ok so_
227	C28:	[and the chickens]
228	C29:	[((inaudible))]
229	C30:	[and chickens hatched em eggs.]
230	T:	we love you they said¿
231	C27:	and ((inaudible))
232		em
233		(0.5)
234	C27:	love and we love to (catch some eggs)¿
235	T:	yes,
236	C31:	<and (0.2) the em the and the chickens em we can make some stuff with the chicken eggs.>
237	C32:	what about my word?
238		(1.0)
239	T:	okay=
240		a::nd okay so_
241	C33:	=and we miss her.
242	T:	yeh.
243	C34:	from protection bay south.
244	T:	from protection bay south?
245		okay.
246		=now that probably would be good at the end.
247		okay?
248		so hold on to that ross,
249		colin now you can go and sit ↑right↓ at miss larne's feet so she
250		can help you listen.
251		we miss you,
252		we love you.
253		you know what I would say?
254		(.)
255		<something exciting happened at kindy.>
256		what do you reckon,
257	C35:	YEP,
258	C36:	YEH,

With five minutes of the activity taken with getting online and establishing a password, the next 90 seconds (captured in Extract 1.1) holds an abundance of interaction from the teacher and children as the teacher elicits many possible ideas from the children that might be included in the email. Beginning with a marked high pitch, which works to get the cohort's attention, she begins with a question about what they might want to say to Miss Sue (line 188), the addressee of the email, and then she moves quickly to question the children about how they will start (lines 189–190). Her self-repair works to shift the focus from what the children want to say to questioning about how they will start. She narrows the question further with "the letter" (line 191), identifying an email as the same type of communication as a letter. The shift to identifying the components of an email is interactionally relevant for the larger activity at hand, the procedural business of composing the email.

The teacher follows the children's lead in taking up possible topics – we miss you and we love you, the chickens hatched some eggs, and the closing salutation of the email. She does this, demonstratively displaying "active listening" (Hutchby, 2005), by repeating what they have said to show that she has heard their suggestion (lines 193, 196), and by suggesting that an idea could come at a particular point in the email, such as in the closing of the email (lines 246–248). The children's responses, however, belong to what might possibly be written within the body of the text, but do not specifically address how an email might start, and so the teacher delays feedback, such as acceptance, of those ideas. The children's original contributions are "kept in the air" while the teacher works at the matter of what needs to come first in writing an email. In this way, she keeps those responses "in play".

It is the teacher who continues to orient to the procedural structure of how to start an email by proposing that "I would start" (line 200). Her reference to herself ("I") (line 200) is emphasised to propose what she would do as distinct from what they (the children) would do. This appears to work to make her suggestion authoritative. She does not complete her utterance, though, as the children continue, in overlap with the teacher and with each other, to continue to call out ideas for what to say in the email. She tries again in 206, 208 and 215 to seek a cohorting request to agree with her suggestion originally proposed in line 200.

Once the opening to the email has been attended to, the teacher returns to what might be possibly written within the body of the text. She returns to the children's original suggestions by asking which child had suggested saying "we miss you" (line 218). This request leads again to the children returning to what might be written within the body of the text, to which the teacher minimally receipts with an "okay" (lines 222 and 226). In 230, the teacher again attempts to pick up on the message "we love you" and again the children without prompting provide a myriad of responses about what else could be said in the body of the email. She minimally receipts these suggestions, and only responds more fully when she fully repeats a child's suggestion "from protection bay south" (lines 243 and 244), a suggestion that has not been introduced until now. She acknowledges this idea, and attends to the procedural matter of where that might belong in an email ("at the end") (line 246), and suggests to the child that he holds on to that suggestion for later. The children again return to calling out their previous ideas.

At this point, the teacher initiates a new topic for the email, of something exciting happened at kindy (line 255). By inviting the children to consider what she would say, twice, she encourages them to come back as a cohort. In displaying her authority to manage the cohort of children, at the same time she proffers a culturally accepted topic for personal communication. The teacher introduces the idea of telling Miss Sue that the chickens have laid eggs. While a child had suggested this as a possible topic earlier (line 229), the teacher does not acknowledge this, and she may not have even heard it with all the children proffering their ideas at the same time. She addresses the procedural matter of "news" in the email by emphasizing what she would say (line 255), shifting the activity along in a timely way to address the components of an email, to display that an email should disclose something to say, information that might be of interest to the reader. She seeks their approval (line 256), to which the children agree.

During this segment of the talk, the teacher directs the children to look at the whiteboard to "watch the letters as they come up" (211) and adds, "as we type" in 212. This is a clear authoritative directive that she proffers to the cohort, attending to procedural matters such as what to look at when reading a text, directing the children to observe the link between what they are suggesting could be said in the email and what text is being typed and displayed on the whiteboard. At this point, the video recording shows Henry keying in words onto the laptop and the teacher aide supports him to do that. At the same time, the teacher is looking to the cohort for displays of understanding where the children's claims would be the preferred response, whereas Henry's task is quite different in that his display of knowing is his demonstration of typing in the correct letters and words (see Koole, 2010, for displays of epistemic access).

Below is a screen capture of what the children are now seeing on the electronic whiteboard. The teacher aide and Henry have been the audience to the talk between the teacher and the other children. The aide in particular has had to hear the "message" from all the talk in order to support Henry to produce the written text through interacting with him.

The next extract occurs about a minute after Extract 1.1 finishes. In Extract 1.2, the discussion among the children and the teacher has followed on from the teacher's suggestion about telling Miss Sue about the chickens laying eggs. The teacher now adds a new technological object, suggesting a candidate course of action for the children's agreement (line 307).

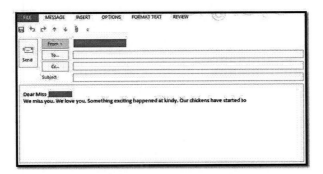

FIGURE 1.1 The email on the whiteboard.

Extract 1.2 Course of action

Time segment: 07:39–08:00

Line	Speaker	Speech
307	T:	do ↑you↓ think we should put some pictures.
308		attach some pictures so she can see the eggs?
309	Chn:	ye::h.
310	T:	okay
311		let's do that.
312		(1.0)

Following this agreement to attach some photos, approximately four minutes of talk occurs as the teacher aide finds the camera, and she plugs the camera into the computer. The screen comes up with the gallery of photos of the hens laying eggs, and the children decide which photos they would like to send Miss Sue. Extract 1.3 shows the teacher's search for the photos as she scrolls through the gallery of photos, which the children can see on the whiteboard.

Extract 1.3 Teacher's search for photos

Time segment: 12:05–13:30

Line	Speaker	Speech
491	T:	where's those ↑e↓ggies.
492		=okay.
493	C92:	em,
494		(0.2)
495	T:	we're going to attach the picture.
496		(1.2)
497	T:	I'll just go up the top and ↓attach↑,
498		=yeh_
499		look at that,
500		and we're going to pick the pictu::re
501		(0.9)
502	C93:	maybe we should do the one that ( ) with.
503	C94:	are we going to talk to miss
504		[s:::::ue?]
505	T:	[(would that be it,)]
506		(3.1)
507	T:	my computer,
508		(2.2)
509	T:	no¿
510		(2.5)
511	T:	gotta ↑find↓ them,
512		(2.2)
513	H:	gotta ↑find↓ it.

514		(3.9)
515	H:	°gotta find them°.
516		gotta f:ind them.
517		gotta f::ind th::em.
518		.hh hh
519		we gotta find them.
520	T:	[can't we just click on there and]
521	H:	[gotta find them.]
522	T:	ah.
523	H:	I've gotta find them.]

In Extract 1.3, the teacher starts by asking where to find the photos of the "↑e↓ggies" (line 491). She then describes the steps she is going through to attach the photos: she finds the picture, and she attaches it. She does this action with two pictures (lines 491–497 and line 500). At the same time, her talk works to direct the cohort's attention to her actions. In line 502, a child proffers a selection and the teacher confirms the choice in line 505. Next, the teacher begins a turn beginning with "gotta find them" with high pitch on "find" (line 511). Her talk is taken up by Henry, sitting at the computer, at first in a quiet voice (line 515) and elongation of word (lines 516–517) over several repetitions. He finally announces the finding of the pictures as his own task. At this point, while the teacher's actions and her talk have cohorted the group, Henry is displaying his own attention towards completing the physical task of finding and clicking on the photos in order to upload them. In the next extract, another issue arises with technology, the time taken to load the photos.

Extract 1.4 Time to load photo

Time segment: 14:44–15:00

Line	Speaker	Speech
592	T:	ah okay
593	Chn:	((inaudible talking))
594	T:	it's still loading
595		(1.9)
596	Chn:	((inaudible talking))
597	TA1:	it must be a big file,
598		(0.8)
599	H:	uh uh uh.
600	T:	so while that's loading we might ↑g:o↓ and have morning tea.

The final excerpt deals with an affordance of technology – the length of time it takes to load photos and have them attached to the email. In line 594, the teacher makes the observation that the file is still loading, to which one of the other teacher aides sitting with the group suggests a possible reason, that the file is big (line 597). At this point, the teacher adjourns the activity with a suggestion for morning tea.

Conclusion

In this 15-minute episode, the teacher's delivery of the task appeared to be closely aligned with the affordances of the technology. In terms of the textual aspects of composing an email for an audience, the teacher suggested the activity of composing and sending an email to a former staff member, the children contributed ideas for the content of the email, and the teacher talked about the structure of an email, including how to start and close one, and the adding of class photos. The teacher initiated most of the ideas for the email in terms of providing information. At the same time, the children were asked to recall classroom activities, such as the hens laying eggs. As well as the teacher's content suggestions, the children's initial suggestions of what they wanted to include (that they miss and love Miss Sue) remain within the body of the email. All the time, the teacher managed the cohort in terms of what to say and what's been said already, and what to key into the email message.

This episode shows in close detail the complexities of the teacher's work as she negotiates the materiality of screen use, and of temporal organisation, as well as the cultural procedures of negotiating relationships via text, both with the children in the class and with the addressee of the email. While her interactions were situated within the local, relationships involving future communication from afar were also being framed.

Evident within the teacher's work was how she oriented to the procedural work of how to write an email. This activity is what would be recognised in curriculum agendas as the teacher initiating a digital literacy experience. What is also evident, but not so immediately recognisable in everyday understandings of digital experiences in the classroom, is the moral work of the teacher. Specific aspects of the moral work of the teacher were shown through her authority as teacher to direct what materials were worth including, such as the photos, and what was important to look at when composing an email, such as openings and closings of an email. Further, the very activity of writing an email as a form of personal communication is a moral action associated with an intention to stay in touch with others. The authority of the teacher was such that she was able to achieve and enforce procedural definitions of how to write an email. In this way, she could be said to be encouraging the children towards culturally appropriate versions of digital personal communication (Freebody, 2013; Heap, 1991). At the same time, we note the separation of keying from talking, such that the teacher aide and Henry complete the physical task on the laptop, displayed on the whiteboard. This is a necessary condition for the successful demonstration of the completed email for the whole group.

The paper contributes new understandings of digitally mediated interactions between teachers and children in early childhood settings, the ways that digital literacy practices are accomplished in a cohorted setting. What we have shown here is how digital technologies can be understood and examined concretely in a specific setting to understand what counts as digital literacy and what personal digital communication looks like in one preschool classroom. The focus here has been on pedagogic practices involving talk about communication regarding the composing of an email, rather than a focus on the digital technology as a device and what its affordances are. Through this concrete example, we can attend to how policies and guidelines become enacted within particular social contexts of everyday classroom activities. More broadly, such considerations encourage further investigations of how understanding digital practices has to move beyond operational skills to broader understandings of digital practices as cultural and situated activities.

Acknowledgements

We thank the Australian Research Council, who awarded funding to Susan Danby, Amanda Spink, Karen Thorpe and Christina Davidson for the project *Interacting with knowledge, interacting with people: web searching in early childhood* (DP110104227). The project has ethical approval by Queensland University of Technology's University Human Research Ethics Committee (Reference No.: 1100001480) and Charles Sturt University's Research Ethics Office (Reference No.: 2012/40). We thank the teachers, children and families of the Crèche and Kindergarten Association for their participation in this study. We also thank Helen Breathnach for transcription, and Sandy Houen for her comments on an earlier draft.

Appendix 1

Transcription notation
The transcription system used to transcribe conversational data was developed by Gail Jefferson (2004). The following notational features were used in the transcripts presented in this chapter. The following punctuation marks depict the characteristics of speech production, not the conventions of grammar.

TABLE 1.1 Transcription notation.

Notation	Speech characteristics
bu-u-	hyphens mark a cut-off of the preceding soun
[	a left bracket indicates the overlap onset
]	a right bracket indicates where the overlapped speech ends
=	no break or gap between turns
(0.3)	number in second and tenths of a second indicates the length of an interval
(.)	brief interval (less than 0.2) within or between utterances
so:::rry	colon represents a sound stretch of immediately prior sound with increases in the number of colons indicating the longer prolongation
you	underline indicates emphasis
↑	shifts into high pitch
↓	shifts into low pitch
DOG	loud talk is indicated by upper case
hey?	a question mark indicates a rising intonation
dog¿	a Spanish question mark indicates a substantial rise that ends up in the mid to mid-high end of the speaker's range
here,	a comma indicates a continuing intonation with a slight rise
did.	a full stop indicates falling, final intonation
boots	underline indicates stress or emphasis via pitch or amplitude. The longer the underline the greater the emphasis
°soft°	softer, quieter sounds
>quick<	talk is speeded up
<slow>	talk is slowed down
.hhh	a dot prior to h indicates an in-breath
hhh	indicates an out-breath
( )	the talk is not audible
(house)	transcriber's best guess for the talk
(do)/(dig)	two equally possible hearings
together!	an exclamation mark indicates an animated tone
_dr-dirt	a single dash indicates a noticeable cut off of the prior word or sound
((walking))	annotation of non-verbal activity

References

Australian Bureau of Statistics. (2012). 4901.0 – *Children's Participation in Cultural and Leisure Activities, Australia, April 2012*: Internet and mobile phones. Retrieved on 25 June 2014 from http://www.abs.gov.au/ausstats/abs@.nsf/Products/4901.0

Baker, C. (1997). Ethnomethodological studies of talk in educational settings. In: B. Davies & D. Corson (Eds), *Encyclopedia of Language and Education. Volume 3: Oral Discourse and Education* (Vol. 3: Oral discourse and education, pp. 43–52). Dordrecht: Kluwer Academic.

Cope, B. & Kalantzis, M. (2009). "Multiliteracies": new literacies, new learning. *Pedagogies: An International Journal, 4*(3), 164–95.

Danby, S., Davidson, C., Theobald, M., Scriven, B., Cobb-Moore, C., Houen, S., . . . Thorpe, K. (2013). Talk in activity during young children's use of digital technologies at home. *Australian Journal of Communication, 40*(2), 83–99.

Davidson, C. (2009). Young children's engagement with digital texts and literacies in the home: pressing matters for the teaching of English in the early years of schooling. *English Teaching: Practice and Critique, 8*(3), 36–54.

Davidson, C. (2010). "Click on the big red car": the social organization of playing a Wiggles computer game. *Convergence: The International Journal of Research into New Media Technologies, 16*(4), 375–94.

Department of Education, Employment and Workplace Relations for the Council of Australian Governments. (2009). *Belonging, Being and Becoming: The Early Years Learning Framework for Australia.* Barton: ACT: Author.

Fenwick, T., Edwards, R. & Sawchuk, P. (2011). *Emerging Approaches to Educational Research: Tracing the Socio-material.* London: Routledge.

Freebody, P. (2013). School knowledge in talk and writing: taking "when learners know" seriously. *Linguistics and Education: An International Research Journal, 24*(1), 64–74.

Garfinkel, H. (1967). *Studies in Ethnomethodology.* Englewood Cliffs, NJ: Prentice-Hall.

Heap, J. L. (1991). A situated perspective on what counts as reading. In: C. D. Baker & A. Luke (Eds), *Towards a Critical Sociology of Reading Pedagogy: Papers of the XII World Congress on Reading* (pp. 103–39). Amsterdam: John Benjamins Publishing Company.

Hutchby, I. (2001). *Conversation and Technology: From the Telephone to the Internet.* Malden, MA: Polity Press.

Hutchby, I. (2005). "Active listening": formulations and the elicitation of feelings-talk in child counselling. *Research on Language & Social Interaction, 38*(3), 303–29.

Jefferson, G. (2004). Glossary of transcript symbols with an introduction. In: G. H. Lerner (Ed.), *Conversation Analysis: Studies from the First Generation* (pp. 13–31). Amsterdam: John Benjamins.

Koole, T. (2010). Displays of epistemic access: student responses to teacher explanations *Research on Language & Social Interaction, 43*(2), 183–209.

Lankshear, C. & Knobel, M. (2003). New technologies in early childhood literacy research: a review of research. *Journal of Early Childhood Literacy, 3*(1), 59–82.

Macbeth, D. (2003). Hugh Mehan's Learning Lessons reconsidered: on the differences between the naturalistic and critical analysis of classroom discourse. *American Educational Research Journal, 40*(1), 239–80.

Marsh, J., Brooks, G., Hughes, J., Ritchie, L., Roberts, S. & Wright, K. (2005). *Digital Beginnings: Young Children's Use of Popular Culture, Media and New Technologies.* Sheffield, UK: Literacy Research Centre, University of Sheffield.

Merchant, G. (2007). Writing the future in the digital age. *Literacy, 41*(3), 118–28.

Plowman, L., Stephen, C. & McPake, J. (2010). *Growing Up with Technology: Young Children Learning in a Digital World.* London: Routledge.

Sacks, H. (1992). *Lectures on Conversation* (G. Jefferson, Trans. Vol. I and II). Oxford, UK: Blackwell.

Sefton-Green, J., Nixon, H. & Erstad, O. (2009). Reviewing approaches and perspectives on "digital literacy", *Pedagogies: An International Journal, 4*(2), 105–27.

Spink, A., Danby, S., Mallan, K. & Butler, C. W. (2010). Exploring young children's web searching and technoliteracy. *Journal of Documentation, 66*(2), 191–206.

Thorpe, K., Hansen, J., Danby, S., Davidson, C., Zaki, F. M., Grant, S., … Given, L. M. (2015). Teachers, Teaching and Digital Technologies: Reports from the Early Childhood Classroom. Early Childhood Research Quarterly, 32, 174–182. doi: 10.1016/d.ecresq.2015.0.00

Waldvogel, J. (2007). Greetings and closings in workplace email. *Journal of Computer-Mediated Communication, 12,* 456–77.

2

TECHNOLOGY AND LITERACY IN THE EARLY YEARS

Framing young children's meaning-making with new technologies

Cathy Burnett and Karen Daniels

Abstract

This chapter examines relationships between technology and literacy in the early years in the light of recent research in the field. It draws on a small group of studies that have investigated open-ended opportunities for young children (aged 14 months to five years) to use digital technologies to mediate meaning-making. This work prompts us to examine how literacy is conceptualised in the early years and specifically highlights the significance of embodiment and materiality to meaning-making using digital technologies. It ends with recommendations for further research.

Introduction

It is a Friday family assembly at a primary school in England, and children and family members have gathered in the school hall to celebrate what has happened during the week. A row of parents, some with babies and toddlers, sit watching as their school-age children present their work. Fifteen-month-old Jessica is there with her dad, the father of older children at the school. Seeing another parent's phone lying on a chair, she climbs down from his lap and picks it up. Tapping it, she finds the owner's bank of photos and starts scrolling through, seeming surprised that these aren't the set of photos she's used to seeing on her dad's phone. Later at home, she is sitting beside her dad as he picks up his phone to send a text message. Jessica takes the phone from his hands and puts it down on the back of the sofa. She then raises her hands, puts one either side of her dad's face, and turns his head so he is looking at her.

These tiny moments in one toddler's life suggest much about what digital tools, and the texts they mediate, mean to her. She knows that devices can carry meaning from place to place: she expects a phone in the school hall to offer as much as it does at home. Her search for the photographs implies that she knows that tools mediate texts, that texts can have permanence (she expects photos to be there), that there are strategies she can use, such as tapping, to conjure up the texts she wants to see, and that these are accessible even when virtually real; she tries to retrieve them not from a bookshelf or envelope of photos but with the tap and swipe of a screen. Perhaps most importantly she knows that these texts can hold meanings that matter to her: she wants to see familiar photos. She knows that texts, or at least the devices that hold them, play a part in social life, sometimes enhancing it and sometimes distracting from things she enjoys.

This brief vignette illustrates how from the earliest years devices are significant for the meanings they mediate and that these meanings are deeply entangled with identity and relationships (Razfar & Gutierrez, 2013). It also suggests how these meanings are located within particular social, cultural and economic contexts (Heath, 1983). In this chapter these themes, and their implications, are explored more fully, drawing on studies identified through a survey of recent research focused on literacy and technology for birth to five-year-olds. It is argued that there is a need to know more about how children make meanings around new technologies, and that early literacy provision needs to build upon the kinds of understandings children develop in their home lives.

Technology, literacy and early years settings

Recognising the pervasive ways in which digital tools are embedded in the "textual landscape" (Kress, 2003) of young children's lives has implications for how early literacy is framed. When they enter educational settings, many young children bring with them extensive understanding and experience of making meanings using digital tools and in digital environments (Levy, 2009; Yamada-Rice, 2011). In the UK, for example, nearly three-quarters of children aged three to five have access to a touch-screen device at home (Formby, 2014a), more than a quarter of three- to four-year-olds use a tablet computer and 12 per cent use one to go online (Ofcom, 2013). In the US, ownership of tablet devices in families with children aged eight or younger increased five-fold from less than 8 per cent in 2011 to 40 per cent in 2013 (Rideout, 2013). In Australia 93 per cent of homes have a device for playing computer games and 73 per cent of parents talk about games with their children (Interactive Games and Entertainment Association, 2014).

Despite these patterns of technology ownership, the literate environments young children encounter in early years settings are largely dominated by paper-based texts. Digital resources are often scarce (Formby 2014b), and many early years educators remain unsure how to integrate digital tools within early years settings (Plowman et al., 2010), or how children's interactions with these tools and environments might "count" for their literacy learning (Burnett, 2011). Moreover, debates continue about the appropriateness of digital technologies for the youngest children: studies of children's practices in the home have explored the playfulness, agency and creativity with which very young children may engage with digital texts (Giddings, 2014; Marsh, 2004), and yet for some the use of screens in early years settings sits uneasily with the principles and practices of early learning. For example, as Bath and Enriquez-Gibson (2014) explore, new technologies have been associated with sedentary activity rather than the active learning recommended for children in the early years, and the pressure to support the development of print literacy can limit what practitioners feel able to intoduce (Lynch & Redpath, 2014).

Children may bridge this disconnect to some extent through how they take up what is offered in early years settings. Wohlwend (2009) described how children in kindergarten imported imagined technologies to a role play area through using folded paper as flip phones, playing a world of mobile phone use into being; while Bjorkvall & Engblom (2010) noted how children spiced up some rather limited school-sanctioned technology use with unofficial techno-literacies. Such learning however cannot be left to chance. Children's confidence and competence in using digital environments is central to their ability to participate fully and critically in the world around them now and in the future. Yet the distribution and use of digital resources such as tablet computers and high-speed internet access remains uneven, patterned by differences in economic wealth as well as practices associated, for example, with gender, ethnicity and class (Black et al., 2014; Rideout, 2013). Moreover, from the earliest years, the digital environments children encounter are deeply entangled with commercial interests, as the discourses of marketisation thread through virtual environments and associated artefacts (Black, 2010), not least the digital tools, toys and texts sold as supporting children's early literacy development (Merchant, in press). As Wohlwend et al. write, "multimodal lessons that powerfully shape children's literate identities occur mostly after school on corporate websites with global distribution" (2011, p.161).

Researching literacy and technology in the early years

Successive literature reviews of research investigating early years literacy and technology have generated very few studies of young children's digital meaning-making (Burnett, 2010; Burnett & Merchant, 2012; Lankshear & Knobel, 2003), and experimental studies investigating the impact of specific digital tools on specific aspects of literacy learning still dominate the field (e.g. Di Stasio et al., 2012; Roskos et al., 2011). Moreover, relationships between technology and literacy in the early years are inflected by different perspectives on early years education and on digital technologies, and are underpinned by different conceptualisations of literacy. In a previous review of studies of literacy and technology focused on 0–8-year-olds between 2003 and mid-2008, one of us (Burnett, 2010) distinguished between studies that focused on technology as a *deliverer of literacy* that investigated the impact of specific programs on print literacy skills and studies of technology as *mediating meaning-making* that considered the use of email, talking books, video and so on.

This second group of studies engaged more directly with the changing literacy landscape by bringing digital texts and environments used at home to early years settings. They demonstrated how digital media generate new possibilities for communication and creativity, for accessing new audiences, collaborating in new ways and using new resources for meaning-making. We could see such studies as *expanding* the boundaries of literacy to incorporate multimedia and multimodality. However, as most studies drew on projects and applications introduced by researchers, the scope and range of children's meaning-making was generally considered in relation to project aims – the quality of emails for example, or the value of talking books to community members. As the vignette that opened this chapter illustrates, however, young children's encounters with digital devices and the texts they mediate are embedded in everyday life. Meanings made through and around texts involve physical interactions with artefacts in particular settings. In understanding these meaning-making processes, and consequently how they may best be encouraged and supported in educational settings, there is a need for open-ended exploratory research.

In what follows we consider a small group of recent studies that investigated more open-ended opportunities for young children to use digital technologies to mediate meaning-making. These were identified through a survey of research on literacy and technology for 0–5-year-olds published between 2011 and 2014. While the survey was not exhaustive it is worth noting that – like previous reviews of technology, literacy and the early years – surprisingly few studies were located. Young children's meaning-making using digital technologies, it would seem, remains under-researched. However, the studies located do highlight some emerging areas of interest and concern that we suggest are significant for how relationships between literacy, technology and early years are framed. They focus respectively on interactions with a YouTube video, with story apps on iPads, and with filmmaking. We explore how this work does not just expand the boundaries of literacy (by extending the range of literacy practices that might be seen as significant to an early literacy curriculum), but prompts us to examine how we conceptualise literacy. Specifically these studies highlight the significance of embodiment and materiality to meaning-making using digital technologies. In doing so, they suggest we do not just need to reframe the boundaries of early literacy but, as we shall explore more fully, see those boundaries as porous.

Young children's meaning-making around digital technologies: perspectives on the significance of embodiment and materiality

It is widely agreed that children develop deeper understandings of the world through moving and doing (Brock et al., 2014) and in particular the moving and doing that takes place as they engage in exploratory play (Moyles, 1989; Vygotsky, 1978). Doherty (2008) proposes that physical, cognitive and perceptual development combine with motivation as a child interacts with the environment. We could therefore see physical development as driven by the desire to make and take meanings from the world. Heuristic play in very young children, for example, is typified by early physical exploratory play with objects in order to discover their properties and potential (Goldschmied & Hughes, 1992). As they develop manipulation skills, such as reaching, grasping and releasing objects, young children develop the physical dexterity needed to handle tools such as books, crayons and touch-screen devices. As young children become increasingly mobile, their exploration extends from objects in one place to larger objects, spaces and places (Brock et al., 2014). Play can include verbal and non-verbal communication and movement, and as a child develops, their repertoires for meaning making and play are extended.

Influenced perhaps by the easy availability of hand-held digital video cameras, growing numbers of studies are using video data to generate detailed accounts of young children's meaning-making. This trend has been accompanied by a focus on material and embodied dimensions in literacy research (e.g. see Dixon, 2012; Kontovourki, 2014). It is hard to know whether the increased focus on materiality and embodiment has been generated by the use of video (researchers now notice things that were less evident previously), or whether an interest in materiality and embodiment has led to increased use of video (researchers use video because they feel that essential dimensions of meaning-making would be lost without it). Or perhaps the mobility and interactivity of digital devices means that researchers are more likely to see new technologies, and the texts they mediate, in relation to the bodies, things and spaces associated with them. Whichever is the case – and we suspect the relationship is reflexive – increased use of video is generating new insights into relationships between embodiment, materiality and literacy.

Interactions around computers have long been the subject of classroom research (e.g. Mercer, 1994). While early studies focused specifically on spoken interaction, however, more recent work has explored talk around digital texts in relation to a range of on- and off-screen actions. Davidson et al. (under review), for example, used conversation analysis to explore child/teacher interactions around a YouTube video in a preschool setting. They describe the ways that shared understandings about the video were negotiated and constructed, partly through non-verbal responses to on-screen actions, such as gesture, gaze and facial expression. Their work highlights the socially situated nature of meaning-making, which is shaped, and helps to shape, the roles, relationships and spaces associated with it. With a similar focus on the social construction of meaning, Kucirkova et al. (2013, 2014) drew on Vygotskian theories of learning to explore parent-child talk during iPad story-sharing using a personalised story app. Again, gesture, gaze, posture and facial expression were central to the meanings and practices associated with the app, as were the size and portability of iPads. The materiality of iPads is also foregrounded in the analysis. Kucirkova et al. (2013) suggest that the physical connection, generated as parent-child dyads gathered round tablets, may be significant to affective dimensions of the story-sharing experience. As such the iPad, and the app it mediated, became a third member of the social group. The process of learning about story-sharing became "trialogical" rather than "dialogic" as the app offered potential for playing with multiple media, which the child and parent took up (Kucirkova et al., 2014).

While the work by Davidson et al. and Kucirkova et al. explores how collaborative meaning-making happens around screens, other studies have focused more tightly on what happens at the interface of body and screen. Again interested in "things in use" (Ihde, 1990), Merchant (2014) draws on a micro-analysis of child/adult/iPad interactions recorded during a study of adults' and toddlers' (14–22 months) use of story-related apps (*Peppa Pig Party Time*, P2 Games; *The Three Little Pigs*, Nosy Crow) on iPads in a nursery setting. He both highlights how the iPads themselves contributed to children's interactions with apps and problematises the tendency to overplay the "intuitive" nature of touch-screen devices, documenting some children's difficulties when using the interface. Mapping out an emerging "gestural vocabulary" of hand/body during iPad interactions, he identifies three broad categories associated with different functions: movements associated with keeping the iPad steady ("stabilizing movements"); movements associated with navigating the on-screen text ("control movements"); and movements associated with a particular part of the text or device ("deictic movements"). In contrast to the kinds of movements associated with print books, Merchant noted some blurring between control and deictic movements. During story-sharing with printed books, control movements and deictic movements are distinct – we turn the pages and then look at and explore what they show, which remains fixed. When exploring story apps, a deictic movement may morph into a control movement, as pointing becomes touching, then tapping, and what appears on screen subsequently changes. This blurring, Merchant suggests, arises from embodied relationships with the materiality of iPads that differ from embodied relationships with paper-based texts.

These recent iPad studies not only highlight how children negotiate interactive texts and devices, but also how interactions are situated within broader social and cultural practices. Noting how story-sharing around iPads maps onto existing literacy practices, Merchant draws analogies between the body movements, gestures and facial expressions accompanying adult-child-iPad interactions and those commonly associated with shared book-reading. The adults in the nursery guided engagement with a story and/or characters just as they might with picture books. Similarly the mother/child dyads Kucirkova et al. describe snuggled comfortably around an iPad as they would during book-sharing.

Importantly, however, meaning-making does not just occur within tightly framed dyadic interactions but across multiple, often hybrid, spaces: children may carry their stories with them using mobile devices, and meanings may travel across modes and media. For example, Daniels et al. (2013) examined activity on and around an iPad displaying *Pepper Pig's Party Time* during the same study as Merchant. They observed how one child, Charlie, who had spent time stirring a pan of ingredients in a role play kitchen area connected this interest with the virtual mixing bowl in the iPad story app by stirring with a plastic spoon from the role play kitchen. Seemingly drawing from an autobiographical intertext (Torr, 2007) and his broader experiences, Charlie seemed to hybridise physical and virtual objects and spaces for a moment, as the spoon became integrated with the iPad app. Digital texts – in this case the story app – exist as resources alongside many other resources (toys, spaces, etc.), and children draw from this broad range in their play.

Like Daniels, Wohlwend (in press) explores how children play across digital and paper-based media and how meaning-making consequently works across "artefacts, tools, rules and roles". Literacy from this perspective becomes play, and play becomes literacy. Wohlwend draws on ethnographic accounts and mediated discourse analysis (Scollon, 2001) to consider how children take up media resources. Foregrounding the embodied experiences of young children's meaning-making, she defines play as a "literacy of possibilities" through which children can explore and experiment with different roles in imagined worlds with their peers. Husbye et al. (2012) exemplify this by describing a project in which groups of children played with a range of resources alongside digital video. They describe the processes through which children created a narrative, drawing on video as one of many media, and how ideas, characters and narratives migrated across media as they played. Wohlwend, Husbye and colleagues argue that a focus on literacy as play also has implications for how we frame critical literacy in the early years. Rather than approaching critical literacy by looking at texts, they focus on the process of production. They suggest that as children play and replay narratives and characters together, they are repositioned as media producers, and that this provides an opportunity to consider "children's relative classroom positioning within the here-and-now conflicts and negotiations that often occur as children play, share materials and work out who should play with what" (Husbye et al., 2012, p. 86). It is children's embodied reenactments and negotiations that become the focus for reflection rather than texts produced by others.

Framing literacy and technology in the early years

Exploratory open-ended studies like the ones summarised previously provide insights into how children make meanings through digital play and consequently how to support and extend this meaning making. Green's (1988) influential framework for distinguishing between operational, cultural and critical dimensions of literacy is useful in sketching the scope of what this might mean for educators. With Green's framework in mind, early literacy provision needs to: address the skills children need to create and access digital texts, such as tapping and swiping (operational); provide opportunities for children to make choices about what they want to communicate and which resources to use (cultural); and encourage reflection on what they and others become through their text-making (critical). As technologies evolve and new possibilities emerge, there is a need to continually revise what matters in each of these dimensions.

Specifically, these studies add to previous research on literacy and technology in the early years by emphasising how meaning-making around digital texts is entwined with bodies and things.

Four overlapping themes emerge as particularly pertinent:

- the multimodality of interaction around digital texts;
- a foregrounding of haptics and gesture in negotiating digital devices (and a need to better understand their role in meaning-making);
- a conceptualisation of literacy as play;
- and related to this, a reframing of the nature of criticality in early literacy.

These four themes highlight how meaning-making through digital technologies is not something that just happens on-screen. It is not the sedentary, decontextualised, individual activity that some early years educators decry. Instead it is (or can be) active, embedded with other activities and often deeply felt. The studies draw on a range of theoretical perspectives to explore how bodies and things are significant: some foreground the object, some the child(ren), some the text. They range from a focus on embodied semiotic resources, including use of gesture and a focus on haptics (in Davidson et al. and Merchant's work), to relationships between touch and affect (Kucirkova et al.), to embodiment of meanings as they translate across media. In doing so, they sketch the scope of literacy slightly differently, some zooming right in to focus on the detail, while some zoom out to see these interactions in relation to broader social forces, which in turn play out in the detail of what children do. However, they all, to some extent, de-centre literacy research from a focus on texts (and screens), and encourage us to see early literacies in relation to bodies and things. Over 10 years ago, Leander and McKim (2003, p. 227) argued that

> the study of literacy practices could pull back from a fixation on isolated texts, authors, and isolated textual practices to consider how such texts are related to actual readers, desks and workspaces, writing technologies, classroom rules, clothing, school lunches, calendars, and a whole host of material, symbolic, and human actants that are active in the construction of social space.

If we return to the vignette at the start of this chapter, we can further consider the pervasive ways in which digital tools are embedded in Jessica's "textual landscape". Jessica draws from and utilises available meaning-making resources to take part in what is significant to her. By focusing on embodiment and materiality we are prompted to look at the kinds of spaces, roles and relationships that inflect Jessica's meaning-making around new technologies, but also to explore how that meaning-making itself works to maintain or transform those spaces, roles and relationships.

Conclusion

The studies explored in this chapter highlight the importance of seeing young children's literacy as happening across multiple modes, moment by moment. We need to understand more about the varied ways in which children, devices, texts and sites intersect and work to construct one another. This leads to questions about how children's literacy practices are embedded in and inflected by wider economic, political, societal and historical forces. The studies described draw in different ways on broader social and cultural contexts in making sense of children's engagement with digital texts, some considering the object/child/text in relation to broader social movements or, as Wohlwend writes, a "dense tangle of discourses" (in press, p. 4). Together, however, they make a compelling argument for seeing meaning-making in relation to a mess of things and embodied relationships, experiences and power relations. There would seem to be a need for further research to better understand the processes, choices and roles associated with meaning-making with and beyond new technologies. This, we suggest, means combining fine-grained analysis of meaning-making processes with divergent explorations that are always open to the unexpected, the unexplored and currently unarticulated, that look down into the detail of children's literacy practices in order partly to look back up again to all the things that help enable and limit the meanings children can make.

References

Bath, C. & Enriquez-Gibson, J. (2014). Incorporating digital technology into the lives of young children. Paper presented at EECERA Conference, 7–10 September, Crete.

Bjorkvall, A. & Engblom, C. (2010). Young children's exploration of semiotic resources during unofficial computer activities in the classroom. *Journal of Early Childhood Literacy*, 10(3), 271–93.

Black, R. W. (2010). The language of Webkinz: early childhood literacy in an online virtual world. *Digital Culture and Education*, 2(1), 7–24.

Black., R.W., Korobkova, K. & Epler, A. (2014). Barbie dolls and Xtractaurs: discourse and identity in virtual worlds for young children. *Journal of Early Childhood Literacy*, 14(2), 265–85.

Burnett, C. (2010). Technology and literacy in early childhood educational settings: a review of research. *Journal of Early Childhood Literacy*, 10(3), 247–70.

Burnett, C. (2011). Pre-service teachers' digital literacy practices: exploring contingency in identity and digital literacy in and out of educational contexts. *Language and Education*, 25(5), 433–49.

Burnett, C. & Merchant, G. (2012). Learning, literacies and new technologies: the current context and future possibilities. In J. Larson & J. Marsh (Eds), *Handbook of Early Childhood Literacy* (pp. 575–86). London: Sage.

Brock, A., Doherty, J., Jarvis, P., Matthews, J. & Stevenson, D. (2014). Born to play: babies and toddlers playing. In: A. Brock, P. Jarvis, Y. Olusoga (Eds), *Perspectives on Play: Learning for Life* (pp. 103–29). London: Routledge.

Daniels, K., Page, J., Yamada-Rice, D. (2013). Toddlers and ipads: young children, story apps, iPads and play. Paper presented at the Children's Media Conference 3-5th July, Sheffield, UK.

Davidson, C. Danby, S., Given, L. M. & Thorpe, K. (under review). Talk about a YouTube video in preschool: the mutual production of shared understanding for learning with digital technology.

Di Stasio, M. R. & Savage, R. (2012). A follow-up study of the ABRACADABRA web-based literacy intervention in Grade 1. *Journal of Research in Reading*, 35(1), 69–86.

Dixon, K. (2012). *Literacy, Power and the Schooled Body*. London: Routledge.

Doherty J. (2008). *Right from the Start: An Introduction to Child Development*. Harlow: Pearson Education.

Formby, S. (2014a). *Parents' Perspectives: Children's Use of Technology in the Early Years*. London: National Literacy Trust.

Formby, S. (2014b). *Practitioner Perspectives: Children's Use of Technology in the Early Years*. London: National Literacy Trust.

Giddings, S. (2014). *Gameworlds: Virtual Media & Children's Everyday Play*. New York: Bloomsbury.

Goldschmied, E. & Hughes, A. (1992). *Heuristic Play with Objects: Children of 12–20 Months Exploring Everyday Objects*. VHS Video. London: National Children's Bureau.

Green, B. (1988). Subject-specific literacy and school learning: a focus on writing. *Australian Journal of Education*, 32(2), 156–79.

Heath, S. B. (1983). *Ways with Words: Language, Life and Work in Communities and Classrooms*. Cambridge: Cambridge University Press.

Husbye, N., Buchholz, B., Coggin, L, Wessel-Powell, C. & Wohlwend, K. (2012). Critical lessons and playful literacies. *Language Arts, 90*(2), 82–92.

Ihde, D. (1990). *Technology and the Lifeworld: From Garden to Earth.* Bloomington and Indianapolis: Indiana State University Press.

Interactive Games and Entertainment Association (IGEA) (2014). *Digital Australia 2014.* Retrieved 26 July 2014 from http://www.igea.net/2013/10/digital-australia-2014/

Kontovourki, S. (2014). Backstage performances: a third grader's embodiments of pop culture and literacy in a public school classroom. *Literacy, 48*(1), 4–13.

Kress, G. (2003). *Literacy in the New Media Age.* London: Routledge.

Kucirkova, N., Sheehy, K. & Messer, D. (2014). A Vygotskian perspective on parent-child talk during iPard story sharing. *Journal of Research in Reading.* Retrieved from http://onlinelibrary.wiley.com/doi/10.1111/1467-9817.12030/abstract.

Kucirkova, N., Messer, D. Sheehy, K. & Flewitt, R. (2013). Sharing personalised stories on iPads: a close look at one parent-child interaction. *Literacy, 47*(3), 115–22.

Lankshear, C. & Knobel, M.(2003). New technologies in early childhood literacy research: a review of research. *Journal of Early Childhood Literacy, 3*(1), 59–82.

Leander, K. M. & McKim, K. K. (2003). Tracing the everyday "sitings" of adolescents on the internet: a strategic adaptation of ethnography across online and offline spaces. *Education, Communication and Information, 3*(2), 211–40.

Levy, R. (2009). "You have to understand words … but not read them": young children becoming readers in a digital age. *Journal of Research in Reading, 32*(1), 75–91.

Lynch, J. & Redpath, T. (2014). "Smart" technologies in early years education: a meta-narrative of paradigmatic tensions in iPad use in an Australian preparatory classroom. *Journal of Early Childhood Literacy, 14*(2), 147–74.

Marsh, J. (2004). The techno-literacy practices of young children. *Journal of Early Childhood Research, 2*(1), 51–66.

Mercer, N. (1994). The quality of talk in children's joint activity at the computer. *Journal of Computer Assisted Learning, 10*(1), 24–32.

Merchant, G. (in press). Moving with the times: how mobile digital literacies are changing childhood. In: V. Duckworth & G. Ade-Ojo (Eds), *Landscapes of Specific Literacies in Contemporary Society: Exploring a Social Model of Literacy.* London: Routledge.

Merchant, G. (2014). Young children and interactive story-apps. In: C. Burnett, J. Davies, G. Merchant & J. Rowsell (Eds), *New Literacies around the Globe* (pp. 121–39). London: Routledge.

Moyles, J. (1989). *Just Playing.* Buckingham: Open University Press.

Ofcom (2013). *Children and Parents: Media Use and Attitudes.* Retrieved from http://stakeholders.ofcom.org.uk/binaries/research/media-literacy/october-2013/research07Oct2013.pdf.

Plowman, L., McPake, J. & Stephen, C. (2010). The technologisation of childhood? young children and technology in the home. *Children and Society, 24*, 63–74.

Razfar, A. & Gutierrez, K. (2013). Reconceptualizing early childhood literacy: the sociocultural influence and new directions in digital and hybrid mediation. In: J. Marsh & J. Larson (Eds), *The Sage Handbook of Early Childhood Literacy* (pp. 52–79). London: Sage.

Rideout, V. (2013). *Zero to Eight: Children's Media Use in America 2013.* Retrieved 30 July 2014 from https://www.commonsensemedia.org/…/zero-to-eight-2013pdf-0/download.

Roskos, K., Burnstein, K., You, B., Brueck, J. & O'Brien, C. (2011). A formative study of an E-book instructional model in early literacy. *Creative education, 2*(1), 10–17.

Scollon, R. (2001). *Mediated Discourse: The Nexus of Practice.* London: Routledge.

Torr, J. (2007). The pleasure of recognition: intertextuality in the talk of pre-schoolers during shared reading with mothers and teachers. *Early Years, 27*(1), 77–91.

Vygotsky, L. S. (1978). *Mind and Society: The Development of Higher Psychological processes.* Cambridge, MA and London: Harvard University Press.

Wohlwend, K. E. (2009). Early adopters: playing new literacies and pretending new technologies in print-centric classrooms. *Journal of Early Childhood Literacy, 9*(2), 119–43.

Wohlwend, K. (in press). Making, re-making and reimagining the everyday: play, creativity, and popular media. In: K. Pahl & J. Rowsell (Eds), *The Routledge Handbook of Literacy Studies*. London: Routledge.

Wohlwend, K., Zanden, S., Husbye, N. & Kuby, C. (2011). Navigating the discourses of place in the world of Webkinz. *Journal of Early Childhood Literacy*, *11*(2), 141–63.

Yamada-Rice, D. (2011). New media, evolving multimodal literacy practices and the potential impact of increased use of the visual model in the urban environment on young children's learning. *Literacy*, *45*(1), 32–43.

3

DIGITAL TECHNOLOGY AND YOUNG CHILDREN'S NARRATIVES

Susanne Garvis

Abstract

This chapter will provide an up-to-date examination of the new directions for contemporary research perspectives on children's voice and digital technology, with a specific focus on young children's narratives. The importance of narrative meaning-making will be explored to allow the communication of sense-making. In this chapter, the narrative genre is the cultural tool concerned with children's appropriation. The cultural tool (narrative genre) is the bridge between the individual and the collective (Säljö, 2005). Using case study research, the chapter reports on children's narratives after the introduction of digital technology devices in a kindergarten. Findings show how digital technology can enhance young children's narrative meaning-making.

Introduction

The concept of "children's voice" has come to be associated with the new social studies of childhood. Until recently, research was based fundamentally *on* children rather than *for* children and *with* children (Darbyshire et al., 2005; Mayall, 2002; O'Kane, 2000). By accessing the otherwise silenced voices of children and presenting these voices to the world, researchers hope to gain a better understanding of childhood. Digital technology is one mode for allowing children's voices to be empowered. Digital technologies include multiple desktop and mobile technologies as well as digital toys (O'Hara, 2011) and internet-enabled technologies that operate as platforms for young children's consumption of digital media and associated popular culture (Gutnick, Robb, Takeuchi & Kotler, 2011).

Engagement with digital technology in early childhood education is an area filled with "few facts and many opinions" (Skeele & Stefankiewicz, 2002, p. 80). While many argue that technology and computers have a place in the hands of young children (Cordes & Miller, 2000), others also argue that those who do not embrace new media may be in danger of losing touch with the popular culture of young children (Yelland, Neal & Dakich, 2008). The need to increase research into young children's computer and technology use has been expressed by many researchers and practitioners.

Using recent case study research, this chapter reports on children's narratives after tablets and computers were introduced into a kindergarten. The children and teacher were involved in the data collection. Findings suggest the children and teacher found new ways of understanding and communicating with digital narratives. Findings are important as they provide critical understandings of how digital technology can enhance narrative stories and improve children's learning dispositions.

The use of narratives in contemporary times

Children's experiences are organised in narrative form within the memory. Narrative is considered a "universal mode of thought" and a "form of thinking" (Bruner, 1986; Nelson, 1998, 2007). According to Hakkarainen et al. (2013, p. 215), "from the cultural-historical perspective, a narrative could be defined as a psychological tool formalising and unifying human thought and knowledge into thematic units – units of thought". Accordingly, narrative is the smallest cell of human thinking, providing insight into the child's experiences. As Vygotsky described (1978, p. 126), "thought undergoes many changes as it turns into speech. It does not merely find expression in speech; it finds reality and form".

The use of narrative as a contemporary research technique allows young children to share their experiences with others. Bruner (1990) tells us that small children are interested in human interaction and activity, the temporal sequences and unexpected turns of events. Narrative descriptions exhibit human activity as purposeful engagement in the world (Polkinghorne, 1995). The research technique is respectful of the child's voice and allows the child to choose what they would like to share with others.

Constructing and co-constructing narratives

Bruner (1986) describes narratives as forms of oral discourse that characterise and facilitate culturally determined ways of communicating lived or imagined events to others. As such, narratives are the way in which individuals represent and make sense of past experience, evaluate experiences in the present and plan and anticipate future experiences.

Constructing and conveying a sequence of events by way of a spoken narrative is a common event in children's daily lives. Children have something to say and are experts at being in the moment. They do not live or grow in a "bubble" but are active participants in their lives. For example, Vivian Paley documented the stories that children tell as part of their daily lives in classrooms. The stories have common themes of questioning fairness and justice, of what transpires with characters in a storybook and the day-to-day activities children take part in (Paley, 1986, 1993, 2000). All children learn through stories while engaging in play and other activities in early childhood settings.

Sharing stories in early childhood and school settings

Many stories are shared by children in early childhood and school settings. Stories in classrooms are more scripted than home environments as educators engage with large groups of children at once (Dickinson, 1991). When a child is at home they may have informal and less structured conversations with adults or with one or a few children. Narratives in school are shared in a different environment and context. At school, the structure of the classroom dictates the types of narratives that are shared in the preschool and the characteristics of the story. Narratives in schools are generally shorter than those shared at home (Dickinson, 1991); however, they are also more diverse in form and expose children to a variety of interactions with other children that may not be experienced at home (Dickinson, 2001). Children experience different topics and different narrative structures.

Educators can also engage in narrative sharing during non-structured activities such as meal time or free play episodes. The role of the educator is to ask genuine questions that can aid the comprehension of the story and help children to become more familiar with diverse narrative practices and traditions (Curenton, 2006).

When a child tells a story (even as a word or a sentence) they not only want to tell the story, they want to tell it to someone (Pramling & Ødegaard, 2011). Utterances are given meaning in human interaction in the way others respond to them (Bakhtin, 1986). The role of the educator is therefore not only to develop the narrative skills of the child, but also to be interested in and communicate that they are interested in the emerging narrative. Through questions, the educator will be able to direct young children's attention towards what they consider worth telling (Aukrust, 1996; Ødegaard, 2006).

Young children and digital technology

Given that there have been rapid advances in the age of digitation and technology (Hobbs, 2010), there is a need for young children to develop "new skills" in reading, navigating and participating in highly digitally mediated environments (Bittman et al., 2011). The role of early childhood education is to support such skills. The current research literature however has focused more on school-aged children's use of technology compared with children in preschool and long day-care settings (Yelland, 2005). However, technology is increasingly available to younger children, including toddlers (Jordan & Woodard, 2001; Robinson, 2003) and infants (Roderman, 2002).

Selwyn (2012) proposes that more in-depth understanding about how technologies are used across social settings is necessary to move educational technology research beyond a focus on how technologies should be used to improve learning (such as literacy or numeracy). He argues that educational technology research should adopt a more critical orientation to thinking about the relationship between technologies, education and the social and cultural experiences (Selwyn, 2012, p. 216). Such an in-depth understanding could be achieved through exploring narrative interactions with young children.

A number of researchers have noted the potential of digital technologies to facilitate dialogue and collaboration, enabling young children's positive learning dispositions (Aubrey & Dahl, 2008; O'Hara, 2008; Roberts-Holmes, 2014; Stephen & Plowman, 2008). For example, O'Hara (2008) found instances of enhancement in problem solving, levels of motivation, concentration, resilience and perseverance. Such studies demonstrate that the development of positive learning dispositions provides important evidence for engagement with digital technologies in early childhood settings.

In order to facilitate young children's positive learning experiences, meaningful social interactions need to be considered for children's knowledge construction. Young children's social interaction with their friends and teachers encourages knowledge construction in developmentally appropriate ways (Colker, 2011). According to Lim (2013), young children's social interactions with peers in computer areas provide opportunities for knowledge construction that allow for inter-psychological and intra-psychological experiences. Previous research suggests when technology is integrated in early childhood education settings, children are more likely to interact with one another when using computer technology as a tool of meaningful technology integration (McCarrick & Li, 2007). Technology integration means that computer activities are interconnected in the classroom (Lim, 2013).

As yet, few studies have explored the concept of combining digital technology and narratives in early years settings. The concept of a digital narrative is emerging and provides new ways for children to express themselves and the world around them.

Focus on digital narratives

The next section focuses on a qualitative case study in which an early childhood setting implemented digital technologies to support young children's narratives. The case study highlights the importance of allowing children to explore narratives with the assistance of digital technology. Of particular focus are the enhanced features digital technology allowed with children's narrative and positive learning dispositions.

The kindergarten accommodated 20 children aged three and a half to four and a half years of age. The children would attend the kindergarten for five days over two weeks.

Activities allowed the young children to engage in digital narration. Children were provided with access to tablets and computers throughout the day. The teacher showed small groups of children how to sketch on the tablets and computer and insert sounds, words and pictures. Children were also shown how to use two applications: DoodleCast and PuppetPals. Both applications allowed children to create animations and record sound in short three-minute videos.

The children were free to create narratives about any topic or experience. Many children chose to create narratives about a recent excursion to a shopping centre. Some children spoke about activities they engaged in with their families outside of the early childhood centre: for example, a party, visiting grandma or a recent holiday. Children would share their narratives with each other and their families. Some children asked for their narratives to be played on the white board through the digital projector.

Observation and interview data was collected throughout the experience. Data was collected from children and the teacher. The data was organized into broad themes using constant comparison analysis (Leech & Onwuegbuzie, 2008). Broad themes were developed and continually reworked to adequately reflect the context under investigation. At the end of the process three themes emerged: (1) narrative representations with digital features; (2) positive learning dispositions; and (3) pedagogical practices of the teacher. A summary of each theme is presented in the next section.

Narrative representations with digital features

The first broad theme to emerge was the different representations of meaning children would use to represent themselves in stories. Engagement with digital technologies appeared to provide alternate realities of representation for the children. Images and photos formed an important part of the digital stories. Many of the children would find photos of places they had visited to enhance their story. For example, a child had been to church to see his baby brother being christened. The child decided to create a story about his experience and found an image of a church, a priest and a baby being christened. He inserted these into his story and then sketched other objects onto the images. With the church image, he sketched his family standing in front of the church. In the image of the baby being christened, he inserted drops from the baby's eyes to represent the baby crying.

Some children preferred to sketch all of their narrative on the iPad in drawings. This small group of children would move between different pages on the application to create a sequenced event in the story. Each new page appeared to provide a new period of time in the story. Page turning was achieved by swiping a finger across the page.

Electronic sound effects featured in the digital narratives of many of the children. For example, one child would use a bell to represent her voice. Every time the child would speak in the story, a bell would ring. The same child would also use a short jazz interlude to represent her birthday party. The child suggested that sounds allowed you to also "hear the story I'm telling. It makes you watch".

The digital narrative also provided opportunities for children to present their story in multiple contexts. Some children would share their story on the iPad, while other children would want their story shown on the digital projector. Some children also wanted their story shown on a plasma TV in the entry of the kindergarten to allow families to see the stories. At all times children were the owners of their narratives and could choose how to communicate and present to others.

The electronic feature of the narratives also allowed the narratives to be played and replayed by the children. Children were able to compare the different stories created and explore the different representations and digital features. Some children would also create alternate endings to their stories after watching and rewatching their narrative. Some children would create a different ending electronically, while other children would verbally provide an alternate ending. One particular child provided his alternate ending with the teacher about the story of a boy who fell down a hole:

Extract 3.1 Alternate ending

1. Carl (aged 4.3 years): That's not what happened! (referring to his digital story)
2. Teacher: OK. What happened?
3. Carl: Tricked ya! The boy woke up and was dreaming. That's what happened.
4. Teacher: Do you like stories with tricks at the end?
5. Carl: I like changing the ending. The story gets better. You can make it a happy or sad story.
6. Teacher: Do you like making stories on the iPad?
7. Carl: My story is better. It's like a story on TV. I can add sound and pictures. You can't do that when drawing. I can take this to Daddy at home.

Overall, the children expressed enjoyment at being able to create their own digital narratives. The children highlighted the extra features that allowed them to embellish their stories and provided more features for the children to draw upon. The children suggested their narratives allowed for easier sequencing of events. The digital recorded features also provided opportunities for the digital narrative to be watched and viewed multiple times, in multiple locations within and beyond the kindergarten.

The teacher also expressed the benefits of digital narratives from her observations and engagement with the children. This included enhanced skills of description by the children, the children understanding the importance of sequencing and allowing the communication of the narratives in different formats. The children were able to share their different topics and narratives structures with one another.

Positive learning dispositions

The teacher reported that engagement with the tablets and computers had motivated and engaged the children both emotionally and cognitively. The children's positive learning dispositions (such as perseverance and self-esteem) were encouraged by watching their own videos with the other children and the teacher. The children took delight in sharing their narration with each other on the screen and explaining what was occurring. In some instances, stories would be told and retold (or played and replayed on the digital technology) numerous times with children predicting what was going to happen next in the story. One teacher commented:

Extract 3.2 Teacher reflection

It has been really interesting to see the changes that have happened. The children want to share more about their own lives and start to co-construct narratives with each other. One child may start a story and the other children will work with that child to finish the story. Sometimes the story will be retold and there are alternative endings. The children are really engaged in learning. I had one group of children spend 2 hours at the computer creating a story! They had worked out how to add sounds and wanted all of the characters in their drawing to have a sound. They are teaching each other.

The teacher was asked to comment on differences observed between children presenting traditional narratives and digital narratives. The teacher commented that digital narratives allowed the story to be captured and replayed again and again. This allowed the children to change the meaning and the perceived realities within the story. The teacher also commented that engagement with the digital technology had allowed the narratives to be more easily shared with the other children. The stories were captured in time and the children were able to have a tool to scaffold their jointly created stories.

The children also commented on changes in their own learning dispositions. A group of three children stated:

Extract 3.3 Changes in learning dispositions

14. Anya (aged 3.6): I come here in the morning and stay (pointing to the tablet area).
15. James (aged 4.1): Yeah – we sit and story.
16. Justin (aged 3.8): We all touch it (referring to the tablet).
17. James: Wait ... no sound (James is trying to show his story).
18. Justin: Touch here! (Justin turns on the sound).
19. James: Watch this – we made this (hands me the tablet).
20. Anya: Let's make a new story about yesterday (the three children begin working together).
21. Justin: What was yesterday?
22. James: Tom's Dad bought in a pipe (bagpipes).

Even though the children worked with the same applications every day, they were able to extend the ways in which they were engaged. The young children in the group above were able to gain new information and apply that information to their own story in order to create new interest areas (Morgan, 2007). O'Hara (2008) suggests such a process influences the development of children's metacognition, regarding the monitoring and control of the classroom project. Children find new functions and new methods within the applications, sharing with other children. In this example, the children have been able to expand on their own knowledge contents and schemas (Morgan, 2010).

In conversations with the children, ideas about teamwork, motivation and perseverance became known. The children also appeared to teach each other new skills and provide support in solving problems. The children were motivated to work together to produce a shared narrative.

Pedagogical practices

The teacher demonstrated an intersubjective awareness of the children's contextual and conceptual understanding of digital video (Fleer, 2010) and extended the children's understanding about digital narratives. This demanded that the teacher make a "double move" (Fleer, 2010) holding onto the children's current understandings and at the same time introducing new concepts about digital narratives. Such scaffolding required the skillful pedagogical framework of working and editing with different groups of children throughout the day. Group sizes would vary and the teacher had to understand all of the different skill levels of the students.

The teacher commented that the digital technology had generated "dialogic spaces" (Wegerif, 2007). The digital narratives became a tool for continual discussion and interaction. By opening up such a space, the dialogue fulfilled the criteria for a sustained shared conversation because both parties were involved and the learning was instructive (Siraj-Blatchford, 2007). Throughout the exchanges, there was also a sense that the children's views were respected.

The teacher also reported that that her own motivational interest for engaging with digital technology in the kindergarten had improved. She suggested that the project had created a "catalytic change agent" (Clark & Murray, 2012) by improving her pedagogical engagement, leading to improvement in the children's learning dispositions. The teacher suggested she would like to further update her own digital technology skills to further support the children.

Conclusion

Digital technology is important for extending children's narratives in early childhood settings. It allows children to represent their understanding of events and experiences in extended ways beyond traditional formats of drawing. Digital technology allows children to integrate sound, photos, images, sketches and voice commentary.

The digital narrative case study presented has also shown that the digital technology implemented allowed young children to broaden and build their knowledge structures (Zevenbergen, 2007). Both the children and the teacher reported positive learning dispositions after engaging in the digital narratives. Children were able to compare their stories and extend each other's understanding via social interaction. Children created shared narratives that built on each other's ideas.

One of the strengths of digital narratives is the ability of a recorded story to be played and replayed, told and retold to provide different meanings. Digital narratives are portable and can be moved around and in and out of a kindergarten space. Digital narratives can be viewed in a private space only by the author, or the author may want to broadcast the story with a bigger audience.

What must be acknowledged from this case study is the understanding of digital technology shown and enacted by the teacher. To allow children to experience digital stories also requires the early childhood teacher to be skilled in digital technology. The teacher needs a working understanding of creating stories, engaging with tablet applications and implementing the sharing of digital stories. In this chapter, the teacher was also aware of the importance of continual professional development.

Future research is needed into the benefits, enablers and barriers of digital narratives in early childhood contexts. Digital narratives allow children to construct and convey a sequence of events, which is a common event in their daily lives. By exploring children's digital narratives, we are able to explore many facets of young children's lives in terms of cognition, development and wellbeing. Digital narratives provide enriched opportunities to provide new meaning of children's lives.

References

Aubrey, C., and Dahl, S. (2008). *A Review of the Evidence on the Use of ICT in the Early Years Foundation Stage*, for British Educational Communications and Technology Agency. Retrieved 10 April 2010 from http://dera.ioe.ac.uk/1631/.

Aukrust, V. G. (1996). Learning to talk and keep silent about everyday routines: a study of verbal interaction between young children and their caregivers. *Scandinavian Journal of Educational Research*, 40(4), 311–24.

Bakhtin, M. M. (1986). The problem of speech genres. In: C. Emerson & M. Holquist (Eds), *Speech Genres and Other Late Essays* (pp. 60–102). Austin: University of Texas Press.

Bittman, M., Rutherford, L., Brown, J. and L. Unsworth. (2011). Digital natives? New and old media and children's outcomes. *Australian Journal of Education*, 55(2), 161–75.

Bruner, J. S. (1986). *Actual Minds, Possible Worlds*. Cambridge, MA: Harvard University Press.

Bruner, J. S. (1990). *Acts of Meaning*. Cambridge, MA: Harvard University Press.

Clark, R. & Murray, J. (2012). *Reconceptualising Leadership in the Early Years*. Maidenhead: Open University Press.

Colker, L. J. (2011). Technology and learning: what early childhood educators have to say. *Teaching Young Children*, 4(3), 25–27.

Cordes, C. & Miller, E. (2000). *Fool's Gold: A Critical Look at Computers in Childhood*. College Park, MD: Alliance for Childhood.

Curenton, S. M. (2006). Oral storytelling: a cultural art that promotes school readiness. *Young Children*, 61, 78–89.

Darbyshire, P., MacDougall, C. & Schiller, W. (2005). Multiple methods in qualitative research with children: more insight or just more? *Qualitative Research*, 5(4), 417–36.

Dickinson, D. K. (1991). Teacher agenda and setting: constraints on conversation in preschools. In: A. McCabe & C. Peterson (Eds), *Developing Narrative Structure* (pp. 255–301). Hillsdale, NJ: Erlbaum.

Dickinson, D. K. (2001). Book reading in preschool classrooms: is recommended practice common? In D. K. Dickinson & P. O. Tabors (Eds), *Beginning Literacy with Language: Young Children Learning at Home and School* (pp. 175–203). Baltimore, MD: Brookes.

Fleer, M. (2010). *Early Learning and Development: Cultural-historical Concepts in Play*. Cambridge: Cambridge University Press.

Gutnick, A. L., Robb, M., Takeuchi, L. & J. Kotler. J. (2011). *Always Connected: The New Digital Media Habits of Young Children*. New York: The Joan Ganz Cooney Center at Sesame Workshop.

Hakkarainen, P., Bredikyte, M., Jakkula, K. & Munter, H. (2013). Adult play guidance and children's play development in a narrative play-world. *European Early Childhood Education Research Journal, 21*(2), 213–25.

Hobbs, R. (2010). *Digital Media and Literacy: A Plan of Action. A White Paper on the Digital and Media Literacy Recommendations of the Knight Commission on the Information Needs of Communities in a Democracy.* Washington DC: The Aspen Institute.

Jordan, A. B. & Woodard, E. H. (2001). Electronic childhood: the availability and use of household media by 2- to 3-year olds. *Zero to Three, 22*(2), 4–9.

Leech, N. L. & Onwuegbuzie, A. J. (2008). Qualitative data analysis: a compendium of techniques and a framework for selection for school psychology research and beyond. *School Psychology Quarterly, 23*, 587–604.

Lim, E. (2013). The factors influencing young children's social interaction in technology integration, *European Early Childhood Education Research Journal.* (published online http://dx.doi.org/10.1080/1350293X.2013.810484), 1–18.

Mayall, B. (2002). *Towards a Sociology for Childhood: Thinking from Children's Lives.* Buckingham: Open University Press.

McCarrick, K. & Li, X. (2007). Buried treasure: the impact of computer use on young children's social, cognitive, language development and motivation. *AACE Journal, 15*(1), 73–95.

Morgan, A. (2007). Using video-stimulated recall to understand young children's perceptions of learning in classroom settings. *European Early Childhood Education Research Journal, 15*(2), 213–26.

Morgan, A. (2010). Interactive whiteboards, interactivity and play in the classroom aged three to seven years. *European Early Childhood Education Research Journal, 18*(1), 93–104.

Nelson, K. (1998). *Language in Cognitive Development.* New York: Cambridge University Press.

Nelson, K. (2007). *Young Minds in Social Worlds. Experience, Meaning, and Memory.* Cambridge: Harvard University Press.

Ødegaard, E. E. (2006). What's worth talking about? Meaning-making in toddler-initiated co-narratives in preschool. *Early Years, 26*(1), 79–92.

O'Hara, M. (2008). Young children, learning and ICT: a case study in the UK maintained sector. *Technology, Pedagogy and Education, 17*(1), 29–40.

O'Hara, M. (2011). Young children's ICT experiences in the home: some parental perspectives. *Journal of Early Childhood Research, 9*(3), 220–32.

O'Kane, C. (2000). The development or participatory techniques. Facilitating children's views about decisions which affect them. In: P. Christensen and A. James (Eds), *Research with Children. Perspectives and Practices* (pp. 120–35). London: RoutledgeFalmer.

Paley, V. G. (1986). *Boys and Girls: Superheroes in the Doll Corner.* Chicago: University of Chicago Press.

Paley, V. G. (1993). *You Can't Say You Can't Play.* Cambridge, MA: Harvard University Press.

Paley, V. G. (2000). *White Teacher.* Cambridge, MA: Harvard University Press.

Polkinghorne, D. E. (1995). Narrative configuration in qualitative analysis. In: J.A. Hatch and R. Wisniewski (Eds), *Life Histories and Narrative* (pp. 5–24). London: Falmer Press.

Pramling, N. & Ødegaard, E. E. (2011). Learning to narrate: appropriating a cultural mould for sense-making and communication. In: N. Pramling & I. Pramling Samuelsson (Eds), *Educational Encounters: Nordic Studies in Early Childhood Didactics* (pp. 15–35). Dordrecht: Springer.

Roberts-Holmes, G. (2014). *Doing Your Early Years Research Project: A Step by Step Guide.* London: Sage Publications.

Robinson, L. (2003). Technology as a scaffold for emergent literacy: interactive storybooks for toddlers. *Young Children, 58*, 42–48.

Roderman, L. S. (2002). Technology and the very young: lapware, smart toys and beyond. Palo Alto, CA: Computer Professionals for Social Responsibility.

Säljö, R. (2005). Lärande och kulturella redskap: Om lärprocesser och det kollektiva minnet [Learning and cultural tools: on processes of learning and collective memory]. Stockholm: Norstedts Akademiska.

Selwyn, N. (2012). Ten suggestions for improving academic research in education and technology. *Learning, Media and Technology, 37*, 213–19.

Siraj-Blatchford, I. (2007). Creativity, communication and collaboration: the identification of pedagogic progression in sustained shared thinking. *Asia Pacific Journal of Research in Early Childhood Education, 1*(2), 3–23.

Skeele, R., & Stefankiewicz, G. (2002). Blackbox in the sandbox: the decision to use technology with young children with annotated bibliography of internet resources for teachers of young children. *Educational Technology Review, 10*(2), 79–95.

Stephen, C., & Plowman, L. (2008). Enhancing learning with information and communication technologies in pre-school. *Early Childhood Development and Care, 178*(6), 637–54.

Vygotsky, L. (1978). *Mind in Society: The Development of Higher Psychological Processes.* Cambridge: Harvard University Press.

Wegerif, R. (2007). *Dialogic Education and Technology: Expanding the Space of Learning.* New York: Springer.

Yelland, N. (2005). The future in now: a review of the literature on the use of computers in early childhood education (1994–2004). *Association for the Advancement of Computing in Education Journal, 13*, 201–32.

Yelland, N., Neal, G. & Dakich, E. (2008). *Rethinking Education with ICT: New Directions for Effective Practices.* Rotterdam: Senses Publishing.

Zevenbergen, R. (2007). Digital natives come to preschool: implications for early childhood practice. *Contemporary Issues in Early Childhood 8*(1), 19–29.

4

YOUNG CHILDREN'S INTERNET COGNITION

Susan Edwards, Helen Skouteris, Andrea Nolan and Michael Henderson

Abstract

In the past five years young children's access to and usage of the internet has burgeoned, mostly due to the availability of internet-enabled, touch-screen and mobile technologies. While this creates exciting learning opportunities for young children, internet activity in this age-bracket raises several issues of practical, research and pedagogical concern. Two of the most pertinent concerns outlined in the literature – conceptions of cyber-safety and digital literacies – are focused on in this chapter. We suggest that an understanding of young children's thinking about the internet – their "internet cognition" – is a necessary precursor to learning about internet safety and digital literacies. Without such knowledge it is problematic to expect teachers to know how and what to teach in relation to both cyber-safety and digital literacies. The chapter concludes by proposing a research and pedagogical agenda for early childhood education in an effort to establish a knowledge base for the field regarding young children's "internet cognition".

Introduction

The availability of touch-screen and internet-enabled mobile technologies in post-industrialised societies is associated with a marked rise in the use of the internet by very young children. Holloway, Green and Livingstone (2013) argue that preschool-aged children increasingly use mobile phones and tablet technologies as a touch-screen portal that takes them directly to a range of online activities including apps, video content sharing, online games, television- and movie-associated websites and communication with peers and family members (e.g. FaceTime, Skype). For the first time in the history of the internet, online access by very young children is not only increasing (Buckleitner, 2008), but also infants and toddlers are already linked with "digital footprints" as parents, guardians and grandparents post images and associated commentary about young children on social networking sites (Holloway, Green & Livingstone, 2013; O'Keeffe & Clarke-Pearson, 2011). Australian Bureau of Statistics (2012) data indicates that 90 per cent of Australian children aged 5–14 years accessed the internet in the previous year. Like international research (e.g. Livingstone et al., 2011), these findings focus predominately on older children, with access levels for preschoolers harder to establish. However, emerging research suggests that approximately 40 per cent of Australian preschoolers go online for at least one hour per day (Johnson, 2010). As an unprecedented occurrence, the internet activity of children in the years prior to school raises several issues of practical, research and pedagogical concern. Chief among those identified in the literature are: a) how to keep young children "safe" when they are online (Ey & Cupit, 2011); and b) how to foster the development of digital and multiliteracy skills in young children (Hobbs, 2010).

In this chapter we reflect on the extent to which conceptions of cyber-safety and digital literacy for very young children presuppose a more basic question regarding young children's understanding of the internet in the first instance. We suggest that how children understand the internet represents a significant concern for the field of early childhood education. This is because without this knowledge it is difficult for teachers to work with children to explain first, how and why the internet might be unsafe and what they need to do to remain safe; and second, how the internet uses digitised information to create multimodal sources of information and therefore how "reading" needs to occur in particular ways.

We begin the chapter with an outline of the research pertaining to internet safety and digital literacies in early childhood education. We then consider the limited research into children's understanding of the internet and propose a research and pedagogical agenda for early childhood education that works towards establishing a knowledge base for the field regarding young children's "internet cognition". From a sociocultural perspective, cognition is understood as the process by which children build knowledge and understand their social and cultural worlds. Knowledge and understanding is built through relationships with social peers and adults using both the physical and conceptual tools of the host community (Daniels, 2008; Vygotsky, 1997). The "internet" for the purpose of this chapter includes a technical and social concept in which the internet is understood as an interconnected network of worldwide computers used by people for both positive and negative social reasons (Yan, 2005). For us, the idea of "internet cognition" therefore represents how very young children construct their knowledge and understanding of the internet through their daily online experiences. For the purpose of this chapter we define "early years" or "early childhood education" as the period from birth to eight years and the provision of education and/or care for children in this age range.

Internet safety and digital literacies in early childhood education

Internet safety or "cyber-safety" focuses on the risks children are likely to experience online. Considerable research conducted in this area consistently identifies risks for children in terms of exposure to inappropriate or illegal content, exposure to extensive advertising for unhealthy food products, opportunities to meet and talk with strangers, downloading content and responding to pop-ups (Livingstone et al., 2011; Snyder et al., 2011). Much of this research focuses on children aged 8–18, with very little attention paid to young children. With the focus on older children, cyber-safety interventions are likewise predicated on primary and secondary education and involve teaching children about the range of risks they are likely to face online (Willard, 2007). In early childhood education, there is now some awareness that young children are online in increasing numbers and that cyber-safety should be part of the early years curriculum. Here, the recommendation is based on the layered approach often used with older children. This approach involves using both tools (such as filters to restrict access to content) and rules (such as children only going online with an adult) to mediate online risks for young children (Grey, 2011).

Digital literacies in early childhood education attracts a stronger body of research specific to the early years than cyber-safety. This is probably because young children's access to the internet has only recently increased due to the widespread availability of touch-screen and mobile technologies, whereas awareness regarding the need for multiple forms of digital literacies in the early years has existed for over a decade (Dyson, 2003; Marsh et al., 2005). The main argument for digital literacies in the early years rests on young children's exposure to, and use of, technologies in their home and community settings (Parette, Quesenberry & Blum, 2010). Necessary "literacies" for young children include "navigating virtual environments, manipulating avatars, interpreting icons, communicating via online messaging systems, and maintaining online relationships" (Black, 2010, p. 19). Marsh (2010) and Wohlend (2010) identify the capacity to navigate, interact with and produce original content that is image-, text- and video-based as important digital literacies for young children. Yelland and Gilbert (2013) suggest these capacities are best developed through "playful explorations" where teachers support children to explore the use of a range of technologies. Despite research identifying the range of digital literacies appropriate for children to learn in early childhood education settings, the uptake of technologies in early childhood education, and children's consequent digital literacy learning, remains limited (Ruckenstein, 2010).

Children's understanding of the internet

Research into children's understanding of the internet is very limited. This is interesting given the plethora of research focused on children's use of the internet in terms of searching strategies (Schater, Chung & Dorr, 1998); parental mediation of internet use (Kirwil, 2009); and/or the relationship between internet use and academic achievement (Jackson et al., 2006). Once again, such research is generally focused on children aged in the primary and secondary years of school, with little attention paid to the experiences of young children in the early years. Of the research conducted into children's understanding of the internet the focus is on older children. This work is situated in what is described as a "new field of inquiry in developmental psychology" (Greenfield & Yan, 2006, p. 391), that is, the internet as a developmental niche evidencing new forms of developmental capacity in children and in adolescents.

Research conducted into children's understanding of the internet focuses on two main concepts. The first refers to a technical understanding of the internet as an interconnected, worldwide network of computers, users and communication protocols (Yan, 2005). The second refers to social understandings of the internet in terms of the benefits (e.g. increased access to information; faster forms of communication; multiple forms of modality) and the risks (e.g. phishing crimes; predatory behaviour; cyberbullying; internet overuse and addiction) associated with internet use (Lindsay et al., 2011; Yan, 2005). Yan's (2009) work suggests primary and secondary school students have "minimal" or "partial" understandings of each concept. For a technical concept of the internet, the minimal and partial understandings are defined as:

> Minimal – representing completely perception-based knowledge about the internet. Perceiving the internet as one computer (Yan, 2009, p. 107)

Partial – representing perception-bounded knowledge about the internet. Perceiving the internet as either several computers with no indication of connections among them or simple connections of several computers (Yan, 2009, p. 107)

For a social concept of the internet, the minimal and partial understandings are defined as:

Minimal – no awareness of social aspects of the internet and expresses little precaution when using the internet (Yan, 2009, p. 108)

Partial – a general but limited sense of the positive and negative consequences of the internet (Yan, 2009, p. 108)

Yan (2009) attributes the developing understandings children and adolescents possess of the technical and social concepts of the internet to the physicality of the technologies that allow children to access the internet. This is because children will typically access the internet through a device such as a phone, a desktop or laptop computer and/or tablet. The technology possibly represents the "internet" for children because when they go online this is the immediate artefact with which they engage.

This suggestion aligns with findings from our own research in which early childhood teachers used technologies in their programming and planning with young children (Edwards, in press). Here teachers reported children's understanding of the internet as strongly associated with the technology itself. For example, one teacher described a conversation held with a four-year-old boy:

None of the kids could differentiate between the internet and the computer. I said to them, "Oh you use the computer". They said, "Yes I go online". I said, "That's the internet". They said to me, "No that is the computer". So they couldn't tell me – they didn't have any understanding about it. It was just "I play games on the computer".

In another example, a teacher described a pretend game of police-people in which the children needed to access a map to further their play. She promptly provided the children with some older style key-pad mobile phones obtained through a recycling outlet. The children immediately rejected these as "not the phones with the maps". One child said, "All you can do on that one is phone – that one does not do anything". Here, the children knew what the technology for accessing a Global Positioning System (GPS)–enabled map would look like, but not necessarily the technical aspects that meant that one type of phone was different from another. As with Yan's (2009) suggestion, the "internet" potentially includes for children a "perceptual dimension" associated with the technology used to connect them with any given online experience or activity.

Against the backdrop of existing research into children's conceptions of the internet our early research suggests to us that children aged five to seven years may not understand the internet in a technical or social way. It is possible that young children understand the internet in a more socially-culturally orientated way that references the practices they are used to engaging in when using the internet, such as a place for searching out information or a tool for completing tasks, like doing email or ordering shopping (Dodge, Husain & Duke, 2011; Johnson, 2010). Here, young children's internet understanding may be more focused on the social practices associated with online activity than with technical or social concepts of the internet. These findings indicate that an early starting point for researching young children's understandings of the internet needs to consider: a) the various technologies they use to access the internet; and b) their social and cultural experiences of going online. This is because the perceptual and social-use aspects of the internet are likely to be the most immediate for young children.

Towards young children's internet cognition

Existing research into very young children's understanding of the internet is so limited as to be almost non-existent. The limited research that is available shows that preschoolers, toddlers and infants now access technologies that promote their internet access (Holloway, Green & Livingstone, 2013). With research showing that older children equate technologies with the internet, and that they are not always aware of the social and/or legal dimensions of their online activity, it is critical that early years researchers and teachers appreciate what children know and understand about the internet. To encapsulate this need we propose the concept of "internet cognition" (Edwards et al., 2014). The concept of internet cognition opens opportunities for exploring how the perceptual aspects of young children's engagement with technologies shape their understandings of the internet (e.g. is the computer the internet?). There is also potential for considering how young children's knowledge and understanding of what the internet is are influenced by the social and cultural practices that guide their online activities. The extent to which young children's understandings of the internet evolve over time and whether or not there are identifiable "markers" of children's internet cognition also requires consideration.

Engaging these research opportunities would inform pedagogical efforts aimed at examining the technical and social dimensions of the internet with young children. For example, the teacher earlier describing how her children equated the internet with the computer could draw on research showing how children understand the internet as perceptually related to the technology they are using. In this case, the teacher could engage with the children to begin early-level conceptual work regarding the internet as a series of internetworked computers that talk to each other to share information. In this way, the immediate conception of the internet as "one device" can be engaged with by children and an understanding of the internet that extends beyond the perceptual begins to be explored. Likewise, Grey (2011) argues that layered approach to internet safety is necessary in early childhood education because children do not understand the internet beyond the immediate device they are accessing. According to this view, filters and rules for use are necessary to protect children. However, pedagogical engagement with children directed towards helping them to understand that the technical dimensions of the internet enable many people to be online provides a context in which it is appropriate to talk with children about why and how they need to practice online cyber-safety. Research-informed pedagogy of this nature is an important step forward for early childhood education because it helps to justify for children *why* parents and teachers might be telling them that the internet is not always safe, or that the internet requires them to "read" information in different ways.

Research and pedagogy directed towards understanding young children's internet cognition is therefore likely to provide a rich basis for informing future practice with respect to cyber-safety and digital literacies in the early years. Researching internet cognition and using the idea of internet cognition from a pedagogical perspective also has the benefit of shifting the existing focus on children's internet understanding from one of limitations, such as "minimal" or "partial" concepts of the internet, to a more strengths-based focus. This is because a research and pedagogical agenda for internet cognition in the early years should not focus on how children's understandings of the internet compare to adult understandings of the internet (Yan, 2005, p. 200), but focus instead on how children experience and make sense of the internet within their given social and cultural contexts. We propose that key questions for this new area of work are:

- How do children perceive the perceptual dimensions of the artefacts that enable them to access the internet?
- What are children's understandings of the activities or experiences they engage in with the internet?
- To what extent does engaging children in descriptions of the technical aspects of the internet influence their thinking regarding the perceptual dimensions of the artefact they use to access the internet and their levels of awareness regarding being "online"?
- To what extent does engaging children in descriptions of the technical aspects of the internet enable conversations regarding social concepts of the internet?

Engaging with these questions has the potential to extend current ideas regarding cyber-safety and digital literacies in early childhood education into a consideration of how children understand the internet. In this way, technical and social concepts of the internet can provide the basis of pedagogical engagements with young children leading towards later consideration of how to be safe online, or what it means to "read" combinations of image, text and video when using mobile internet-enabled devices.

Conclusion

Touch-screen and internet-enabled mobile devices have made access to the internet prevalent for very young children. For the first time in the history of the internet, infants, toddlers and preschoolers are creating digital footprints and actively engaging in online activity. This raises a consequent need in early childhood education for teachers to engage children in learning about internet safety and digital literacies. A key aspect of effective internet safety and digital literacy learning in the early years may be associated with the extent to which young children understand the internet according to their social and cultural contexts. This is particularly the case given research suggesting that older children align the internet with the perceptual dimensions of the technologies they use when participating in online activities. In this chapter, we have suggested the idea of young children's "internet cognition" as a way of beginning to comprehend how children understand the internet and how these understandings can be fostered in early childhood settings as an appropriate basis for engaging children in internet safety and the learning of digital literacies.

References

Australian Bureau of Statistics (2012). *Children's Participation in Cultural and Leisure Activities. Internet and Mobile Phones.* Retrieved 27 April 2014 from http://www.abs.gov.au/ausstats/abs@.nsf/Products/4901.0~Apr+2012~Main+Features~Internet+and+mobile+phones?OpenDocument

Black, R. (2010). The language of Webkinz: early childhood literacy in an online virtual world. *Digital Culture and Education, 2*(1), 7–24.

Buckleitner, W. (2008). *Like Taking Candy from a Baby: How Young Children Interact with Online Environments*. Yonkers, NY: Consumer Reports WebWatch. Retrieved 3 February 2011 from http://consumersunion.org/wp-content/uploads/2013/05/kidsonline.pdf.

Daniels, H. (2008). *Vygotsky and Research*. New York: Routledge.

Dodge, A., Husain, N. & Duke, N. (2011). Connected kids? K-2 children's use and understanding of the internet. *Language Arts, 89*(2), 86–98.

Dyson, A. (2003). "Welcome to the Jam": popular culture, school literacy, and the making of childhoods. *Harvard Educational Review, 73*(3), 328–61.

Edwards, S. (in press). Technologies in early childhood education. In: M. Henderson & G. Romeo (Eds), *Teaching and Digital Technologies: Big Issues and Critical Questions*. Cambridge: Cambridge University Press.

Edwards, S. Skouteris, H., Nolan, A. & Henderson, M. (2014). *Internet Cognition in the Early Years*. Retrieved 26 September 2014 from http://acu-au.academia.edu/SusanEdwards/Posts

Ey, L. & Cupit, C. (2011). Exploring young children's understanding of risks associated with internet usage and their concepts of management strategies. *Journal of Early Childhood Research, 9*(1), 53–65.

Greenfield, P. & Yan, Z. (2006). Children, adolescents, and the internet: a new field of inquiry in developmental psychology. *Developmental Psychology, 42*(3), 391–94.

Grey, A. (2011). Cyber-safety in early childhood education. *Australasian Journal of Early Childhood, 36*(2), 77–81.

Hobbs, R. (2010). *Digital Media and Literacy: A Plan of Action. A White Paper on the Digital and Media Literacy Recommendations of the Knight Commission on the Information Needs of Communities in a Democracy*. Washington DC: The Aspen Institute.

Holloway, D., Green. L. & Livingstone, S. (2013). *Zero to Eight. Young Children and Their Internet Use*. LSE, London: EU Kids Online.

Jackson, L., von Eye, A., Biocca, F., Barbatsis, G., Zhao, Y. & Fitzgerald, H. (2006). Does home internet use influence the academic performance of low-income children? *Developmental Psychology, 42*(3), 429–35.

Johnson, G. (2010). Young children's internet use at home and school: patterns and profiles. *Journal of Early Childhood Research, 8*(3), 282–93.

Kirwil, L, (2009). Parental mediation of children's internet use in different European countries. *Journal of Children and Media, 3*(4), 394–409.

Lindsay, D., de Zwart, M., Henderson, M. & Phillips, M. (2011). Understanding legal risks facing children and young people using social network sites. *Telecommunications Journal of Australia, 61*(1), 1–18.

Livingstone, S., Haddon, L., Görzig, A. & Ólafsson, K. (2011). *Risks and Safety on the Internet: The UK Report*. LSE, London: EU Kids Online.

Marsh, J. (2010). Young children's play in online virtual worlds. *Journal of Early Childhood Research, 8*(1), 23–39.

Marsh, J., Brooks, G., Hughes, J., Ritchie, L., Roberts, S. & Wright, K. (2005). *Digital Beginnings: Young Children's Use of Popular Culture, Media and New Technologies*. Literacy Research Centre: University of Sheffield.

O'Keeffe, G. & Clarke-Pearson, K. (2011). Clinical report. The impact of social media on children, adolescents, and family. *Pediatrics*. doi: 10.1542/peds.2011-0054

Parette, H., Quesenberry, A. & Blum, C. (2010). Missing the boat with technology usage in early childhood settings: a 21st century view of developmentally appropriate practice. *Early Childhood Education Journal, 37*, 335–43.

Ruckenstein, M. (2010). Toying with the world: children, virtual pets and the value of mobility. *Childhood, 17*(4), 500–13.

Schater, J., Chung, G. & Dorr, A. (1998). Children's internet searching on complex problems: performance and process analyses, *Journal of the American Society for Information Science, 49*(9), 840–49.

Snyder, I., Jevons, C., Henderson, M., Gabbott, M. & Beale, D. (2011). More than chatting online: children, marketing and the use of digital media. *English in Australia 46*(3), 32–40.

Vygotsky, L. S. (1997). Research method. In: R. W. Rieber (Ed.), *The Collected Works of L. S. Vygotsky* (Vol. 4). New York: Plenum Press.

Willard, N. (2007). *Cyber-safe Kids, Cyber-savvy Teens: Helping Young People Learn to Use the Internet Safely and Responsibly*. San Francisco: Jossey-Bass.

Wohlend, K. (2010). A is for Avatar: young children in literacy 2.0 worlds and literacy 1.0 schools. *Language Arts, 88*(2), 144–52.

Yan, Z. (2005). Age differences in children's understanding of the complexity of the internet. *Journal of Applied Developmental Psychology, 26,* 385–96.

Yan, Z. (2009). Limited knowledge and limited resources: children's and adolescents' understanding of the internet. *Journal of Applied Developmental Psychology, 30,* 103–15.

Yelland, N. & Gilbert, C. (2013). *iPlay, iLearn, iGrow*. Melbourne: Victoria University.

5

YOUNG CHILDREN PHOTOGRAPHING THEIR LEARNING TO SHARE THEIR LIVED EXPERIENCES OF THE LEARNING ENVIRONMENT

Narelle Lemon

Abstract

Young people are capable users of technology in the early years setting. When trusted and scaffolded to use a digital camera, the hand-held and portable nature of this technology enables young people to become digital image-makers. This chapter illuminates how the voices of the young photographers, through reflections, form visual narratives that communicate their lived experiences. The four cases shared demonstrate how the digital camera can be meaningfully integrated into the early years learning environment to support learning skills such as reflective and metacognitive thinking, communication and problem solving.

Introduction

A digital camera is a common digital tool in early childhood learning environments (Northcote, 2011). Although they have had a regular history with teachers and visiting adults using them to document moments and learning experiences (Carr, 2001; Lemon, 2007, 2014; Pasor & Kerns, 1997), more student-centred practices are now promoted within the learning context (Lemon, 2007, 2014; Northcote, 2011; Yelland, 1999). When children are invited to use the technology there are many beneficial results in regards to developing competency in digital technology, communication, thinking and problem-solving skills while they also share and extend their learning experiences (Lemon, 2008; Lemon & Finger, 2013; Richards, 2009). It has been argued that digital cameras also enable personalised reflection in a manner that other technical devices do not (Chen, 2005; Hargreaves, 2003; Moyle, 2010). Conversations that occur during and after the creation of images can provide opportunities for young learners that move beyond simply writing about the photograph (Ewald & Lightfoot, 2001; Lemon, 2008). Working within a constructivist framework (Denzin & Lincoln, 2000; Guba & Lincoln, 1994; Schwandt, 1994), young children's visual narratives (photographs paired with narrative in written or oral form) are understood to reveal insights into their lived experiences and their existing schemas of knowledge and understanding (Lemon, 2008, 2014).

In this chapter I explore an approach that builds on the work developed by Bach (2007) and Moss (2008) to explore visual narrative as methodology to investigate student and teacher learning in the early childhood environment. The generation of digital visual narratives by children, in this case early years children aged between five and six years, demonstrates that they are capable users of digital technology (Lemon, 2008; Lemon & Finger, 2013) and illuminates how young children use digital photographs to capture the "*unsayable* stories they hold" (Leitch, 2008, p. 37). It is from this perspective they become digital image-makers of their lived experiences.

The four cases presented in this chapter illustrate how student-generated visual narrative provides an alternative strategy for reflective learning by encouraging independence and accountability while engaging children in authentic learning experiences. Visual narratives produced digitally promote an opportunity for the young people to develop communication skills, as shown by the cases of James and Stan. The chance to reflect on past learning opportunities and problem-solve through inquiry is evident in the cases of Mark, Jane and Rachel. All cases highlight how digital technology has the advantage of supporting young children to share their lived experiences to allow for the promotion of voice (Burns, Dimock & Martinez, 2000; Dillner, 2001; Lemon, 2007; Moyle, 2010). Collectively the cases show how it is possible to integrate the digital camera into the early years setting and allow young children to be digital image-makers.

Digital cameras and young children

In the context of the early years setting, digital literacy is changing (Hopkins, Green & Brookes, 2013). As Moyle (2010, p.1) reminds us, "building innovation with technologies in school education is providing Australian educators with the opportunity to reconceptualise teaching and learning in the 21st century". The Melbourne Declaration on Educational Goals for Young Australians (Ministerial Council for Education, Early Childhood Development and Youth Affairs [MCEECDYA], 2008) further reiterates this. Such approaches require teachers to support students in learning how to work with others and also how to use technology to communicate in order to create new knowledge or share insights (Moyle, 2010). Highlighted also is the pressure that exists for teachers to maintain awareness and skills in being able to rethink the concepts of digital literacy and how they can inform meaning-making, social and emotional development while providing opportunities to engage with the new technologies of information and communication (Anstey & Bull, 2006; Baker, 2010; Cloonan, 2010; Cope & Kalantzis, 2000; Lemon & Finger, 2013; Pahl & Rowsell, 2005).

In thinking about the place and value of technology in the early years environment there is a need to extend past what Plowman and Stephen (2005) acknowledge as practitioners generally referring to "children playing with the computer" (p.145). Acknowledgment needs to be made and celebrated that young learners enter the learning environment already immersed in interactive digital environments and engaging with digital devices (Edward-Groves & Langley, 2009). It is the skills of the young learners in interpreting, considering, decoding, deciphering, transmitting, transforming and creating information visually, verbally and aurally in networked and interlinked ways (Tayler et al., 2008) that can be enhanced with and through technology (Lemon & Finger, 2013). Opportunities exist for teachers to facilitate learning as well as promote the young children to peer-teach those with different skills, experiences or knowledge (Hopkins, Green & Brookes, 2013). It is here that the early years learning space can provide opportunities for meaningful integration of technology to support continuity of learning experience across different scenarios or contexts (Chan et al., 2006).

This chapter shares how the digital device of a mobile hand-held digital camera can acknowledge both familiar and unfamiliar learning opportunities; specifically, to support the development of reflective skills, as well as much broader outcomes such as communication and problem solving, as unpacked throughout the chapter. The cases presented demonstrate how early years learners can be engaged in their learning settings as they interact with and without technology to negotiate their own understanding of the world around them through their lived experiences (see Table 5.1 for outline). The mobile technology becomes an example of how the digital camera can be a device for the children not only to interact with hands-on learning specific to technology, but also to support development in engagement with peers, teachers and other people in their learning community (Barron, 2006; Chan et al., 2006; Looi et al., 2010; Squire & Klopfer, 2007). Most importantly the teacher is afforded the opportunity to facilitate student-centred pedagogies and integrate interdisciplinary skills such as problem solving, communication, thinking, reflection and metacognitive thinking through the promotion of digital camera use.

Visual narratives produced digitally allow for the capturing of the learning environment, which allows the technology to support "anytime" and "anywhere" teaching and learning possibilities (Snyder, 1999). Digital technology has the advantage of supporting young children to share their experiences (Dillner, 2001). Conversations that occur during and after the creation of images can provide opportunities for young learners that move beyond simply writing about the photograph. Working within a constructivist framework (Denzin & Lincoln, 2000; Guba & Lincoln, 1994; Schwandt, 1994), young children's visual narratives are understood to reveal insights into their lived experiences and their existing schemas of knowledge and understanding. Photography is not about a flat or linear view of the world; rather, photography depicts and allows for a sharing of perspective and insight into life, lived experiences that can be interpreted and represented on multiple levels.

A digital camera is seen as an accessible, portable, hand-held and usable digital technology for young people to engage with (Lemon, 2008, 2014) and a valuable device in the educational setting. The digital camera as a technology gives easy access to visually produced data. It is from this perspective that the cases shared in this chapter were a part of a study that honoured the "content and structure of young children's narratives [as they] are often different in important ways from that which typically engages adults [in the learning context]" (Wright, 2011, p.162). Thus giving the young children an opportunity to create narratives through

TABLE 5.1 Outline of why digital camera was integrated into early years setting shared in this chapter.

Case	Digital camera use	Main reason for use
Year 1 class (5–6 years of age, in second year of school)	By all students in the class for the whole school year. A timetable that enables one-on-one use was developed as a class.	• Facilitate student voice and promote sense of community • Promote alternative strategy for reflection and metacognitive thinking • Integrate portable digital technology as a part of curriculum • Listen to children's perspectives on learning and teaching • Promote confidence in use of mobile digital technology

digital visual methods enables further possibilities for voice to be shared (Lemon, 2008, 2014; MacNaughton, 2003; Moss et al., 2007; Prosser, 1998).

A strength of using visual digital technology in education is the capacity to slow down and repeat observations of the learning environment (Prosser, 1998). This allows for multiple opportunities for deeper reflection, different perspectives, interruptions, questions, inquiries and the complexities that occur in the learning environment to be noticed.

The digital camera integrated into the early years setting

The digital camera was introduced to the young children as a device that they would use to share their stories of learning and teaching. The aims of this study, with five- and six-year-olds, was to show how young children are capable image-makers: they can engage productively with portable digital technology and generate digital photographs that share lived experiences of teaching and learning. In doing this, careful scaffolding had to occur in order to safely use the digital camera (for example, to wear the strap around their wrist in case of an accidental bump), to take turns in sharing one camera in the learning environment and to show mutual respect towards what peers decided to photograph and thus share as part of their visual narratives.

In designing the research (as the teacher-researcher of 28 students) I wanted this project to be a part of the learning environment, not an extra element on the side but an integral part of the teaching and learning environment. The children were collaborators in the process. They photographed throughout the calendar year and were invited to use a digital camera to record events that were important to them.

FIGURE 5.1 Celia holding the digital camera with the camera strap around her wrist, modelling how to use the camera (taken by Hannah).

There was a timetable that was decided together by all learners for a specific time when each child could use the camera (times rotated each week). At other times the camera was free from specific use, allowing opportunities for the children to photograph new discoveries that were unplanned. No limitations were set in regards to how many images were generated, rather inviting children to capture learning around them. The children themselves identified the importance of not posing or taking "silly photos that would not make sense". After the child finished taking photos, the images would be downloaded onto a computer where the child photographer would share his/her narrative, allowing for another child to use the camera. Eventually after scaffolding from the teacher, children learnt how to download images and began to teach each other. Some students explored attaching photographs to emails to send to family and other programs that allowed for inserting images and typing reflections about the photograph's intentions as a way to extend their interest in digital technologies. In the sharing of photographs and the narratives that emerged, close connections were made to ongoing reflection, with links made to opportunities to assess learning.

Following scheduled sessions within the curriculum, where photographs were taken independently, the child was invited to discuss and reflect on why they had taken the photograph(s) (intention) and what it/they meant to them. These discussions took the form of either a written reflection (reflective journal entry, graphic organizer such as a mind map or a graffiti wall entry) or a conversation one-to-one with myself as their teacher, a peer, a small group of classmates or the whole class. The children always had a choice about whether they would reflect, how they would do this and with whom. This is where the intertextuality of photographs and text, that is, the shaping of a text's meaning by another text, was honoured. It is the stories of learning created by the student-generated visual narratives that enabled the lived experience to be shared.

The digital camera provided opportunity for reflection in the early years learning environment. Verbal responses to photographic visuals became a regular occurrence in the classroom. The young children built on the process of using a digital camera and reflected on their own photographs in a variety of situations. Each time, the children were encouraged to offer their photographs for learning experiences that promoted reflection through mediums such as child-directed class discussions, digital stories, vignettes of learning published in the learning environment newsletter, wall displays, graffiti walls or graphic organizers. Photographs were used for reflection, with sentence starters being used as both prompts and as a modelling strategy. Reflection was undertaken in written, verbal or visual modes, providing the children with an opportunity to use their preferred mode of reflection.

In the next section of this chapter four cases are shared that illuminate how five children responded to using the digital camera in the early years context. Visual narratives generated by the children are shared, with their own digital images and the narratives paired with the photographs, to show how young people are capable photographers of their lived experiences of the learning environment. Through this sharing of lived experiences there was the opportunity for reflective and metacognitive thinking, problem solving, communication and peer teaching.

Voices from the learning environment

James – a young man developing confidence to communicate

As an English as second language student, James was a young man who struggled to find his sense of belonging. Introducing James to the digital camera provided him with a tool to practice his new language skills and communicate these to his teacher, peers, integration aide and family. Over time the digital camera became a mobile technology for him to use that instilled confidence to share his lived experiences. The kinaesthetic nature of using the digital camera – that is, physically placing the camera close to the eye, focusing on content to be captured and moving around the learning environment – contributed greatly to his capacity to communicate his feelings about his learning environment and about his own learning skills. Previously he had been frustrated at times and displayed a mixture of anger or withdrawal. When he learnt to use the digital camera, and was trusted to use it to capture what he was interested in, the authentic nature of the integration of the digital camera assisted James to move towards learning opportunities that interested him. This way of being enabled him to celebrate his skills and his learning preferences. There was a shift from focusing on learning how to speak English towards learning how to use the technology that then required him to communicate what he had photographed. For James, movement associated with using the digital camera and being a photographer enabled observation and interaction with others.

> That's the grade six classroom [learning environment]. [See Figure 5.2.¹] I took it because my buddy [friend] used to be in it. I'm friends with some grade sixers like Thomas, Jordan and Monty. Do you know Jordan Miss Lemon? [teacher-researcher] He's good at kicks. He has glasses. (James)

It was intended that the use of the digital camera, the generation of digital photographs and the sharing of lived experiences would be inclusive (Sapon-Shevin, 2007). This was demonstrated, for example, as James's confidence grew with using the digital camera, generating photographs of his learning experiences. His sharing of his photos with others allowed him to realise he would be listened to and that he could communicate what he was experiencing. Most importantly, his narratives, spoken in English rather than his mother tongue, developed over time to be intricate and detailed (see Figure 5.3). His oral language skills supported reading and writing skills, and produced a shift from frustration with learning to speak English and communicate with others to a more positive experience.

FIGURE 5.2 That's the grade six classroom [learning environment].

FIGURE 5.3 Joy [learning support aide] gave me silkworms to look after.

Joy [learning support aide] gave me silkworms to look after (Figure 5.3). I have to take them home everyday and feed them and care for them. I have to get leaves from the tree outside our room.

One's Spike [naming the silkworm] and he's six centimetres. This is Delicious cause he eats too much [referring to the mulberry leaves]. This is Fight cause he has a bruise on the back. See. He was fighting with another silkworm. This morning I put new leaves in because they ate so much when I was out.

Yesterday they went to bed late because they were sneaky and wouldn't stop eating. We left the light on and then we turned it off. One climbed up the wall [of the shoe box] and then pushed the leaf down. Now they are lazy because they were so full. (James)

Stan – self-awareness of learning behaviour

The digital camera ignited an enthusiasm in Stan that was contradictory to past behaviour where low motivation, tiredness and refusal to participate in learning activities often dominated. With the digital camera in hand, Stan explored his learning experiences with a new-found confidence.

There's you [teacher] helping Max to find another one [another word] [see Figure 5.4]. He's getting it and he's being a risk taker. You're helping and that's really good since sometimes he forgets.

For Stan the slowing of time through the generation of the photographs encouraged him to slow down and communicate the story he wished to share. Of particular focus for Stan was the ability to observe social behaviour that was more desirable when working with others (see Figures 5.4 and 5.5). His visual narratives enabled a self-awareness of reflection of others that he could then apply to himself.

Brad and Mark are working together like a team. They are doing really well and when they finish it may be Miss Lemon might let them do whatever they want to build.

FIGURE 5.4 There's you helping Max to find another one.

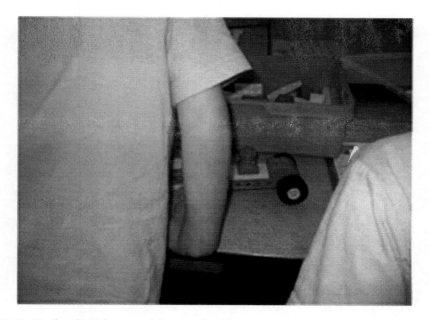

FIGURE 5.5 Brad and Mark are working together like a team.

Over time Stan's language developed, as did his confidence and desire to write his stories. Previously he would actively avoid writing activities. Communication was closely connected to his development in emotional and social skills. Stan soon realised his peers enjoyed and appreciated his expression of joy during image-making and encouraged him to continue to do this during non-camera activities.

Jane and Rachel – being environmentally conscious

When given the opportunity to photograph outside the physical constraints of the learning environment's four walls and into the learning space of the school grounds, Jane and Rachel's photographs gave insight into their intentions behind the stories that are connected to their visual narratives. Hedges (2004) presents the concept that reflection can be knowledgeable and contribute to learning and thinking about environments. In the following photographs (see Figures 5.6 and 5.7), the children's narrative supports an interest in environmental aspects associated with the actual learning setting, providing insights into the learning of the macro- rather than the micro-environment

> I took this bin photo because we could have more bins around the school. They could be littler so we don't have to waste plastic or metal. (Rachel)

In using visual narrative in the learning environment, opportunities are provided to evoke memories around which we construct and reconstruct life stories. For Rachel and Jane, the visual narratives shared in this chapter provide examples of how they reflected upon the environment, as well as specific units of inquiry and learning activities that had been experienced previously.

FIGURE 5.6 I took this bin photo because we could have more bins around the school. (Rachel)

FIGURE 5.7 This one is the environment. And not to litter on anything. (Jane)

Mark – engaging with family

Mark introduced visual narratives to his family while on their holiday. As an example of life-long learning, Mark shared his engagement with taking photographs in the classroom with his family. He was able to use and share his newly developed skills and interest in a different context. Mark then returned to the classroom and shared the interaction with his peers. The dialogue between Mark and myself was only brief, but is one of many examples of the digital camera's impact beyond the classroom.

Extract 5.1 Engaging with family

Mark: On my holiday I was allowed to take photos on my mum and dad's camera.

Narelle: Haven't you done that before?

Mark: No. I wasn't allowed to use it. [Pause]. Mum saw my photos I took with you. She thought they were good and wanted to see what I would take on our holiday.

Narelle: Did you talk about your photos?

Mark: Yeah of course! … like I do with you. Mum said I saw things she didn't. Dad said I talked a lot about the photos, more than I talk at home sometimes. My sister wanted to have a go as well. She liked pointing things out on the photos. I liked sharing what I think. Now everyone can see what I see … see by the photos [points to the images].

This transference of new skills with digital technology from the learning environment at school to within his family highlights how working with the digital camera supports authentic learning opportunities. Mark's experiences afford him the opportunity to continually develop and extend his communication skills, ability to reflect and problem-solving skills across multiple sites. His willingness to explore digital visual narratives and technology supported his ability to share his voice.

Conclusion

The digital camera is seen as a portable and accessible technology that young children can engage with. With a digital camera integrated into the learning environment, as teacher-researcher I was able to establish a community of learners in which the young children could explore their sense of belonging by the honouring of their lived experiences and voice. Through the promotion of mutual respect for both the use of the digital camera and sharing of experiences, the children were encouraged to be insightful contributors to learning and teaching.

The cases in this chapter use visual narrative inquiry to explore and make "meaning of experience both visually and narratively" (Bach, 2007, p. 282) that is empirically robust (Guillemin & Drew, 2010; Penn, 2000). "When used instrumentally, photographs can [lead to] deliberate learning, reflection and growth" (Lemon, 2007, p. 183), "reinforcing concepts and having the capacity to extend learning to teaching others" (Lemon, 2006, p. 7). Photography is a powerful research method due to its unique capacity to capture "details, memories, emotions, and meanings" (Loeffler, 2004, p. 2). The cases demonstrate how reflection and metacognitive thinking can be developed through the construction of visual narratives. Highlighted in the chapter is how young people, when trusted, are capable digital image-makers who can confidently share their lived experiences to explore their own learning needs in an authentic way.

Note

1   Please note that all visual narratives are generated by the early years children and are representational of how they communicated their lived experiences; as a result some grammatical errors are present.

References

Anstey, M. & Bull, G. (2006). *Teaching and Learning Multiliteracies: Changing Times, Changing Literacies*. Kensington Gardens, South Australia: Australian Literacy Educators Association.

Bach, H. (2007). Composing a visual narrative inquiry. In: D. J. Clandinin (Ed.), *Handbook of Narrative Inquiry: Mapping a Methodology* (pp. 280–308). London: Sage Publications.

Baker, E. (2010). *The New Literacies: Multiple Perspectives on Research and Practice*. New York: The Guildford Press.

Barron, B. (2006). Interest and self-sustained learning as catalysts of development: a learning ecologies perspective. *Human Development, 49*(4), 193–224.

Burns, M., Dimock, V. & Martinez, D. (2000). Storytelling in a digital age. *Tap into Learning, 3*(2), 6–9.

Carr, M. (2001). *Assessment in Early Childhood Settings: Learning Stories*. London: Paul Chapman Publishing.

Chan, T. W., Roschelle, J., Hsi, S., Kinshuk, Sharples, M., Brown, T., Patton, C., Cherniavsky, J., Pea, R., Norris, C., Soloway, E., Balacheff, N., Scardamalia, M., Dillenbourg, P., Looi, C., Milrad, M. & Hoppee, U. (2006). One-to-one technology-enhanced learning: an opportunity for global research collaboration. *Research and Practice of Technology Enhanced Learning* 1(1), 3–29.

Chen, H. L. (2005). *Reflection in an Always-on Learning Environment: Has It Been Turned Off?* Retrieved June 2008 from http://campustechnology.com/articles/40502/

Cloonan, A. (2010). *Multiliteracies, Multimodality and Teacher Professional Learning.* Melbourne: Common Ground Publishing.

Cope, B. & Kalantzis, M. (Eds) (2000). *Multiliteracies: Literacy Learning and the Design of Social Futures.* London: Routledge.

Denzin, N. K. & Lincoln, Y. S. (Eds) (2000). *Handbook of Qualitative Research* (2nd ed.). Thousand Oaks, CA: Sage Publications.

Dillner, M. (2001). Using media flexibly to compose and communicate. *Reading Online, 5*(1). Retrieved 22 July 2013 from http://www.readwritethink.org/resources/resource-print.html?id=985

Edward-Groves, C. & Langley, M. (2009). i-Kindy. Responding to home technoliteracies in the kindergarten classroom. Paper presented at the National Conference for Teachers of English and Literacy. Hobart: English Literacy Conference

Ewald, W. & Lightfoot, A. (2001). *I Wanna Take Me a Picture – Teaching Photography and Writing to Children.* Boston: Center for Documentary Studies (in association with Beacon Press).

Guba, E. & Lincoln, Y. (1994). *Naturalistic Inquiry.* Beverly Hills, CA: Sage Publications.

Guillemin, M. & Drew, S. (2010). Questions of process in participant-generated visual methodologies. *Visual Studies, 25*(2), 175–88.

Hargreaves, D. (2003). Personalising learning: next steps in working laterally, *Journal of Educational Policy, 17*(4), 399–430.

Hedges, H. (2004). A whale of an interest in sea creatures: the learning potential of excursions. *Early Childhood Research and Practice, 6*(1), 1–6.

Hopkins. L., Green, J. & Brookes, F. (2013). Books, bytes and brains: the implications of new knowledge for children's early literacy learning. *Australasian Journal of Early Childhood, 38*(1).

Leitch, R. (2008). Creatively researching children's narratives through image and drawings. In: P. Thompson (Ed.) *Get the Picture: Visual Research with Children and Young People* (pp. 35–58). London: RoutledgeFalmer.

Lemon, N. (2006). Using visual narrative for reflection. Refereed abstract for Australian Association for Educational Research Annual Conference (pp. 1–17). December 2006, Adelaide.

Lemon, N. (2007). Take a photograph: teacher reflection through narrative. *Journal of Reflective Practice, 8*(2), 177–91.

Lemon, N. (2008). Looking through the lens of a camera in the early childhood classroom. In: J. Moss (Ed.), *Research Education: Visually-Digitally-Spatially* (pp. 21–52). Rotterdam: Sense Publishers.

Lemon, N. (2014). Image making as a way to build a sense of belonging and wellbeing in young people. In: S. Garvis & D. Pendergast (Eds), *Health and Wellbeing in the Early Years* (pp. 206–21). Sydney: Cambridge University Press.

Lemon, N. & Finger, G. (2013). Digital technology. In: D. Pendergast & S. Garvis (Eds), *Teaching Early Years: Rethinking Curriculum, Pedagogy and Assessment.* (pp. 141–64). Crows Nest: Allen & Unwin.

Loeffler, T. A. (2004). A picture is worth … capturing meaning and facilitating connections using outdoor students' photographs. Paper presented at the International Outdoor Education Research Conference, Latrobe University, Bendigo.

Looi, C., Seow, P., Zhang, B., So, H. J., Chen, W. & Wong, L. H. (2010). Leveraging mobile technology for sustainable seamless learning: a research agenda. *British Journal of Educational Technology, 41*, 154–69.

MacNaughton, G. (2003). Eclipsing voice in research with young children. *Australian Journal of Early Childhood Education, 28*(1), 36–42.

Ministerial Council on Education, Employment, Childhood Development and Youth Affairs. (MCEECDYA) (2008). *Melbourne Declaration on Educational Goals for Young Australians.* Canberra: Ministerial Council on Education, Employment, Training and Youth Affairs.

Moss, J. (Ed.) (2008). *Educational Researchers Working – Visually-Digitally-Spatially.* Rotterdam: Sense Publications.

Moss, J., Deppeler, J., Astley, L. & Pattison, K. (2007). Student researchers in the middle: using visual images to make sense of inclusive education. *Journal of Research in Special Educational Needs, 7*(1), 46–54.

Moyle, K. (2010). *Building Innovation: Learning with Technologies*. Camberwell: Australian Council for Educational Research.

Northcote, M. (2011). Step back and hand over the cameras! Using digital cameras to facilitate mathematics learning with young children in K-2 classrooms. *Teaching with Technology, 16*(3), 29–32.

Pahl, K. & Rowsell, J. (2005). *Literacy and Education: Understanding the New Literacy Studies in the Classroom*. London: Paul Chapman Publishing.

Pasor, E. & Kerns, E. (1997). A digital snapshot of an early childhood classroom. *Educational Leadership, 55*(3), 42–45.

Penn, G. (2000). *Semiotic Analysis of Still Images, Qualitative Researching with Text, Image and Sound*. London: Sage Publications.

Plowman, L. & Stephen, C. (2005). Children, play, and computers in pre-school education. *British Journal of Educational Technology, 36*(2), 145–57.

Prosser, J. (Ed.) (1998). *Image-based Research: A Sourcebook for Qualitative Researchers*. London: Falmer Press.

Richards, R. D. (2009). Young visual ethnographers: children's use of digital photography to record, share and extend their art experiences. *International Art in Early Childhood Research Journal, 1*(1), 1–16.

Sapon-Shevin, M. (2007). *Widening the Circle: The Power of Inclusive Classrooms*. Boston: Beacon Press.

Schwandt, T. A. (1994). Constructivist, interpretivist approaches to human inquiry. In: N. Denzin & Y. S. Lincoln (Eds), *Handbook of Qualitative Research* (pp. 729–49). London: Sage Publications.

Snyder, I. (1999). Using information technology in language and literacy education: an introduction. In: J. Hancock (Ed.), *Teaching Literacy Using Information Technology: A Collection of Articles from Australian Literacy Educators' Association* (pp. 1–10). Newark, DE: International Reading Association.

Squire, K. & Klopfer, E. (2007). Augmented reality simulations on handheld computers. *Journal of the Learning Sciences, 16*(3), 371–413.

Tayler, C., Ure, C., Brown, R., Deans, J. & Cronin, B. (2008). Victorian early years learning and development framework and the Victorian essential learning standards. Draft discussion paper. Melbourne: The University of Melbourne.

Wright, S. (2011). *Children Meaning-making and the Arts*. Brisbane: Pearson.

Yelland, N. (1999). Technology as play. *Early Childhood Education Journal, 26*(4), 217–20.

6

SHARED CURIOSITY, TECHNOLOGY AND MATHEMATICS

Exploring transitions between two and three dimensions

Geir Olaf Pettersen, Monica Volden and Elin Eriksen Ødegaard

Abstract

This chapter will investigate what happens when teacher-researchers invite a group of children to an activity with the aim of providing children experiences with mathematics. Two selected episodes from a series of video observations over time in one kindergarten in Norway afford rich descriptions of activities that combine digital artefacts with non–digital. Both activities are planned as a shared curiosity-driven inquiry following a sociocultural framework for didactic practice.

Introduction

Today there is both a presumption and an antagonism about the connection between digital technology and children's learning. In kindergartens, materials such as wooden and plastic blocks in three dimensions (3D) and mathematical shapes in two dimensions (2D) have played an important role in children's explorative and playful learning for centuries. Our outset is the fact that there are connections between the material world and the models of it, which is central to the kindergarten tradition.

When tablets and interactive devices become more common in kindergartens and are used as supplements to material artefacts, activities can be varied in new ways. Children have often been portrayed as passive recipients when watching television or playing computer games. The premise of this study, however, portrays children as actors and participant explorers when using digital and material artefacts in kindergarten activities.

The aim of the study was to develop knowledge about children's use of and explorations with tablets with touch screens, particularly in relation to material for construction and mathematical understanding and learning. Empirical data was collected and created through describing descriptive (narratives), visual and auditive data (video and stills) from explorative situations where adults and children explore transitions from 2D to 3D and vice versa.

The case consists of two selected empirical activities that will form the basis for analysis and reflection. The questions first investigated are as follows:

- What happens in activities where children are given the opportunity to explore by combining digital and non-digital artefacts?
- What happens when children switch between digital and non-digital artefacts?
- Do the artefacts add something to each other?

This chapter will provide descriptions of explorative activities in order to illuminate how children and teachers can explore a mathematical problem together. The case will explain how the teacher-researchers created activities characterised by endurance and how the children contributed to the activity with motives and curiosity for explorative activities.

Children participating in the exploration of artefacts – a theoretical framework

Friedrich Fröbel recognised the importance of the activity of the child in play and learning. By introducing "toy gifts" for children, he argued that they were enabled to explore mathematical and scientific concepts (such as numbers, shapes and sizes) through direct manipulation of physical objects. As children grew older, he introduced more complex patterns (models) and more blocks of various shapes. This should enable the child to manipulate and explore the world of mathematics in more advanced combinations and progression (Fröbel & Hailmann, 2005).

Following a Froebelian approach, digital technology such as programmable building blocks can serve as a variation in explorative activities. Digital technology can enable young children to experience and differentiate between different shapes and, as a consequence, help them learn concepts that previously were considered too advanced for them (Resnick, 1998).

Looking into the field of early play research, we can see that a distinction was made between play and exploration (Hutt, 1966). Children will either explore or play in completely unfamiliar surroundings with unfamiliar issues, but in familiar surroundings they will be content to explore new things. According to Hutt (1966), familiar surroundings with familiar issues constitute favourable conditions for play. Exploration can be said to be a form of play activity that generally occurs when children encounter new objects, materials or toys and as they become familiar with the features, forms and materiality of these new things.

The term "artefact" is of Latin origin: *arte* or *art*, meaning art, and *factum* or *facereto*, meaning to make or create (Ødegaard, 2012). Here we use the term "artefact" for blocks, tablets and models of mathematical shapes. We will occasionally use the term "tool" as a synonym.

The Russian philosopher Marx Wartofsky believed that human experience and insight are intertwined with cultural artefacts. He argued further that it is inappropriate to create a distinction between artefacts that are tangible, such as a block, and artefacts that are based on signs, language and models, which are more or less abstract. By developing three categories, i.e. primary, secondary and tertiary artefacts, he revealed that various forms of artefacts create conditions for what is possible to do and think. Blocks as tactile objects can be considered a primary artefact because they can be used as a tool to build with. When the block is used as an imaginary artefact – for example, when a child pretends that the block is something else – one can say that the block is now a secondary artefact mediating an insight or understanding, or an attempt to arrive at such understanding. This could be considered an explorative activity.

The tablet is also a tool for many different activities. In this study, tablets are used for the purpose of variation in the activity. With certain educational applications, shapes can be manipulated with colours; different angles and shapes can be unfolded and packed together into two- and three-dimensional shapes. The tablet is thus a primary artefact. The application used in the activity offers representations and models of mathematical shapes and is thus also a secondary artefact (certain characters and icons make things happen) showing a tertiary artefact, i.e. a model.

The empirical study is inspired by a sociocultural framework. More specifically, we use the term "activity" with reference to activity theory, a theory derived from the dialectical materialism of Marx and the psychological works of Vygotsky (Sam, 2012). Activity theory is a framework to study the actions of people on both an individual and a societal level simultaneously. The unit of analysis is an activity, a conscious action directed at a goal, and this conscious action includes context as well as relations to tools and people (Hedegaard, Edwards & Fleer, 2012). In our study an activity is seen as events initiated by teacher-researchers in a kindergarten. Two activities are selected for analysis. Each activity consists of interacting components and their relationships to one another. Such sociocultural theoretical concepts are well suited to researching children's and teachers' activities in an institutional setting.

Mariane Hedegaard follows Marx Wartofsky's philosophical idea of human's dynamic relation to objects. The starting point here is not the child's primary need, rather humans' general relation to the world. According to Hedegaard's approach to children's activities in institutional practice (2012), activity settings are often structures of traditions. Activities can be analysed as a situation in process where certain dynamic aspects will be revealed. The concept of motive can open analysis for how the dynamic in human activities evolves around objects (Hedegaard, 2012). Change in a child's development and learning happens when the child is introduced to a new kind of practice. Variations and new activities extend the child's activities. A child's activity can be understood as directed towards the transformation of an object that could satisfy a need. The child will, as a consequence, not only adapt to a task and demand, but will also contribute to the development of the activity.

Visualisations of shapes

Geometric content can be divided into the following four categories: shape and properties, transformations, locations and visualisations. The recognition of shapes in the environment and the relationships between two-dimensional and three-dimensional shapes are included in the visualisations category (Van de Walle et al., 2012).

Spatial visualisation is about making and manipulating mental pictures of two- dimensional and three-dimensional shapes (Føsker, 2012). This includes the ability to rotate an object mentally. This means the ability to see what an object will look like after being rotated around its own axes. It also includes the ability to mentally transform a shape from two dimensions to three dimensions and to recognise it after this transformation (Føsker, 2012). These parts of the spatial visualisations do not require children's physical movements.

Levels of geometric thinking

Van Hiele (1999) developed a five-level hierarchy of geometric thinking, which consists of the following levels: 0, visual level; 1, descriptive level; 2, informal deduction level; 3, formal deduction level; and 4, rigor level. In the kindergarten settings, level 0 and level 1 are the most relevant ones.

Level 0 begins with non-verbal thinking, where children recognise shapes without having words for them (van Hiele, 1999). Children can sort shapes by comparing their appearance, and argue that they are in the same group "because they look alike". The shapes are recognised as wholes and are given name from their appearance, and what they look like. For example, children might call a shape a 'rectangle' because 'it looks like a door' or a sphere might be called a ball.

At the next level children can recognise, characterise and sort shapes by their properties (van Hiele, 1999). At this descriptive level language is important to describe shapes. Each shape has different properties, for example a square is a plane figure with four equal sides and four equal angles. A child at this level is able to identify such properties for a shape, both 2D and 3D. Understanding and explaining relationships between classes of figures, such as why a square is a special type of rectangle, and informal deductive argument about shapes and their properties are characteristic of level 2.

The development from one level to another is dependent on the children's experience and teaching, not on their age (van Hiele, 1999). Van de Walle et al. (2012) have developed teaching activities to help children move from one level to another based on van Hiele's geometric thinking. Clements and Sarama (2007) argue that use of different concrete models will help children develop spatial skills. In the present study we have used activities from Van de Walle et al. and adapted them to be used together with an iPad and concrete shapes.

Empirical case study

To obtain in-depth knowledge about the activities, a case study approach was chosen (Cohen, Manion & Morrison, 2007). The aim was to explore the situation where children, together with kindergarten teachers and researchers, are exploring new artefacts. The children in the examples are four to six years of age. The research project was approved by the Norwegian Social Science Data Services (NSD).

Data was collected with video of the situation. Two cameras were placed in a bird's-eye perspective facing the floor. The video from both cameras was synchronised in Adobe Premiere CS6 and was transcribed using Inqscribe (v.2.2.1). All three researchers were involved in selecting the two cases presented in this chapter from the empirical data. The transcription is presented as a narrative/rich text in order to describe the activity in a more detailed and readable way. Excerpts from the case are marked with increased indent and dialogs are marked with numbers. The presentation of the cases is broken into smaller parts with comments in between.

The goal in the activity described was to direct the children's attention to mathematical subjects like the transition between 2D and 3D, problem solving and cooperation. In the descriptions of the selected didactic events, the focus will be on the children's explorations and interactions with the artefacts and the teacher-researchers.

Artefacts

The artefacts used in this study were chosen to give children the opportunity to investigate the relationship between 2D and 3D.

Shapes – 3D Geometry Learning

Shapes – 3D Geometry Learning was released in 2012 under the name *Solid Elementary HD*.[1] *Shapes* shows different solids. By touching the screen one can unfold and fold the solids. This gives an opportunity to investigate which 2D shapes a 3D shape consists of.

Polydron

Polydron building set contains different shapes like squares and triangles that can be clicked together to form cubes, prisms and three-dimensional shapes. This present study uses square frames. By clicking the edges together it is possible to make a cube. However, the edges must align right in order to be put together.

Folding 2D/3D Geometric Solids

These are hands-on 3D shapes. Each of the shapes has both a clear plastic container and a folding net housed inside. There are 11 different shapes and six different colours. The shapes give children the opportunity to feel and touch the shapes both in two and three dimensions. This means that children can explore this transformation through both tactile and visual senses.

Activities

This present study contains two cases where the activities are planned by the researchers together with the pedagogical staff in a kindergarten. The aim of the activities with the children was to focus on the properties of shapes.

In the first activity, kindergarten children were given different three-dimensional traditional shapes in combination with an iPad application. The aim for the activity is that children should be able to experience how these three-dimensional shapes are transformed into a net, which is a two-dimensional representation of a three-dimensional shape.

The second activity is called "Face matching, find a shape with these faces" and addresses the transformation between two-dimensional and three-dimensional shapes (Van de Walle et al., 2012, pp. 428–29, activity 20.27).

First, we showed a paper sheet with six square faces, and three three-dimensional shapes, including a right cylinder, triangle prism and cube (see Figure 6.1). The children should recognise which of the three-dimensional shapes this could represent. We also showed them

FIGURE 6.1 Face matching.

a three-dimensional shape and then asked them to pick the two-dimensional shapes they needed to make the three-dimensional shape.

After spending some time exploring similar tasks the iPad was introduced with the application *Shapes*. The iPad provided an opportunity to investigate further the transformation between two-dimensional and three-dimensional shapes.

Ida explores the cube[2]

The activity presented here is an open explorative, albeit organised activity in a kindergarten. The excerpt is an overview of the activity. It lasted for about 50 minutes from the beginning to the point where Ida had put together her cube with help from Tiril and an iPad.

Monica and Geir Olaf (two of the researcher teachers) sit down on the floor and pick up a prism built from squares. The box in front of them has several squares in different colours. Together with the children, Monica and Geir Olaf start to investigate the prism. They wonder what it looks like, what it can be used for and how many squares you need to make one. All the children start to count faces. "Five" and "seven" can be heard. "Yes, it is seven", says Ida. Then they count together, two blue, two red and two yellow sides. "It has to be six!" The children now have to build their own prism. This one is called a "cube".

In the beginning of the activity Monica and Geir Olaf ask questions to make the children curious about the cube. In the dialog they are indirectly focusing on the properties of the cube, i.e. asking what it can be used for. Will it roll? The cube is built from six squares and three colours. Three different colours are used to help the children count. Before they start to count, the children have to make assumptions about how many faces they believe it has. As we can see from the excerpts, their assumptions varied from five to seven faces.

Ida gets six pieces and starts to put two and two together. She holds up one of the pieces and says, "I can't do this". The girl next to Ida turns around and puts the pieces together. Now, Ida takes a break; she looks into the camera, at the other children and at Janne (kindergarten teacher). The other children now have managed to put together their cubes. Janne helps Ida so that she also gets a cube. It fits on her wrist. "Look", she says to Janne.

After about 45 minutes, Ida has decided to make her own cube and asks Monica for help. They have also invested the cube with some spatial properties, i.e. one can put something inside it or use it as a bracelet. They have also used the iPad to investigate the transitions from two-dimensional shapes to three-dimensional shapes. However, they did not use the application to understand the polydron and vice versa in a very clear way.

At the very end of the activity Tiril is using the application to show Ida a net that will turn into a cube. Even though they did not build the net exactly like the one on the iPad, it is obvious that they are using it like building instructions. They build a T instead of a cross with the polydrons.

According to van Hiele (1999), the development of understanding and the ability to discriminate between shapes and properties are dependent on experience. The way of learning in this open-framed activity will offer opportunities to explore shapes and properties in a variety of materials. The activity is framed in a way that allows the children to touch, see, listen and switch between artefacts, which seems to motivate the children to explore.

The next activity has a stronger framing than the previous activity. In this activity the teacher-researchers have designed several opportunities for problem-solving and discovering. However, the children are free to leave the activity at any point. In that way the activity could also be seen as an open activity.

Open activity about shapes

Monica is sitting on the floor. Together with Geir Olaf, she has brought some foldable solids and two iPads. Together with four five-year-old children, they want to explore the relationship between 2D and 3D shapes. One of the kindergarten boys has already entered the room. Monica and this boy are talking about the shapes. The examples are in chronological order from the organised activity.

Extract 6.1 Stephen talks about shapes

1. Monica: You have done this before, haven't you? Last year? We explored these shapes.
2. Stephen: Which shapes?
3. Monica: These shapes.
              She takes out four of the shapes and staples them like a tower.
4. Stephen: Which one do you think is the best?
5. Monica: Which one is the best? Maybe this one. Because it can roll far.
              She takes the cylinder and shows how it can roll over the floor.
6. Monica: Which one do you like the best?
7. Stephen: The triangle?
              He is pointing to a prism with a triangular top and bottom shape.
8. Monica: Do you like the triangle best?
              She takes out the prism.
9. Monica   But it doesn't only have triangles.
              She points at the sides of the prism. In the meantime, the last three children, Martin, Isabel and Sarah, have entered the room.
10. Isabel: Has it already started?

This is the opening of the activity. Instead of gathering the children and introducing the activity, the adult is already sitting on the floor waiting for the children. This might raise their curiosity about what will happen next. The talk between Monica and Stephen is an example of this. Isabel acknowledges that she knew about the visit in her question (turn 10) when she asks "Has it already started?" Without being told what to do, the children take their place in front of Monica in a small circle. She reminds them that about one year ago they did a similar activity. Monica arranges four prisms in front of her.

Extract 6.2 Monica talks about shapes

11. Monica: What is the name of these shapes?
              She picks up the right cylinder and points to the top and bottom of it.
12. Isabel: A rounding.[3]
13. Monica: It is a rounding, yes.
14. Martin: And circle.

15. Monica: Yes, because it is totally round, and then we can say it's a circle. What about this then?

          She picks up a triangular prism with square faces.

16. Isabel and Stephen: A triangle.

          Sara is nodding but she didn't say anything.

17. Monica: And it also has?

18. Stephen and Isabel: A quadrilateral.[4]

19. Monica: Are there different quadrilaterals?

20. Martin: Hmm.

21. Monica: This one is totally quadrilateral. Do you know the name?

          She waits for about five second before she says, "A square".

22. Monica: What about this?

          She picks up a square prism.

23. Martin: Quadrilateral.

          She picks up the last prism again.

24. Monica: It is also a quadrilateral. Do you see that they are the same, but one is …?

          She compares the two faces.

25. Martin: Bigger, one is bigger.

          He points at the faces of the first prism.

          Monica puts down the first prism and holds the last one up, pointing at the rectangular faces.

26. Sarah: A rectangle.

27. Monica: It's a rectangle, yes, and it is a kind of quadrilateral, isn't it? Because it has four sides.

          Monica puts her finger on each side as she counts one, two, three and four.

In this excerpt Monica is asking more closed questions, i.e. what is the name of this shape? The children use their vocabulary to answer the questions. Martin says a "rounding". Monica repeats the word "rounding", but also explains the term "circle".

Here Monica is trying to focus on properties. She compares two different quadrilaterals and shows that they both have four sides. The children are focusing on appearance. This can be seen in turn 23 when Martin calls a square a quadrilateral and in 25 when he only compares size when Monica is asking for the differences. This could indicate that Martin is at level 0 in van Hiele's model (van Hiele, 1999). As a consequence, Martin gains more experience by being a part of the explorative activity.

Extract 6.3 Find the corresponding 3D shape

Monica takes an A3 paper sheet with pictures of two circles and one rectangle. This is the second task for the children. From the given faces, they should find the corresponding 3D shape (See Figure 6.2).

28. Stephen: A smile.
29. Isabel: No, an angry mouth.
30. Martin: Eye, eye, mouth (dragging his finger along the rectangle).
31. Monica: If I put this together?
        Both Isabel and Martin point to the cylinder
32. Monica: Will this one be?
        She takes the cylinder and puts it in front of herself.
33. Monica: Do you agree? Why?
34. Martin: Because they are roundings. (He points at the circles.)
35. Monica: What about that one? (She points at the rectangle on the paper sheet.)
        Martin takes the square prism with rectangular faces and lifts it up.
        Isabel points at another prism and says, "That one".
36. Monica: Could it be around here (moving her fingers around the cylinder)?
37. Monica: Should we try? And see if we are right.
38.   Oh (Martin, Stephen and Isabel unfold the shape.)
39. Stephen: It doesn't work, because it will be too long.
40. Monica: It fits quite well?
41. Geir Olaf: Does the circle fit?
42. Martin: No.
43. Geir Olaf: Try.
44. Martin: (Looking at Geir Olaf) It doesn't fit. Because then it will be like that.
        He shows that the circle doesn't fit on the circle on the paper at
        the same time.

In the beginning of this excerpt the children interpreted the circles and the rectangle as a smile. This indicates van Hiele level 0. Martin (turn 34) identifies the circles but uses the term "roundings". One indication that the children are focusing on appearance occurs in turn 38. Monica wants them to say that the rectangle is wrapped around the right cylinder. It is not obvious to see that two circles and a rectangle compose a right cylinder, so they start to look for other three-dimensional shapes. Martin is picking up a square prism with rectangular faces and Isabel is pointing to the box containing the rest of the Folding 2D/3D Geometric Solids.

After unfolding the cylinder they see two circles on both sides of the rectangle. This confuses the children because the foldable cylinder does not look like a face when they

FIGURE 6.2 Find the corresponding 3D shape.

unfold it. They try to match it on the paper sheet, but in addition to being in different positions, the circles and rectangles are also a different size than they originally were on the paper. In turn 39, Stephen states that the rectangle would be too long.

Extract 6.4 iPads and shapes

About 12 minutes into the activity, Monica introduces the iPads. There are two iPads available. She starts the application *Shapes* and then gives the iPads to the children and tells them to find a pentagonal prism they have been exploring.

45. Monica:	Do you find a shape that looks like this (holding the pentagonal prism)?
46. Stephen:	What are we really supposed to do? (He poses the question again.)
47. Stephen:	It is a quadrilateral. (He only sees one face of the prism.)
48. Geir Olaf:	Is it? Try to turn it around.
	Stephen uses two fingers to rotate the shape on the iPad.
49. Martin:	It is not a quadrilateral.
50. Stephen:	It is not a quadrilateral.
51. Monica:	Is it correct that it is a pentagon? (Both of the boys agree.)
	Geir Olaf says that it is possible to make it a bit bigger and shows how to enlarge the image, dragging two fingers away from each other. Monica explains how they can drag a finger to open the 3D shape and transform it into a 2D shape, i.e. a net.
52. Monica:	Now you can see that it opens.
53. Martin:	Cool.
	Monica, Geir Olaf and the children are exploring the shapes on the iPad. After a while, Stephen is still not sure what to do. He and Isabel are colouring the shapes.
54. Stephen:	Now we are done.
	He says that about 15 minutes in to the activity. He continues for half a minute and then he says the following:
55. Stephen:	Are we going to do something else?
	Monica responds with a "yes" but does not follow up, and Stephen goes back to moving the shape around on the iPad. Monica waits for 40 seconds before she asks them if they should do something else. She tells them to put away the iPads.

The iPads and the application were not introduced into the activity for almost 12 minutes. After the iPad introduction the children ask what to do for the first time. This could indicate that they have trouble focusing on the activity because of their concentration, or it could also indicate that they do not see the connections between the application and the shapes they have been working on. Monica does not respond in full to the question, instead giving them some time before she tells them to put away the iPads and gives them a new task with the single-face cards.

FIGURE 6.3 Application shapes.

Extract 6.5 Yellow square pyramid

They now explore a yellow square pyramid. From a collection of single-face cards, Monica asks them to pick which one goes with the square pyramid. Isabel says it has to be triangles because of the vertex. Martin suggests a square. After unfolding the square pyramid to check themselves, the children are asked to get the iPads and to find the shape in the application. Stephen is scrolling fast through the shapes on the iPad.

56. Martin:	There it is (stopping at a triangular prism). It is the pyramid.
57. Geir Olaf:	Is it the same one?
58. Stephen:	No, it's longer.
	He does not find it and has to start all over again in the application. He presses the pyramid section in the application. Monica shows him how to mark the edges red so that it is easier to identify the different shapes that make the pyramid. Finally he finds a square pyramid. He opens it up, but it does not look like the one he expected.
59. Stephen:	It doesn't look the same.

Stephen is surprised that the net does not look like he expected. Monica is giving him some technical advice. The reason why it does not look the same is that the application gives all the possible nets that will make this specific pyramid.

Extract 6.6 Colour the pyramid

60. Martin:	Can we colour it?
	Martin turns to Sarah and wants her to colour together with him, and she colours one face of the pyramid yellow.
61. Martin:	Now we have it. (He says to Monica)
	Stephen has also found the square pyramids and he says it looks like lightning.

In turn 60, Martin asks if he can colour. He also wants Sarah to be a more active partner and colour together with him. Finally, in turn 61, Martin tells Monica that he has found the pyramids.

> Geir Olaf asks Stephen if he can explain why he thinks it is the same net on the iPad as the concrete shape in front of him.

62. Stephen: Because it is one quadrilateral and three of those (pointing to the triangles) – no, four of those.
63. Geir Olaf: Four of what?
64. Stephen: Triangles.

> Now the children fold the shape almost into a net and laugh. Geir Olaf wants them to tell him what it looks like. A bonfire or a crown, they answer. Martin has coloured it completely yellow.

65. Stephen: Now we are done.

Stephen is being challenged by Geir Olaf to justify why he thinks it is the same shape. He uses the term "quadrilaterals" but points at the triangles. Geir Olaf follows up on this with a question in turn 63. Stephen answers it with the term "triangles", which is correct.

Extract 6.7 Does a cone contain a rectangle?

After about 23 minutes, Stephen wants to try the circular cone. This shape was not in the original plan for the activity: first, because it is built from a circle and a circle-sector. We found the circle-sector a bit too difficult at this level. Second, the application did not unfold it into a net. Instead, it rotated it around a line from the top of the cone to the centre of the circle. After unfolding it we will have one right triangle left.

FIGURE 6.4 Does a cone contain a rectangle?

66. Stephen: Now I will try that one. (He points at the cone.)
67. Monica: How do you think this will look like? What do you think I need?
68. Martin: A circle.
69. Monica: What about this shape around here?
70. Martin: I don't know.
71. Stephen: A quadrilateral. A long one.
72. Monica: Like the one we had a while ago.

73. Martin:	I think so too.	
74. Stephen:	It has to be.	
75. Monica:	Why does it have to be that one?	
76. Stephen:	Because I can see it.	

        Monica addresses Martin and asks him if he can also see it; he nods back.

        Stephen and Isabel open the shape. When they see that it is not built from a rectangle they burst out: "No?"

77. Isabel:	It was not that one.
78. Martin:	What is that?
79. Monica:	Yes, what can we call that shape? It looks like a cornet. You know, like the one we have ice cream in.
80. Stephen:	A nail.

In this last example there are a number of observations that indicate that they are at level 0. They argue that they can see that it has to be a rectangle. Maybe they are building on their previous experiences with the right cylinder, and then overgeneralising from that.

    The activity continues with a small task for about 50 minutes. After about 40 minutes, we were about to close the activity, but Stephen wanted to continue. When the rest of the children heard that we were about to close, they also wanted to continue. When we finally closed the activity, Stephen protested.

Findings and conclusion

In this study two episodes were chosen for a microanalysis. The activities took place according to kindergarten traditions of open-ended actual shared activities. These activities will differ from more formal activity practice where time, place, number of children and teachers are regulated, often seen with older children in schools. Our episodes are staged; the teacher-researchers bring new artefacts to the kindergarten, define a place on the floor, take the objects and start to explore them together with the children. The activities were analysed as a situation in process and certain dynamic aspects revealed.

Pedagogical findings

The two selected episodes describe how teacher-researchers and young children's activities can be driven by curiosity and a motive or drive to explore. To sum up we have identified some interesting conditions for activities that drive motives for exploration and discovery in kindergarten:

TABLE 6.1 Artefacts and activity.

Artefacts	Activity
Tangible artefacts (bricks and shapes)	Open ended (time)
Changeable artefact (models on applications)	Shared explorative (relation)
Variations of artefacts (patterns on the sheet, the boxes and the iPad)	Staged on the floor (place)

Technical findings

We found that the children were familiar with the iPad and navigation in and out of applications. The introduction from the researcher-teachers was about specific features, i.e. how to colour, unfolding and folding shapes and how to get different nets. After this introduction the children managed to use the application.

Geometric thinking

The children were able to figure out which two-dimensional shape they needed to get the three-dimensional shape in front of them. The cube was the easiest to pick. It was also the one that was only built from congruent two-dimensional shapes, six squares. During the activities they experienced both transformations from two-dimensional to three-dimensional and vice versa.

According to van Hiele's model the children were mostly on level 0. They were typically focusing on the appearance of the shapes more than the properties. When they were presented the two-dimensional shape of the cylinder, they saw a face. They also tried to match the unfolded right cylinder with the shape on the paper sheet, and were a bit unsure since the right cylinder was a tiny bit bigger.

There are some indicators that the children might be about to develop to the next level, level 1 description. Stephen is talking about a long quadrilateral when he is thinking about a rectangle. The data is not clear if they talk about appearance or properties because this could be interpreted both as an appearance, the shape looked long, and a property, the shape has two sides that are longer than the short ones. Isabel says that the pyramid has to contain triangles and not rectangles because it has a vertex, where Stephen says it's a nail.

During the activity the children switched between mathematical concepts like circle, rectangle and triangle to more everyday language like roundings and quadrilaterals. A "quadrilateral" in everyday language in Norway is understood as a general form for shapes with four sides, but also used for the term *square*.

Our findings indicate that the combination of technology and traditional collapsible folding shapes can give children richer experiences when they use the iPads to understand how to fold and unfold 3D shapes. We observed that this iPad application can help children investigate several shapes more effectively than with traditional solid shapes. Despite this, the tactile aspect must not be underestimated. Holding and touching the physical shapes are important for children's investigation of shapes.

Notes

1 http://shapes.learnteachexplore.com
2 Empirical data about Ida and the cube is also published in the article Ida and the cube – playing modus in exploring mathematics and iPads [Ida og Kuben – lekende modus i utforskning av matematikk og nettbrett](Volden, Pettersen and Ødegaard 2014).
3 The term "rounding" corresponds to the Norwegian word *runding*. This is everyday language for shapes that are round. Norwegian children sometimes use the word *runding* for a circle.
4 In the Norwegian transcript Martin says *firkant* for quadrilateral. In Norway quadrilateral is used as a collective term for all shapes that have four sides. Sometimes Norwegian children also use *firkant* for a square.

References

Clements, D. H. & Sarama, J. (2007). Early Childhood Mathematics Learning. In I. K. Lester (Ed), *Second handbook of research on mathematics teaching and learning* (Vol. 1, pp. 461–556). Charlotte NC: Information Age Publishers.

Cohen, L., Manion, L. & Morrison, K. (2007). *Research Methods in Education.* London: Routledge.

Fröbel, F. & Hailmann, W. N. (2005). *Menschenerziehung.* Mineola, NY: Dover Publications.

Føsker, L. I. R. (2012). Grip rommet! In: T. Fosse (Ed.), *Rom for matematikk – i barnehagen* (pp. 61–89). Bergen: Caspar forlag.

Hedegaard, M. (2012). The dynamic aspect in children's learning and development. In: M. Hedegaard, A. Edwards & M. Fleer (Eds), *Motives in Children's Development – Cultural-Historical Approaches* (pp. 9–28). Cambridge: Cambridge University Press.

Hedegaard, M., Edwards, A. & Fleer, M. (Eds). (2012). *Motives in Children's Development – Cultural-Historical Approaches.* Cambridge: Cambridge University Press.

Hutt, C. (1966). Exploration and play in children. In: P. A. Jewell & C. Loizos (Eds), *Play, Exploration and Territory in Mammals.* Zoological Society of London, New York: Academic Press.

van Oers, B., Wardekker, W., Elbers, E., & van der Veer, R. (2008). *The Transformation of Learning: Advances in Cultural-Historical Activity Theory.* Cambridge: Cambridge University Press.

Resnick, Mitchel (1998). Technologies for lifelong kindergarten. *Educational Technology Research and Development. 46*(4), 43–55.

Sam, C. (2012). Activity Theory and Qualitative Research in Digital Domains, Theory into Practice, 57, 83–90.

Spitzer, M. & Heyerdahl, C. (2014). *Digital demens: alt om hvordan digitale medier skader deg og barna dine.* Oslo: Pantagruel.

van Hiele, P. M. (1999). Developing geometric thinking through activities that begin with play. In: *Teaching Children Mathematics*, 5(6), 310–16.

Van de Walle, J. A., Karp, K. S., Bay-Williams, J. M. & Wray, J. (2012). *Elementary and Middle School Mathematics*, 8th ed. Harlow, Essex: Pearson Education.

Volden, M., Pettersen, G. O. and Ødegaard, E. E. (2014). Ida og Kuben – lekende modus i utforskning av matematikk og nettbrett. In: T. Hangaard Rasmussen (Ed.), *På spor etter lek – lek under moderne vilkår.* Bergen: Fagbokforlaget.

Ødegaard, E.E. (2012). Meningsskaping gjennom bruk av artefakter. In: E.E. Ødegaard (Ed.), *Barnehagen som danningsarena.* Bergen: Fagbokforlaget.

7

"I THINK IT SHOULD BE A LITTLE KIND OF EXCITING"

A technology-mediated story-making activity in early childhood education

Ewa Skantz Åberg, Annika Lantz-Andersson and Niklas Pramling

Abstract

In this chapter we study a pair of six-year-old children taking on the task of collaboratively making a story using a digital-story program named *Storybird*. The program allows children to choose images, thematically organised, as a basis for telling (and writing) a story. Theoretically, the study takes a sociocultural perspective on learning. From this point of view, the structuring resources utilised by the children in negotiating and producing their joint story are analysed. The results show that there are a number of structuring resources employed, facilitating and delimiting the children's story-making, such as the children's play, media and genre experience, what the teacher focuses on in the activity and the design of the software.

Introduction

Historically, reading and writing have been seen as fundamental competences in most Western societies. In the contemporary digital era, we not only read and write more than ever before but also in a greater variety of ways, in both official and private contexts. This has resulted in media debates among politicians and researchers about what is currently implied by the phrase "to be literate". These discussions have resulted in a common expansion of the concept into multiple literacies, in which digital literacy is incorporated (cf. Aarsand, Melander & Evaldsson, 2013). A recent report from NMC Horizon (2014), which focuses on European educational systems, outlines challenges for schools regarding the integration of digital technology in education with the purpose of increasing all pupils' digital competence to meet future societal needs. The most demanding challenge reported is for schools to "shape learners who have complex thinking skills" that include "using data visualisation, new forms of imagery, succinct narrative, and other communications tools" (p. 32). These future imperative competences are primarily discussed in relation to school contexts. However, we suggest that they are also of great relevance for early childhood education (ECE) since the adoption of digital technologies among young children has increased substantially. Currently, many children from an early age have access to computers, digital cameras, tablets, mobile phones and other technical devices provided in their homes and in educational practices (Marsh, 2010). Recent statistics in Sweden report that the daily use of the internet among five- to eight-year-olds has trebled since 2010, especially via smart phones (Swedish Media Council's Annual Report, 2012/13).

Through technology, children encounter and handle different sorts of texts that include semiotic modes such as written symbols, sound and images (Kress, 2003; Marsh et al., 2005). These experiences constitute bases for digital competences and communicative skills, which generate crucial questions on how to provide meaningful technology-mediated learning activities as a part of literacy education for preschool children.

This chapter focuses on the use of digital technologies in children's story-making activities in an early childhood setting. The study scrutinises the interactions of two six-year-old girls as they create a story together using a digital story-making application based on images. Taking the children's collaborative activities as the starting point, the study analyses the nature of the emerging activity when six-year-olds are instructed to narrate with digital technologies. We have a particular focus on what *structuring resources* (Lave, 1988) are utilised by the children.

Contemporary demands on new literacy competences

Early writing instruction in school in the nineteenth and twentieth centuries was formalised and characterised by reproduction (Gillen & Hall, 2013). In contemporary education, as argued by van Oers, literacy still tends to be reduced and decontextualised into "versions of reading and writing" (2007, p. 301). Such literacy practices stand in contrast to what it means to become literate as seen from a Vygotskian perspective, that is, to develop the "ability of using sign systems for personal and interpersonal purposes within specific cultural practices" (van Oers, 2007, p. 303). These sign systems are symbolic and function as mediators for an abstract way of thinking, which is necessary for being literate, van Oers maintains. Thus, from a sociocultural perspective (Vygotsky, 1978; Wertsch 1998, 2007), as employed in the present study, literacy denotes social and communicative practices that include writing (Brice Heath, 1983/1996). From this reasoning, reproductive education is no longer sustainable to meet contemporary demands on new literacy competences. Instead, education has to embrace an explorative approach and be oriented to tasks of a problem-solving nature since this allows for making use of previous experiences and knowledge, which is necessary for developing "higher-order thinking skills in a rich way" (Yelland, 2011, p. 37). This kind of educational practice reflects children's contemporary ways of knowledge building. Therefore, Yelland suggests, for children to master literacy, such innovative task design is needed for motivating purposes.

The OECD-research program, DeSeCo, reasons in a similar way by writing that contemporary literacy competency has to be structured around demands and tasks. That is, for fulfilling complex demands of modern life, basic reading, writing and calculating are critical components for reaching numerous competences that go beyond merely knowledge and skills, to also include for instance attitudes, motivation and values. These competences are needed by the individual for the purpose of "interacting effectively with the environment: both physical ones such as information technology and socio-cultural ones such as the use of language" (2005, p. 5).

Digital technology and early childhood literacy

In mapping the research field of digital technology and early childhood literacy it becomes clear that it parallels the changing epistemological view on literacy and literacies discussed earlier.

Initially, studies on technology that supported existing print-based literacy, in the form of decoding/encoding skills, were foregrounded (cf. Labbo & Reinking, 2003), with a movement towards a more explorative approach on children's engagements with digital technologies and texts in their lives (Burnett, 2010). However, more extended and systematic research on how young children make meaning beyond the technology is required (Burnett & Merchant, 2013). That is, research encompassing a focus on what becomes important in activities where technologies are utilized, rather than a focus on merely the way participants operate technologies.

By grounding the study in a sociocultural perspective on learning, and in line with Burnett (2010), a premise is that digital technologies do not simply act upon children. This implies that every activity is seen as offering structuring resources that participants may use but also material conditions that put limits to what is possible to do in an activity (Lave, 1988). Structuring resources in terms of various means of communication that activities enable give children opportunities to explore and develop literacy beyond individual knowledge and sense-making (Barton, Hamilton & Ivanic, 2000). Thus, children make use of and practice different modes of communication, such as verbal and non-verbal (tactile and auditive) in order to make sense. As Wells Rowe points out, "While digital composing frequently involves page- and screen-based writing and reading, print skills comprise only part of what children know and learn as they compose in digital environments" (2013, p. 440). Thus, print-based educational practices are challenged by new contexts of literacy learning (Säljö, 2010) where, for example, narrating is accomplished with support of digital technology.

Narrative as a part of literacy

Literacy events are from a sociocultural perspective viewed as observable situated sequences deriving from a wider literacy practice wherein they occur as repeated activities (Barton, 2007; Barton, Hamilton & Ivanic, 2000). This chapter will present one example of a literacy event where narrative is used in education as a means for children learning how to read and write. In Swedish ECE, narrative is commonly employed as a vehicle for writing. However, it fills many functions, for instance as an essential communicative and meaning-making practice, and as a mediator of culture. Therefore, narrative should be considered an aspect of literacy, and as a highly relevant competence to develop in educational settings (van Oers, 2007). In conceptualising narrative we draw upon Bruner (1996), who delimits narrative to include an agent who acts in a setting to achieve a goal, often encountering a problem to be solved. With an interest in learning, we suggest narrative competence to be understood as the ability to arrange these components in an intelligible way. In van Oers' definition (2007), narrative competence is more generally described in terms of the ability to produce a system of oral or written utterances into a coherent whole.

From a sociocultural perspective, literacy development means, *inter alia*, to appropriate different narrative genres and to master the communicative aspects in varieties of genres. Wells Rowe (2013) summarises research by stating that children six to seven years of age show extensive knowledge of narrative and information genres, in sense of cohesion, tense, word order, spatial arrangements and the use of images. However, their ability to produce genre-appropriate texts orally surpasses their ability to write them down. The discrepancy between children's oral and written language development is discussed by Vygotsky (2004), who maintains that the reason for this is the difference in the degree of difficulty between these two modes of communication. In a study conducted in ECE practice, this tension was particularly visible in instructional tasks where children were expected to produce a story with written words on the basis of their oral telling (Skantz Åberg, Lantz-Andersson & Pramling, 2014).

Narrative competence is increasingly important in an information technology-intense society where we encounter a wide variation of multimodal texts. In addition, we also produce short narratives when participating in, for instance, social media on the internet, which consequently demands communicative skills in order to be understandable for readers. Bagga-Gupta and Säljö (2013) describe this contemporary phenomenon in terms of collective authorship.

A sociocultural perspective on learning

This study is, as already mentioned, informed by sociocultural theory on human learning and development. Learning is understood as a social process, dependent on engaging participants, and contingent upon cultural, institutional and material conditions. What are referred to as cultural tools include both psychological (sign/language, writing and number systems) and physical tools or artefacts developed through history by people as means of solving problems and carrying out various actions (Säljö, 2009; Vygotsky, 1978). In relation to this metaphor for learning, another central concept in this tradition is mediation, meaning that people are not in direct contact with the world, but perceive it by means of mediational tools. For the present study, the unit of analysis is a technology-mediated activity (cf. Säljö, 2009), implying that the digital technologies used, actually being both physical and psychological tools, may provide opportunities for developing higher-order thinking, in terms of problem solving and abstract reasoning.

Everything that interplays with what happens in an activity could also be referred to as *structuring resources* (Lave, 1988). Structuring resources are what participants in an activity evoke to make sense. This could be knowledge of the specific setting, previous experiences, assumptions, expectations, the way the technologies are utilised and the interaction with other participants. Hence, in line with Lave (1988) and Wertsch (2007), we premise that when introducing a new sign or tool into an activity or an action, the tool transforms and interplays with participants' actions in carrying out an activity.

Communication as the mechanism of learning constitutes a link between the individual and the social (Wertsch, 1985). As the main communication tool, language can be characterised as, on the one hand, being highly contextual, or linguistically deictic. On the other hand, language can be used in a decontextualised way, which is expressed through abstract thoughts or generalisations (Wertsch, 1985). However, pointing in opposite directions, both dimensions are normally present in a discourse, although one or the other is dominating. As Vygotsky stated from his empirical studies of children, initially words related to objects solely have indicatory meaning for children, although in semiotically mediated social interaction children eventually learn how to generalise and categorise word meaning. This is made possible not only by verbal speech but by extra-linguistic resources, such as gestures, bodily movement or the use of tone of voice. Thus, social interaction importantly allows for people to communicate beyond the situated context that is significant for developing higher-order thinking or complex thinking. From this reasoning and translated to contemporary conditions, structuring resources that people make use of in social interaction enable sense-making through various semiotic-mediational tools provided by, for example, computers or software applications.

The educational setting, participants and data generation

The setting where the empirical material was generated is a school located in a middle-class area outside a small town, with mainly Swedish native speakers. The choice of school was made on the basis of its involvement in a municipal writing project – learning how to read through writing with digital technology. Consequently, the children were used to handling computers and some software applications before our observations. From a sample of 16 (constituting two groups) participating six-year-old children enrolled in a preschool class, which is a preparatory year of schooling, two girls' story-making activity was selected for analysis in this study. The reason for choosing this particular session was that it serves as an example of how all the observed activities more generally were conducted. The preschool teacher was trained in handling the technologies used.

The data was generated during two occasions in April and June 2012 and during three occasions in February and March 2013. The selected activity for this study was filmed with two cameras, one directed towards the screen and the other towards the faces. This story-making activity lasted approximately 35 minutes, which was the average amount of time for the sessions.

The research adheres to the ethical guidelines of the Swedish Research Council for protecting the rights of the participating children. Before conducting the observations the parents were informed about the purpose of the study and gave their written consent. To acknowledge the children's voluntary participation, they were informed about their rights to abort participation at any time, if they so wished, during recording. To ensure the anonymity of the children, their names have been changed.

Analysis

The analysis aims to illuminate what structuring resources are utilised by the children in taking on the task given in the followed activity. A tool-mediated activity is multimodal in nature; therefore the interactional and semiotic modes the children employ to create a digital story have been the focal point of the analysis for understanding how they engage with the task. By employing the method of Interaction Analysis (Jordan & Henderson, 1995) the focus has been directed towards verbal as well as non-verbal communication (gestures, gazes and bodily orientation) in the activity in relation to the software used. As Interaction Analysis shares the premise of sociocultural perspective that learning can be understood as distributed and embedded in social and material contexts (Jordan & Henderson, 1995; Lantz-Andersson, 2009), the sociocultural concept of structuring resources is employed in the analysis of the video-recorded data. However, our research question requires a sensitive analysis of how the distribution of the children's sequential turn-taking unfolds in order to delineate what structuring resources they use, and for that reason we have used certain transcription conventions of Conversation Analysis (CA) (see Table 7.1 at the end of the chapter). On a more detailed level we have marked out and analysed lengths of pauses, intonation and prosody (e.g. Sidnell, 2010), which may be significant for the dynamic interaction between the participants.

The transcription was initially conducted in a multimodal three-column transcription model, where first the speech was transcribed. Second, the gestures were focused on, and third the activities on the screen were carefully included in the model. However, for better readability this work was then transferred into a vertical script-like format. The transcripts have been translated into English. In doing so, we have paid particular attention to modelling the children's ways of speaking.

Negotiating a narrative theme

Initially, the preschool teacher introduced four children to the software *Storybird* (see Figure 7.1), which is an internet-based application for creating stories offering a large sample of illustrated images. The images are organised by artist and theme, such as love and dogs. The process of creating a story starts with selecting an initial image included in a theme. The story-maker then decides the number of pages and images s/he wants in the story before writing.

During the introduction of the software, the preschool teacher focused on showing the children how to handle the application. Together the group made a narrative by selecting four images, which each child told a short story about while the preschool teacher wrote the sentences on the keyboard. Later on she will write down on paper what the children verbally tell in relation to the images, for them to copy on the keyboard since they have not yet mastered the conventions of writing. After the exercise the children were expected to narrate in pairs decided by the preschool teacher, and the teacher walked around the room and helped the children (see Figure 7.2).

FIGURE 7.1   *Storybird* software.

FIGURE 7.2   Narrating in pairs.

The first excerpt displays the initial phase of the story-making activity. In the sequence, the two girls, Vera and Selma, have just started looking at the images and are about to select a number while negotiating what narrative theme to have for their story. Vera handles the keyboard and scrolls up and down rapidly, and as a consequence all the images occasionally disappear from the screen.

Extract 7.1 Story-making activity

13	Vera:	we'll have some <u>nice</u> images here, ↑ho ((scrolls fast, opens her eyes and recoils)) ★the images shortly disappear★
14	Teacher:	is there anything special you think of Vera
15	Vera:	ah, something there (.) good stuff ((the gaze concentrated on the screen))
16	Teacher:	hm but there are a <u>lot of images</u> here you see
17	Selma:	I think it should be a little kind of ((waves with one forearm)) exciting and so
18	Teacher:	mm, but that you could do, you could make it exciting
19	Selma:	that cat maybe ((points quickly towards the screen)) ★several images including a black cat★
20	Vera:	it we saw an exciting thing, a girl up here
21	Teacher:	but you can take it gently as you ((puts the hand on Vera's arm)) scroll
22	Vera:	<u>that</u> <u>one</u> that one ((points with the cursor on the image becoming the first in the story))
23	Selma:	it was actually rather exciting

Initially, Vera is searching for a nice image (turn 13). However, in an attempt to find a topic for the narrative, Selma suggests the story should be a little exciting (turn 17). Vera responds to the suggestion with a smile, supporting Selma's idea, and the teacher confirms that this is a satisfactory suggestion for a story by positively uttering and repeating the adjective, "mm but that you could do, you could make it exciting" (turn 18). Their mutual previous experiences of hearing exciting stories, together with the teacher's confirmation that this is a good choice, become a structuring resource for the continuing activity. As a result, the story framework is roughly established and the image of the cat that Selma suggests is rejected since it does not completely fit in. Furthermore, Vera seems to already have an image in mind that they have seen while scrolling. In turn 22, Vera utters "that one" with emphasis as she sees a particular image (see Figure 7.3). While pointing out the image verbally, she also moves the cursor to the middle of the image as to strengthen her choice. Here the pointing, which is enabled by the cursor sharpens the focus of their attention. Selma accepts (in turn 23) by saying that the image is actually rather exciting, and thereby the children have reached a temporary consensus and the narrative theme is established.

After Selma initiates the semiotic mediator *exciting* (Wertsch, 1985), the word is mentioned additionally three times in the extract, functioning as a structuring resource, which includes a confirmation of the suggested narrative theme and an indication of a mutual understanding. Put differently, the participants coordinate their actions to establish temporarily sufficient intersubjectivity to go on with a joint activity (Rommetveit, 1974), rather than engage in parallel ones. In this sequence, the participants use indexical terms, that is, deictic references (Ivarsson, 2003) with locally produced meaning, for instance *that* or *here*.

FIGURE 7.3 Making a story.

Talk about the narrative

The activity continues and the excerpt below displays the interaction taking place between the girls during the selection of the second image (see Figure 7.4). This extract illustrates how the children talk about events in their story, that is, how they negotiate the narrative content while looking at the images appearing on the screen and eventually selecting the second image for the story.

FIGURE 7.4 A scary story

Extract 7.2 Talking about stories

31	Vera:	choose someone that is <u>scary!</u>, kind of monster-like 'cause we will do a scary film ((raises her hands and brings them together. Swings her head and closes her eyes))★large screen surface with small images on the right and left side★
32	Selma:	or not a film
33	Vera:	but you know story that's <u>s::cary!</u> Like dark (inaudible) ((moves her hands together in monster-like way)).
34	Selma:	(inaudible)
35	Vera:	that one maybe ((sees an images in the upper-left corner, grabs the computer
36	Selma:	no screen. The girls look there))
37	Vera:	that was scary, that was monster]
38	Selma:	[yes but it should start a bit [mother-like] and so ((pulls an image into the screen surface, which is placed on page two)) ★the image becomes large★
39	Vera:	[monster-like] yes ((looks at Selma and then on the screen))
40	Selma:	mother-like and
41	Vera:	ah mother-like
42	Selma:	((places the image on the left side of the surface))so it should be there I think, so they lived and so and then it will be an <u>adventure</u> and so right (0.4) now we write(inaudible) ((The image is placed to the left and the writing surface to the right. A dropdown menu becomes visible and Vera removes it. However, a dialogue box turns up and the researcher assists in removing the box. Consequently, these incidents caused by the technologies interrupt the story-making.))
43	Vera:	so so it becomes like this <u>mo:ther</u>-like! ((sing-talks)) o then become like this woaw! monster!

Research within the field of play has indicated that children often to a large extent are more engaged in preparing the play, such as inventing and distributing roles, building up settings and rules, than actually enacting the play (Schwartzman, 1978). This becomes a structuring resource in the girls' actions in the sequence displayed above. Initially, Vera urges Selma to select an image suitable for their narrative by referring to the established theme (Extract 7.1). The exciting theme is expanded here by Vera's introduction of new predicates such as scary and monster-like (turn 31). Additionally, she talks about their product as a film, which could be understood as her referring to previous experiences of media and this genre. However, Selma responds dispreferably by an other-initiated repair as she utters "or not a film" (turn 32), whereby Vera makes a self-repair by uttering story. Additionally, Vera repeats scary with a greater prosody and gestures in a playful way, indicating a positive use of the adjective (turn 33).

Selma continues the planning by suggesting how the plot could begin as she utters, "[yes but it should start a bit [mother-like] and so" (turn 38). With an onset-overlapped turn Selma says yes to Vera's suggestion of a scary image she has found in turn 37, but she then introduces the new element. Mother-like could be a mediator for safety. However, in turn 39, Vera overlaps Selma's utterance "mother-like" with "[monster-like]yes" (commencing with the same first letter even in Swedish), indicating insufficient intersubjectivity between the girls; although, after Selma's repetition of mother-like in turn 40, Vera adjusts by uttering "ah mother-like" (turn 41), and thereby sufficient intersubjectivity is established.

Selma shows awareness of the fact that stories within the adventure genre typically start with a presentation of the main character, his or her home or a safe environment before introducing an event (a problem or challenge) leading to the character's departure and ensuing adventure. Thus, Selma's utterance in turn 38 and 42 could indicate her knowledge of this genre characteristic, and this knowledge functions as a structuring resource. In turn 43, through a mixture of singing and talking, Vera summarises the negotiated plot. Selma has marked a transition from the act of *talking about* the narrative to actually starting to produce the text by uttering "now we write" (turn 42), meaning writing down with the keyboard what they have negotiated.

The girls observed use various structuring resources in their talk about the narrative, such as play, a common structure of an adventure story, and their experience from media. Moreover, as a mediator the image functions as a structuring resource for sense-making in that it depicts people with houses in the background, implying Selma's suggestion of a mother-like beginning. Her utterance could be viewed as starting in the context of the image. However, the girl's talk is expanding beyond the imagery to include a forthcoming adventure.

Formulating the narrative

The negotiation now changes character as the girls shift focus from discussing the plot to actually producing the narrative. Note that the girls are formulating sentences as if it were the beginning of the story although the second image is visible on the screen. The following extract is one example of how the participants change perspectives by "going in and out" of the narration (cf. Vygotsky, 1978).

Extract 7.3 Producing the narrative

44	Selma:	now you should write
45	Vera:	yes then I write (.) this this was a castle and it liv- ((takes over the keyboard from Selma and glances at her))
46	Selma:	nah, this was a town that had no life, they have no life and so ((looks at Vera and frowns, and then looks at the screen and sweeps her hand up and down in front of it))
47	Vera:	nah this was a tower all of which they had a life and they would go out on adventures ((looks at Selma))
48	Selma:	nah (inaudible) ((looks at Vera))
49	Vera:	and then you would
50	Selma:	I don't think you should tell that
51	Vera:	nah so now we'll do our story come on ((both smiles))

52	Selma:	yes come on
53	Vera:	it's not that ((bends forward and focuses on an image))
54	Selma:	I think so, nah there I think
55	Vera:	we write like this
56	Selma:	this was a town or this was a village where there was no life
57	Vera:	D D D
58	Selma:	this was a town that had no life
59	Vera:	but how do we write it ((strikes out her hands))
60	Selma:	write

First, the transition from *talking about* to producing the narrative is again marked by Selma (turn 44) in urging Vera to start writing. The girls are leaving the negotiation about the narrative to start formulating the story. Vera responds positively by repeating Selma's word, and simultaneously as she takes over the keyboard she uses the deictic expression "this was" (turn 45) to indicate the beginning of the story. However, they have not fully established the plot and are not coordinated in their opinion of the setting and consequently have to continue negotiating. In turn 46 Selma introduces a new predicate, a town that had no life. In addition to the verbal utterance, she sweeps with her hand up and down in front of the screen as if to legitimise the idea mediated by the imagery. However, Vera responds dispreferably by contrasting with, "nah this was a tower all of which they had a life" (turn 47). This discrepancy is probably due to the girls' effort to make sense of what they perceive to be depicted in the image, although Vera, in the same turn, picks up Selma's previous suggestion of an adventure in turn 42.

Vera then utters something that makes Selma react by stepping out of the narrating, "I don't think you should <u>tell</u> that" (turn 50). Vera agrees and directs them back to the story-making. Selma returns to narrating in turn 56 by clarifying how she wants the first sentence to be phrased. Vera begins to sound the first letter D D D (turn 57), but is puzzled by how to write down the letters. She clearly shows this by bursting out her hands while asking "but how do we write it" (turn 59).

Even if the girls occasionally discuss on a metalevel what should be included in the narrative or not, they do not coordinate perspectives. Their negotiation includes several levels: the preparation as well as the formulation of the narrative, and further, the transition from the oral narration to the written by handling the technologies, which all structure the activity. The extract is an example of how a story-making activity may provide opportunities for reasoning beyond the digital technology. Analytically, this is understood by the girls' elaboration with nouns, such as castle, tower, town and village, implying an evolving decontextualized use of language (Wertsch, 1985).

Selma suggests the beginning of the plot to be about a town where there is no life, which she continues to suggest throughout the story-making activity (turn 46). The utterance implies a language borrowed from the computer-game genre (cf. Linderoth, 2004), which becomes a resource for structuring the narrative. Younger children are found to mix genres or use decontextualised elements from media in order to create something new (cf. Nicolopoulou, 2011).

Un-coordinated perspectives

The story-making activity continues and in the following extract the girls narrate to the third image (see Figure 7.5), which also becomes the last image of their story.

FIGURE 7.5 The third image.

Extract 7.4 The last image

172	Selma:	in the country in the town where there was no life
173	Vera:	no that we have already written
174	Selma:	yes but in the town by the harbour
175	Vera:	the man had fallen into and [then] he
176	Selma:	[then] one called for that one had fallen into
177	Vera:	ah and then a a shark bit him in the ((points at the man's finger finger))
178	Selma:	yes maybe
179	Teacher:	let's see here
180	Vera:	he fell into the water
181	Teacher:	a man had fallen into the water ((the girls agree))
182	Selma:	and one called for help?, so that he would come up
183	Teacher:	in the water and one called ((writes while reading aloud))
184	Vera:	he is not in the water ((looks at Selma))
185	Selma:	no
186	Teacher:	so
187	Selma:	but one has fallen in so he call for
188	Vera:	no he's not in the water he stands on ((points at the tower)) that and there are all the boats
189	Selma:	yes but one has fallen in there ((points at the water))

Both girls are trying to make sense of what they see in the image and at the same time create a story, events that could be connected to the image. The lack of clarity in what the image depicts becomes a structuring resource for their talk. On the one hand it becomes difficult for the girls to figure out what the image illustrates and on the other hand it enables them to speculate and fantasise. Selma initially maintains her idea about the town without life. However, Vera states that they have already written that. In response, Selma changes her mind and utters "yes but in the town by the harbour" (turn 174), arguably because a harbour is seen in the image. Then, with a short phrase, Vera suggests that a man has fallen into the water and Selma fills in the sentence (with an overlap) that someone calls for (probably attention) (turn 176). However, now Vera introduces, verbally and by pointing at the screen, a new predicate to the plot that is not visible in the image: a shark that bit the man's finger (turn 177), arguably in an attempt to adhere to the exciting theme.

While the girls negotiate, the teacher approaches to help them to write down their oral telling. As the teacher summarises and writes, Vera discovers that she might not be co-ordinated with Selma, as she needs to clarify he is not in <u>the water</u> (turn 184) with an emphasis on the water. Thus, an uncertainty appears concerning who has fallen into the water, the man in the tower or someone else. The reason for this confusion could be found in their use of pronouns, in terms of *he* or *one*, and the noun *man*, instead of naming the characters. In order to clarify what they mean and to coordinate perspectives, Vera and Selma use not only language but also gestures by pointing to different objects on the screen (turns 188 and 189). Accordingly, in the sequences the girls' language-use shifts from what could be a reasoning beyond the imagery, to be linguistically deictic, in terms of the use of *that* and *there*.

Ending the story-making activity

When the children have been working with the images and finished the narrative, the preschool teacher again approaches and encourages them to read their story. However, she leaves for a few minutes during which Vera makes an effort to read the first sentence.

Extract 7.5 Ending the story-making activity

312	Vera:	they jump, ehu they they T R Ä F F A E, ähu so, ehu ehu they H A H ade ((sound träffae [Swedish for 'met'] scrolls to page two))
313	Teacher:	are you satisfied
314	Vera:	[ye::s]
315	Selma:	[mm]
316	Teacher:	have you seen it all did you see everything
317	Vera:	can't remember what it said
318	Teacher:	should I read to you (.)
319	Vera:	[ah]
320	Selma:	[m] then scroll back to monster story (.) now it's me that, here they jump and meet monster, they had been out on adventures now they would shower, a man had fallen into the water and called for help, that was the end of the story ((clicks to the left on the TouchPad=browse back)) *displays the cover page*

321 Vera: mm
322 Teacher: are you satisfied
323 Vera: yes

Vera and Selma are at first reluctant to read, claiming they do not have the ability. However, Vera gives it a try using both reading by memory and sound technique (turn 312). The preschool teacher returns and asks if they are pleased with the story, upon which the girls respond yes, but Vera then says she cannot remember what they have written (turn 317). The preschool teacher browses back to the first page and reads the text to each image, and adds, "that was the end of the story" (turn 320), which is a canonical marker to end a (particular kind of) narrative. At this point, the preschool teacher does not comment on the structure or content of the girls' story nor does she evaluate it.

Discussion

The analytical interest of this study concerns a literacy event in the form of an instructed technology-mediated story-making activity, with a particular focus on what structuring resources come into play in the activity.

The institutional frame set by the school environment, the introduction given by the preschool teacher and her anticipation of the children's collaboration with each other, together with the digital technology, structure the overall conditions for how the children take on the task. Thus, the result shows that the formalised story-making task constitutes the main structuring resource (Lave, 1988) for the children's narration with its embeddedness in a social and cultural context. Primarily, the preschool teacher mediates the activity to a large extent through her planning of the task and her introduction of the digital software application *Storybird*. At the forefront, during the introduction and the following activity, her focus is on selecting images and writing a short story to each of them. An example of the preschool teacher's scaffolding is when she summarises the girls' oral telling and transfers it to written symbols on a paper for them to copy on the keyboard (Excerpt 4). In this sequence, the preschool teacher does not indicate her awareness of the girls' uncoordinated perspectives concerning who-does-what in the imagery. Nor does she discuss the misunderstandings or suggest alternative ways to formulate a plot inspired by the image. The preschool teacher's scaffolding could be understood as if she considers the girls' disagreement on a text to be subordinated to the overall aim of succeeding in completing the task. An example of the preschool teacher's scaffolding is when she summarises the girls' oral telling and transfers it to written symbols on paper for them to copy on the keyboard (Extract 7.4).

However, while the instructed task constitutes the main structuring resource, the narration itself also structures the activity by the distinct ways the working processes continue due to the children's narrative knowledge. As Lave (1988) argues in her studies on diverse mathematical activities, the sum of the calculation will always be the same regardless of context, although the calculation will be differently structured, arranged and divided into units and relations depending on context and the actor's intention. Lave points out that an activity is multilayered and many things are going on simultaneously, and consequently multiple resources are in play. Thus, translated into this research, the instructed task is expected to result in a digital story, but the path towards the final product may differ depending on what structuring resources are utilised by the children.

During the observed activity, the girls use different resources such as language, the digital technology, knowledge of adventure genre and other previous experiences. In the empirical data it is evident that the children's story-making changes character during the work: selecting images and negotiating the narrative theme (Extract 7.1), preparing the narrative by talking about it (Extract 7.2), formulating the narrative (Extract 7.3), negotiating the plot in relation to how they understand the image (Extract 7.4) and finally rounding up the activity by reading the story (Extract 7.5). These changes could to some extent be paralleled to the children's known pattern of play and therefore constitute a structuring resource for guiding the narration. The initial talk about theme and setting is also accompanied by playful elements such as an animating voice and gestures, for example in Extract 2. Research has indicated that young children use play as an important resource to explore language and literacy knowledge through their everyday social activities (Saracho & Spodek, 2006). Thus, social interaction is a source for meaning making and literacy learning (Säljö, 2012), and literacy-related play conveys possibilities for appropriating new concepts and the use of literate ways of thinking, for instance, in writing and narration (Saracho & Spodek, 2006). In the analysis we show that the observed children do the opposite by bringing patterns of play into a formalised story-making task, indicating unclear boundaries between the institutional activity and their play.

Introducing a new physical tool in an educational practice does not automatically lead to improved education, but creates different contexts for learning (Lantz-Andersson, 2009; Säljö, 2010). The use of a new artefact, such as a computer or software, may entail new activities that qualitatively transform psychological functions and practical operations (Wertsch, 2007), although this requires a dynamic interplay between technology and user. From this premise, digital technologies are seen as supporting the development of abilities such as thinking, communicating and acting (Lantz-Anderson & Säljö, 2014). However, the computer materiality determines what is possible to do in an activity, in terms of its design (Aarsand, Melander & Evaldsson, 2013). Hence, the inbuilt possibilities and constraints provide structuring resources, for, in this case, narration. The software application selected by the preschool teacher for the observed story-making activity constitutes a motivating tool for the children, although they occasionally have difficulties in operating the technologies (Extracts 7.1 and 7.2). However, as accounted for in the analysis, when the girls have decided on a narrative theme, the numbers of selectable images decrease, since the design does not allow for selecting images across themes, thus becoming a structuring resource for their narrative. The images function as mediators for the girls' sense-making, although occasionally providing ambiguity in what they depict. This becomes especially evident in Extract 7.4, where the negotiation deviates from the narrating to focus on clarifying the image.

In the empirical material analysed here, findings show that the narrating is conducted primarily with the use of language as a mediating tool and as a structuring resource. However, to some extent the language used by the children in the study is deictic. Deixis is a linguistic construct that changes meaning continuously (e.g. *here*, *that*, *now*), and therefore is highly contextual. In his study, Ivarsson (2003) found that deictic references were used to a large extent in a computer-supported learning environment. Ivarsson maintains that the reason for this is that the visual and interactive aspects of the technology facilitate this kind of language.

In the present study, we have identified a similar pattern in the girls' use of *that*, *here* and *there*, but also in their use of pronouns such as *he*, *man* and *one*. These are expressed verbally in addition to pointing gestures (by finger and cursor) for pragmatic reasons, as the girls orient themselves towards the visual representations on the screen when they need to coordinate their perspectives while narrating. However, the girls also use other forms of language, but they do not go from a deictic use to a more expansive language in any linear manner as the activity proceeds. By referring to or describing various phenomena, as the girls do by using nouns as semiotic resources, such as *adventure, castle, town* and *tower* (Extract 7.3), they refer in terms that point beyond the present. This more decontextualised language-use becomes necessary in the coordination of perspectives, and is, Wertsch (1985) argues, required for developing higher-order thinking.

Conclusion

The findings of this study imply that the instructional story-making activity is complex, with multiple things taking place at the same time that the girls need to relate to. In taking on the task, the children employ a series of structuring resources. However, it is the educational practice and the preschool teacher that become the overall structuring resources for the activity, together with the possibilities and constraints of the technologies. The story-making task offers the children opportunities for reasoning and negotiating meaning mediated by the images provided by the software application. In addition to their language use, the girls employ or relate to the other structuring resources, such as patterns of play, awareness of the possibilities the technologies enable and genre knowledge, in managing the task. Consequently, collaborative technology-mediated story-making activities provide possibilities for communicative interactions, in terms of opening up for exploration of language and development of higher-order thinking. This is fundamental for developing literacy and digital competences important for participation in contemporary society.

TABLE 7.1 Transcription key.

[	point of overlap onset
]	point at which utterance terminates
(0.0)	lapsed time in tenths of a second
,	comma indicates a gap between utterance which is too short to time, more like a very short pause
(.)	a gap of approximately one-tenth of a second
<u>word</u>	underline indicates speaker emphasis
↑↓	marked shifts in higher or lower pitch in utterance immediately following arrow
!	animated and emphatic tone
?	rising intonation, not necessarily a question
:	prolongation of immediately prior sound
::::	the more colons the longer the sound is drawn out e.g. ye::ar
(....)	indicates a fading away which is unintelligible
( )	inability to hear what was said
(word)	dubious hearings or speaker identification
(( ))	transcriber's descriptions rather than or in addition to transcriptions
★ ★	screen activity

References

Aarsand, P., Melander, H. & Evaldsson, A.-C. (2013). Om media literacy-praktiker i barns vardagsliv. In: S. Bagga-Gupta, A.-C. Evaldsson, C. Liberg & R. Säljö (Eds), *Literacy-praktiker i och utanför skolan* [Literacy practices in and out of school] (pp. 41–63). Stockholm: Gleerups.

Bagga-Gupta, S. (2013). Literacies som handling. Den språkande människan och praktikgemenskaper. In: S. Bagga-Gupta, A.-C. Evaldsson & R. Säljö (Eds), *Literacy praktiker i och utanför skolan* [Literacy practices in and out of school] (pp. 19–40). Stockholm: Gleerups.

Bagga-Gupta, S. & Säljö, R. (2013). Inledning [Introduction]. In: S. Bagga-Gupta, A.-C. Evaldsson & R. Säljö (Eds), *Literacy praktiker i och utanför skolan* [Literacy practices in and out of school] (pp. 9–17). Stockholm: Gleerups.

Barton, D. (2007). *Literacy: An Introduction to the Ecology of Written Language*, 2nd ed. Oxford: Blackwell.

Barton, D., Hamilton, M. & Ivanic. R. (2000). *Situated Literacies: Reading and Writing in Context*. London: Routledge.

Brice Heath, S. (1983/1996). *Way with Words: Language, Life, and Work in Communities and Classrooms*. New York: Cambridge University Press.

Bruner, J. S. (1996). *The Culture of Education*. Cambridge, MA: Harvard University Press.

Burnett, C. (2010). Technology and literacy in early childhood educational settings: a review of research. *Journal of Early Childhood Literacy 10*(3), 247–70.

Burnett, C. & Merchant, G. (2013). Learning, literacies and new technologies: the current context and future possibilities. In: N. Hall, J. Larson & J. Marsh (Eds), *Handbook of Early Childhood Literacy* (pp. 575–86). London: Sage.

Gillen, J. & Hall, N. (2013). The emergence of early childhood literacy. In: N. Hall, J. Larson & J. Marsh (Eds), *Handbook of Early Childhood Literacy* (pp. 3–17). London: Sage.

Ivarsson, J. (2003). Kids in Zen: computer-supported learning environments and illusory intersubjectivity. *Education, Communication & Information, 3*(3), 383–402.

Jordan, B. & Henderson, A. (1995). Interaction analysis: foundations and practice. *Journal of the Learning Sciences, 4*(1), 39–103.

Kress, G. (2003). *Literacy in the new media age*. London: Routledge

Labbo, L. & Reinking, D. (2003). Computer and early literacy education. In N. Hall, J. Larson & J. Marsh (Eds), *Handbook of Early Childhood Literacy* (pp. 338–54). London: Sage.

Lantz-Andersson, A. (2009). *Framing in Educational Practices: Learning Activity, Digital Technology and the Logic of Situated Action* (Doctoral thesis. Gothenburg Studies in Educational Sciences, 278). Göteborg, Sweden: Acta Universitatis Gothoburgensis.

Lantz-Andersson, A. & Säljö, R. (2014). Inledning: Lärmiljöer i omvandling – En yrkesroll i utveckling. In: A. Lantz-Andersson & R. Säljö (Eds), *Lärande i den uppkopplade skolan* [Learning in the Internet-connected school] (pp. 13–41). Malmö, Sweden: Gleerups.

Lave, J. (1988). *Cognition in Practice: Mind, Mathematics, and Culture in Everyday Life*. New York: Cambridge University Press.

Linderoth, J. (2004). *Datorspelandet mening. Bortom idén om den interaktiva illusionen* [The meaning of gaming: beyond the idea of the interactive illusion] (Gothenburg Studies in Educational Sciences, 211). Göteborg, Sweden: Acta Universitatis Gothoburgensis.

Marsh, J. (2010). Childhood, culture and creativity: a literature review. Newcastle: Creativity, Culture and Education. Retrieved 2 June 2014 from http://www.creativitycultureeducation.org/wp-content/uploads/CCE-childhood-culture-and-creativity-a-literature-review.pdf

Nicolopoulou, A. (2011). Children's storytelling: toward an interpretive and sociocultural approach. *StoryWorlds: A Journal of Narratives Studies, 3*, 25–48.

NMC Horizon Report Europe (2014). 2014 schools edition. Retrieved from http://www.nmc.org/publications/2014-nmc-horizon-report-europe-schools

OECD. (2005). DeSeCo Definition and selection of competencies: Theoretical and conceptual Foundations. The Definition and selection of key competencies Executive summary. Retrieved from http://www.deseco.admin.ch/bfs/deseco/en/index/02.html.

van Oers, B. (2007). Helping young children to become literate: the relevance of narrative competence for developmental education. *European Early Childhood Education Research Journal, 15*, 299–312.

Rommeveit, R. (1974). *On message structure: A framework for study of language and communication.* London: Wiley.

Säljö, R. (2009). Learning, theories of learning, and units of analysis in research. *Educational Psychologist, 44*(3), 202–08.

Säljö, R. (2010). Digital tools and challenges to institutional traditions of learning: technologies, social memory and the performative nature of learning. *Journal of Computer Assisted Learning, 26*(1), 53–64.

Saracho, O. N. & Spadek, B. (2006). Young children's literacy-related play. Early Child Development and Care, 176(7), 707–721.

Schwartzman, H. B. (1978). *Transformations: The Anthropology of Children's Play.* New York: Plenum.

Sidnell, J. (2010). *Conversation Analysis: An Introduction* (Language in Society). Chichester: Wiley-Blackwell.

Skantz Åberg, E., Lantz-Andersson, A., & Pramling, N. (2014). "Once upon a time there was a mouse": Children's technology-mediated storytelling in preschool class. *Early Child Development and Care, 184*(11), 1583–98.

Swedish Media Council's Annual Report (2012/13). *Småungar & medier. Fakta om små barns användning oh upplevelser av medier.* Retrieved from http://www.statensmedierad.se/Kunskap/Ungar--Medier/Statistik-pamedieanvandningen-hos-barn-08-ar

Vygotsky, L. S. (1978). *Mind in Society: The Development of Higher Psychological Processes.* Cambridge, MA: Harvard University Press.

Vygotsky, L. S. (2004). Imagination and creativity in childhood. *Journal of Russian and East European Psychology, 42*(1), 7–97.

Wells Rowe, D. (2013). Recent trends in research on young children's authoring. In: N. Hall, J. Larson & J Marsh (Eds), *Handbook of Early Childhood Literacy* (pp. 423–47). London: Sage.

Wertsch, J. (1985). The semiotic mediation of mental life: L. S. Vygotsky and M. M. Bakhtin. In: E. Mertz & R. J. Parmentier (Eds), *Semiotic Mediation: Sociocultural and Psychological Perspectives* (pp. 49–71). Orlando, FL: Academic Press.

Wertsch, J. (1998). *Mind as Action.* New York: Oxford University Press.

Wertsch, J. (2007). Mediation. In: H. Daniels, M. Cole & J. V. Wertsch (Eds.), *The Cambridge Companion to Vygotsky* (pp. 178–92). New York: Cambridge University Press.

Yelland, N. (2011). Knowledge building with ICT in the early years of schooling. He Kupu, 2(5), 33–44.

8

MULTIMODAL MEANING-MAKING FOR YOUNG CHILDREN

Partnerships through blogging

Marni J. Binder, Reesa Sorin, Jason Nolan and Sarah Chu

Abstract

The authors describe an arts-based collaborative research project with four- and five-year-old children in Canada and Australia to generate perceptions and awareness of environments. Children constructed postcards, providing them with opportunities to make meaning of their and others' worlds. These were shared on a blog over a 10-week period. Blogs offer multimodal, peer-to-peer conversations between communities of learners that extend beyond the classroom walls. The online format encouraged the children to search beyond the postcards to find out more about their own and others' environments and to begin the discourse on issues of sustainability.

Introduction

There is an ever-growing discourse around environmental sustainability issues in early childhood education (Hacking, Barratt & Scott, 2007). In examining notions of play and children's sense of place in their natural world, Louv (2008) stresses that open-ended play in the natural environment is a way for children to explore, stimulate and develop awareness of the world around them. Knowledge construction is important, as is coming to an understanding of the significance of nature and place (Duhn, 2012), to help develop an ethos of care (Noddings, 2011) that comes from connecting with the world (Binder, 2011).

Though children should begin with their own physical environment to develop context and relationships, our project builds on the child's personal experience, using arts-based methods to share and learn about both local and global environments (Sorin, 2014). Kress (1997) suggested that children translate from one mode to another through exploration before they enter into print, and this is how they make meaning and situate themselves in and make sense of the world. In this chapter we look at how multimodal theory shows the integration of these multiple sign systems, or modes such as image, song, sound, gesture, text (traditional and online) and language (Flewitt, 2013), broadening how children socially construct meaning in their lives. Visual narrative (Binder & Kotsopolous, 2011; Wright,

2010) in the form of digital postcards, enabled children in Canada and Australia to share their local environment and understandings of the world around them (Sorin, 2014).

Letters have traditionally been used to maintain connections across distances, and pen pal programmes have been used in elementary classrooms to enhance literacy skills (Moore & Seeger, 2009) and increase students' exposure to international and cross-cultural worldviews (Shandomo, 2009). Validating children's existing competencies in creating drawings and verbalising narratives, digital postcards exchanged through blogs offer the opportunity and platform for children to share their stories with multiple global audiences. For this project, we used blog posts, drawings, paintings, collage, photographs, stories, songs and text as tools to support children's multimodal meaning-making (Sorin, 2014), advocating for the use of online learning environments as another mode supporting children's thoughts, views and how they situate themselves as content producers in the world.

Conceptual framework

Several intersecting frameworks informed this research: learning and play with digital media; blogging in the early years; multimodal meaning-making across digital contexts; and using drawings to foster understanding. They are discussed as follows.

Young children's learning and play with digital media

Young children are increasingly exposed to and engaged with digital media and technology at home and in learning environments (McPake, Plowman & Stephen, 2013). Much research has emerged in recent years building on previous work that investigated the possibilities of online digital media and technology to foster children's technical, communicative and collaborative skills, in both formal and informal learning contexts (Burnett, 2009; McPake, Plowman & Stephen, 2013; Nolan & McBride, 2014, Nolan & Weiss, 2002). Among these new literacies that take into account children's increasingly sophisticated technology practices is "digital literacy", which is constituted by the competencies and skills involved in locating, evaluating, selecting, sharing and creating materials and information using technology, particularly on the internet (Buckingham, 2006). The participatory culture shaped by the convergence of contemporary media and young people's digital creations (Jenkins, 2006) calls for educators to consider how they may adapt to and further refine their students' existing competencies – their multiple literacies (Buckingham, 2006).

Driven by the popularity of technology, a growing number of educators have sought to leverage young children's existing interests around digital media and the productive potential of these media to stimulate student learning. Numerous studies illustrate the successes of integrating technology into classroom activities, demonstrating evidence of learning improvements through harnessing meaningful engagement with technology (Burnett, 2009). However, the implementation of technologies like games have also given rise to pedagogical challenges in bridging the disconnect between educators' agendas for dialogic meaning-making and students' deep attention to the technology as a medium (Vangsnes, Gram Økland & Krumsvik, 2012).

Blogging with young children

Implementing blogs into learning environments has emerged as one method adopted by teachers to bridge traditional classroom activities, utilising children's existing understandings and practices around creating and sharing content on the internet (Davison, 2013). As an online publishing platform, blogs allow individuals or multiple authors to share written content, images and multimedia (Nolan, 2003). Shearer (2010) suggests that the practice of blogging in the classroom expands students' collaborative and communication skills by offering another way to facilitate dialogue between students and teachers. Integrating blogs into learning environments has also been argued to promote students' higher order thinking (Zawilinski, 2009) and critical thinking (Lee, 2011).

Students' motivation to participate in blogging activities is said to be increased by the understanding that the teacher is not the sole reader of their blogs, but that a broad audience has access to their work as well (Lee, 2011). With the capacity of blogs to create cross-cultural online learning communities (Lee, 2011) and expand on traditional pen pal letter and postcard exchanges (Shandomo, 2009), digital postcards exchanged through blogs offer a platform for children to share their stories with worldwide audiences promptly and efficiently. Significant is how blogs connect to curriculum and pedagogy and involve young learners in critical and multimodal literacies through using text, images and video (Vasquez & Felderman, 2013).

Teachers and administrators have also utilised blogs to keep parents and guardians informed of their children's learning activities at school. While teacher-created web pages (Nelms, 2002) and emails (Tobolka, 2006) have helped strengthen school–parent communication in the past, blogs today offer the chance for parents to make threaded comments on student and teacher blog posts, engaging multiple families and teachers in rich discussions online (Powell & McCauley, 2012). And while communication between teachers and parents in the past was often initiated by teachers' observations and feedback, creating a personal blog for each student has allowed children to share their own photos and insights, or to dictate what they want the teachers to write (Powell & McCauley, 2012). This gives them agency to own and reflect upon their learning, and to potentially co-construct a virtual learning community through the stories they share (Nolan & Weiss, 2002).

Multimodal meaning-making in digital contexts

Blogs and other digital media cultivate spaces that invigorate multimodal learning and meaning-making. Drawing on a rich body of scholarly work on multimodal literacy (Jewitt & Kress, 2003; Kress, 2003), researchers studying young children's learning and meaning-making argue that "texts" are constituted by multiple forms of communication and representation that include print, imagery, sound and movement (Arya & Feathers, 2012). The integration of multiple sign systems enhances the meaning-making capacities of children (Binder, 2011; Binder & Kotsopolous, 2011) through offering different opportunities to represent multimodal texts (Kress, 2003).

Research on multimodal learning across digital contexts has focused on the intersection of various media forms to represent information, with specific attention paid to children's ability to read, create and share digital information (Shuker & Terreni, 2013). Researchers in the field maintain that engaging in digital media practices means that children must draw on their traditional literacy practices to decode not only print, but to negotiate diverse interactive and participatory modes of representation that frequently include images and videos and are authored by individuals from a broad range of backgrounds, locales and expertise. The connection between print and image in the digital postcards shared through a blog afforded children the opportunity to practice making sense of multimodal texts and also to create texts of their own through expressing and responding to a receptive audience.

Using drawings to foster understanding

Interpreting and conveying ideas in images is associated with the development of visual literacy (Bamford, 2003). Visual literacy and visual communication skills have been suggested to enhance children's understanding of science (Britsch, 2013), mathematics (Fesakis, Sofroniou & Mavroudi, 2011) and environment (Boulay & Lynch, 2012) topics. Making room for children to draw helps them to further develop their visual literacy (Hopperstad, 2010) and has been found to support children's investigation and understanding of their lived experiences, as well as allow them to reflect and expand on their sociocultural environments (Binder, 2011).

It can be argued that through drawings, children's capabilities and lived experiences are represented as interconnected modes of communication and expression (Binder & Kotsopolous, 2011) to be examined. Kind (2010) suggests that drawings "may be seen as visual constructions and representations of children's thoughts, ideas, and theories" (p. 121) that shift adult thinking away from looking at children's artwork as just creative expressions of communicating and meaning-making. Drawing presents a critical lens into the minds of children (Knight, 2008). Combining images with oral text also allows for a deeper understanding of children's "funds of knowledge" (González, Moll & Amanti, 2005) and as each form of expression augments the other (Wright, 2010).

Research design

This arts-based research was emergent, transdisciplinary and diverse (Bamford, 2003; Leavy, 2011; Rose, 2007). It took on the parameters of action research as it progressed through pedagogical cycles of reflection and action (MacNaughton & Hughes, 2009). Examining samples of children's artwork, stories, group work and class extensions that emerged throughout the project allowed for a more holistic view, providing understanding of the experience and process. The visual narratives of the children were the data and became the texts of meaning-making.

The interface between arts-based methods and practices affords a holistic theoretical framework to transdisciplinary research (Leavy, 2011) and to expand interpretation and process in new learning (Barone & Eisner, 2012). Data were collected with 19 four- to five-year-old children (kindergarten) in Canada and 22 four- to five-year-old children (pre-prep) in Australia over a 10-week period. Drawings with stories, group murals with stories, songs, paintings, photographs, videos; observations from researchers and teachers in the form of field notes and research diaries; and pre and post interviews with the children and teachers were collected in both settings to generate cross-cultural data about children's understanding of local and global environments. At the end of data collection, the *Postcards across Borders* blog site contained 48 posts and 339 images. Researchers at both locations visited the classes once a week for two to two and a half hours. We employed the WordPress (version 4.0) content management system (blog) installed at Ryerson University. In accordance with our ethical protocols, and in order to secure the privacy of the children's work, something they have the right to expect (Nolan, Raynes-Goldie & McBride, 2011), the entire site was behind a firewall and password protected using the university's authentication protocols, and only the teachers and researchers were able to log into the site. Children could view the content only in the classroom.

During the first few weeks, children and teachers at both sites were interviewed about their understanding of their local environments. At the end of the project, similar questions were asked. In between the two interviews, the children were engaged in arts-based inquiry approaches of drawing and storytelling in creating three postcards that were scanned and uploaded to the blog by the researchers to share with children in the other location. The adults functioned as cultural tools, implementing their methods and process of visualising their voices (Soto, 2005).

As the project progressed, other methods emerged, including teacher and researcher scaffolding of learning through sharing of books (e.g. picture books such as *Over in Australia* by Berkes, 2011), mural making, photographs of the children and learning spaces, letter writing, word charts and mapping. These artefacts were also shared on the blog for both classes to view. Including this rich visual data highlighted the importance of using visual texts to contribute to interpretation and inform understanding (Rose, 2007).

Data were analysed using arts-based methods and multimodal approaches, including content analysis, interpretive analysis and grounded theory. Content analysis supported the interpretation of the visual communications and how often certain themes emerged (Rose, 2007). Interpretive analysis examined elements of design, mood and what is expressed and communicated through images and stories (Krenz, 2004). Theron, Mitchell, Smith and Stuart (2011) point out that drawing is "a visual participatory methodology" (p. 34) to be examined using a combination of representation and talking and/or writing. It is this synergistic way of looking at the issues (Leavy, 2011) that unfolds the complexity of meaning-making. A grounded theory approach using a constructivist design (Creswell, 2008) focused on meaning-making, the experiences and overall process of the research. Using this approach allowed for emergent categories to be examined and refined and informed the findings.

Findings

Findings from this research demonstrate the effectiveness of arts-based methods for collecting and interpreting data. Using multimodal approaches, such as online postcards shared through blogs to engage young children in making meaning of self, others and the world, are not prevalent in early learning. The postcards, constructed by drawing and storytelling, followed by sharing them with children across the globe, proved to be engaging and motivational for both the children and their teachers. Other initiatives – such as drawing, book reading, murals, show and tell of artefacts from the other place and practicing the song "Over in Australia" (Berkes, 2011; Gollmick & Dunkley, 1918) – between visits further demonstrated the significance of the connections made between the two groups of children. This section addresses two significant themes that emerged from the research: partnerships of meaning-making and multimodal approaches. Use of blogs is woven through the discussion of these two findings.

Partnerships of meaning-making

Creating the postcards provided opportunities to deepen children's understandings of their lived experiences (Binder, 2011). As the project progressed, the children became more empowered to make their thoughts visible through their drawing and stories (Kress & Selander, 2013) and to share their work with others. Using blogs to share their postcards provided a more immediate opportunity for the children in both countries to connect with each other (Nolan, 2003). This also supported collaboration and communication between children, teachers and the researchers (Shearer, 2010).

The idea of a "pen pal" generated excitement as the children chose what they wanted to draw and tell the children in the partnered country. These illustrated introductions and stories showed their families, where they lived, their pets or other things of importance to them in their worlds. The following figures reflect important information the children chose to share initially.

Figure 8.1 illustrates a multitude of information and questions at the end when a Canadian child shared:

> My name is_____. My house is in Canada. Canada is a fun place. It is fun to play in the park. I drew the picture by myself. It is my house. My school is fun to play and my best friend if Maya J. Do sharks live in Australia? Mountains live in Canada. Raccoons live in Canada. I am four years old. Seashells and rocks live in Canada.

This child demonstrates an understanding of his surroundings and aspects of his environment. What is interesting is his animistic portrayal of natural objects living in his country. It would appear he wants to include everything he sees as having a home, as he does. Based on discussions about creating the first postcard, this child has tried to give as much information as he can, including geographical aspects. His drawing depicts many of the images he speaks of in his story.

Figure 8.2 reflects an important moment in this Canadian child's life as she had just moved. She shares, "This is my moving place. My windows are very nice. There is music in my house. It is a beautiful place. I really love it because I love it". She reflects a sense of joy in her drawing as she shares this event. The bright colours mirror the beauty she describes. One can look out the windows in her drawing and see the sun. While there are no questions asked in this postcard, she has chosen to share what is happening in her life at that moment.

FIGURE 8.1 My house is in Canada.

FIGURE 8.2 This is my moving place.

In Figure 8.3, an Australian child draws and tells about where he lives, focusing on his pet dog and his favourite TV show. Both Canadian and Australian children depicted their everyday lives and what was important to their worlds. This validated the contextual choices children made and reflected the developing agentic qualities observed throughout the project.

These first postcards posted on the blog generated much discussion in both countries. Discussions generated questions about climate and the kinds of animals that lived in each country (see Figure 8.4). The Australian teacher reported the children's fascination with living in apartments, which is quite uncommon in the city where the Australian children lived. To follow this up she read a story about different kinds of dwellings around the world, and reported:

> That's been threaded through some of the books I've read. Someone will say, "Oh that's like in Canada". They would make comments on it. Difference in weather. They really switched on about that.

Sharing this information empowered the children over time as they continued to take more ownership not just over the postcards, but over the project itself. The Canadian children, for example, selected where they wanted their stamp to be placed. In both countries, much discussion took place during the drawing of the postcards and storytelling. The postcards offered visual and textual cues for response.

Having pen pals provided an audience for the children. The stories became more detailed and more questions were posed. This not only situated them as agentic, but also created an engaging learning environment. Illustrative of this partnership are the pictures and dialogue between two children from each country who discussed houses, pets and travel. The Australian child chose to respond to the Canadian child's first postcard as follows in Figure 8.5.

I live in C▬▬. I live near
▬▬'s house. I play with my dog.
His mame is Jet. He jumps on me
and he licks me. He barks. I like
being inside. I sometimes watch
TV. I like Barby. I have 10 Barbsy
dolls.
From ▬▬

FIGURE 8.3 An Australian story.

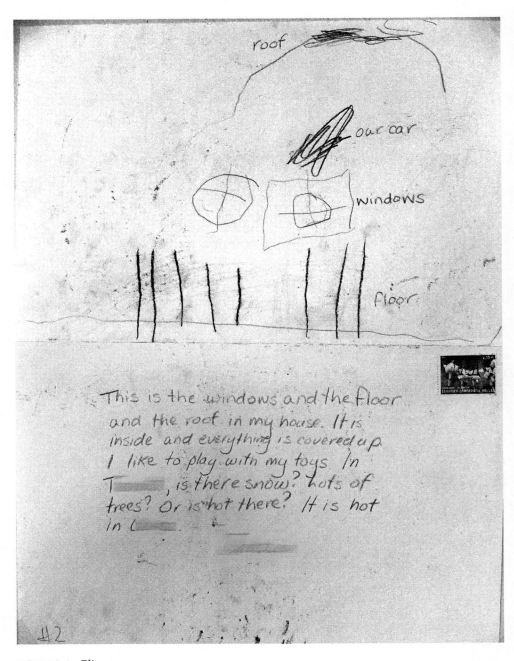

FIGURE 8.4 Climate.

Hello
I am ____, I have two dogs. Kuntha is the boy dog and Sarah is the girl dog. I have a pool. I swim up the deep end and the shallow end. I saw some cows at a farm. I went on a holiday to a big hotel. Do you live in a big, tall house? The dogs play in the yard.

FIGURE 8.5 Postcard from Australia.

Hello __. I am ___. I have two dogs. Kuntha is the boy dog and Sarah is the girl dog. I have a pool. I swam up the deep end and shallow end. I saw some cows on a farm. I went on holiday to a big hotel. Do you live in a big tall house? The dogs play in the yard.

In response to the Australian child's question, "Do you live in a big tall house?" the Canadian child responded, "I don't live in a tall house. There is a big kitchen and there is a bedroom for me, my mom and my dad. And there is an office. My house is wide".

A sharing of information about each child's personal life appears to have been initiated. This was the beginning of a partnership. This is supported by the Australian child stating that he has two dogs, a pool and went on a holiday to a big hotel. The Canadian child reciprocates by stating he went trick or treating for Halloween and got decorations (see Figure 8.6).

The Canadian child responded (see Figure 8.7) with a further postcard reiterating that he lives in a "short house" and contributes to his Australian friend's description of his pets and his travels with a depiction of his cat and a further question about his friend's travels. He ends by inviting his Australian friend to travel to visit him in Canada.

Also observed was the children's acceptance of each other's efforts. In Canada, the children would chat with each other as they created the postcards for their long-distance friends. Though they worked on the postcards individually, there was a collaborative conversation about the postcards and how they were looking forward to receiving a new one. Partnerships were forged between countries, but also within the individual classrooms.

The children gained more confidence and empowerment of voice was observed as they created more postcards through added detail and information sharing. The online postings and being able to observe the postcard exchanges seemed to augment children's growing agency.

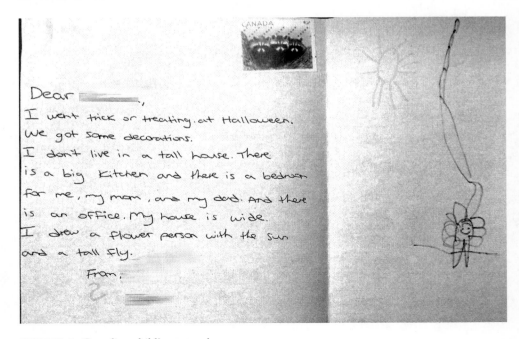

FIGURE 8.6 Canadian child's postcard.

FIGURE 8.7 Invitation to visit.

Multimodal approaches

In our research, children were offered multiple modes of expression, such as drawing, painting, storytelling and photography (Arya & Feathers, 2012). While the postcards themselves and the blogs as a way of sharing the postcards were researcher-initiated, other modes were child-initiated, such as the Canadian children learning and performing the song "Over in Australia" (Berkes, 2011; Gollmick & Dunkley, 1918) and Australian children wanting to have cameras, and teacher-initiated. Taking a multimodal approach, largely arts-based, allowed children both choice of modes of expression and a voice that may not have otherwise been heard (Binder, 2011; Sorin, 2014).

The postcards were created using both visual images and stories. For example, in Figure 8.8 an Australian child used bold colours and organic lines in her visual representation of her outdoor environment. Identifiable features include a sun, a dark sky and a flower.

Her story further expresses her ideas. She said,

> It is dark. The sun went down. I said to Mum, "Can we go to the park soon?" There were flowers and sunflowers. It was very, very dark and I could see the stars and the moon. Mum said, "Dinner is ready". We had fish and chips. In the middle is my house. The brown part is the lounge room. Down below is the shed and the playroom.

The combined visual representation and story convey a richer meaning than the image or story would if only one was created on its own. Her work demonstrates how much a four-year-old may actually understand about her world as described in her story. In this research, multimodality took a number of forms beyond the actual postcard creation. Some children undertook life drawings of their class environments, particularly the class vegetable garden (see Figure 8.9).

FIGURE 8.8 Australian child's environment.

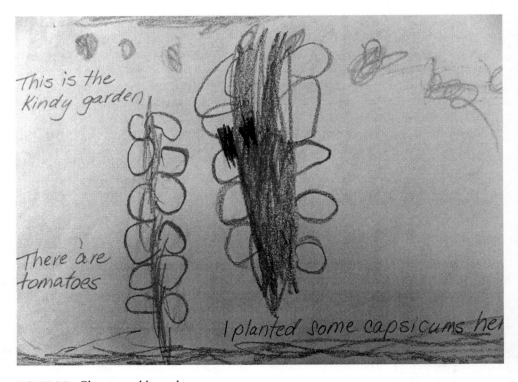

FIGURE 8.9 Class vegetable garden.

As stated earlier, in Australia a number of children wanted to use a camera to document their environment. They were given access to a camera, choosing what they wanted to photograph to share with their Canadian counterparts. Figure 8.10 shows a photograph of the Australian playground.

With parental permission, children in both countries also shared photos of themselves, putting faces to the names on the postcards. The use of blogs, in this particular instance, allowed for the sharing of personal information that would not normally be appropriate. The software, running on a secure university server, was implemented to comply with university research ethics policies. The researchers, who had password access, only knew the URL of the blog. This level of privacy was sufficient to protect children's identity while allowing them to share more information about themselves with others in a "safe" manner. This gave the children an important visual of their pen pal. Time zones made video chatting too much of a logistical challenge.

The researcher in Canada read the children *Over in Australia* (Berkes, 2011), modelled after and meant to be sung to the tune of "Over in the Meadow" (a traditional poem, adapted for picture books and illustrated by many, for example, Keats, 1999). From this experience, the Canadian children chose to learn the story/song, and an audio recording was made of them singing it. Children not only learned the song, but also drew pictures and counted the number of animals described in the story. The song was performed for parents at their annual holiday celebration and the drawings were displayed. Figure 8.11 reflects one child's interpretation of the song.

On a number of occasions, small groups of children at both venues decided to create murals of their environment and the other environment. Figure 8.12 shows a mural of the Australian environment, created by Canadian children. The mural, constructed with pencil and markers, depicts the garden, playground and images that resonated with the children,

FIGURE 8.10 Australian playground.

FIGURE 8.11 "Over in Australia".

FIGURE 8.12 Mural of Australian environment.

such as the duck-billed platypus. The cassowary is also included and is significant as it is a large Australian bird that is the kindergarten mascot. The Canadian children were fascinated by this large creature and wanted to learn more.

The cassowary was also featured in a story written by the Australian children to their Canadian friends. Figure 8.13 shows the cassowary mascot adopted by the Kindergarten children.

We want to tell you about a special bird that lives only near our place. He is called a Cassowary. The Cassowary is the bird on our Kindergarten T Shirts and his picture is on our Kindergarten. He lives in the rainforest and eats the fruit from the forest so if we cut down the forest he would die. We have waterfalls in the rainforest, they tumble over the rocks and trees so the Cassowary can get a drink. We read a story called 'Calvin' and learned that the Dad Cassowary sits on the eggs until they hatch. ____ told us that a Cassowary crashed into her Grandma's car at Kurrumine Beach. It ran off so we hope it was O.K. It rains a lot here and sometimes we have big storms.

FIGURE 8.13 Cassowary mascot.

Other forms of multimodal expression included a word list of Australian birds, dramatisations of life in the other environment (e.g. putting on scarves and mittens for Canadian winters), writing class "farewell" letters (see Figure 8.14) to each other at the end of the research and bringing in artefacts, such as a toy raccoon from Canada. In Australia, several of the children wrote the following (in their writing):

Dear _____ friends,

We play Angry Birds here in _____. We have birds outside. They are cocatoos, Rainbow Lorikeets, Butcher Birds (peck our birdss), Pelicans, Bush Turkeys, Bats, Red Tailed cocatoos, Sunbirds, Willy Wagtails, Cassowaries, Minah birds.

From your friends in _____

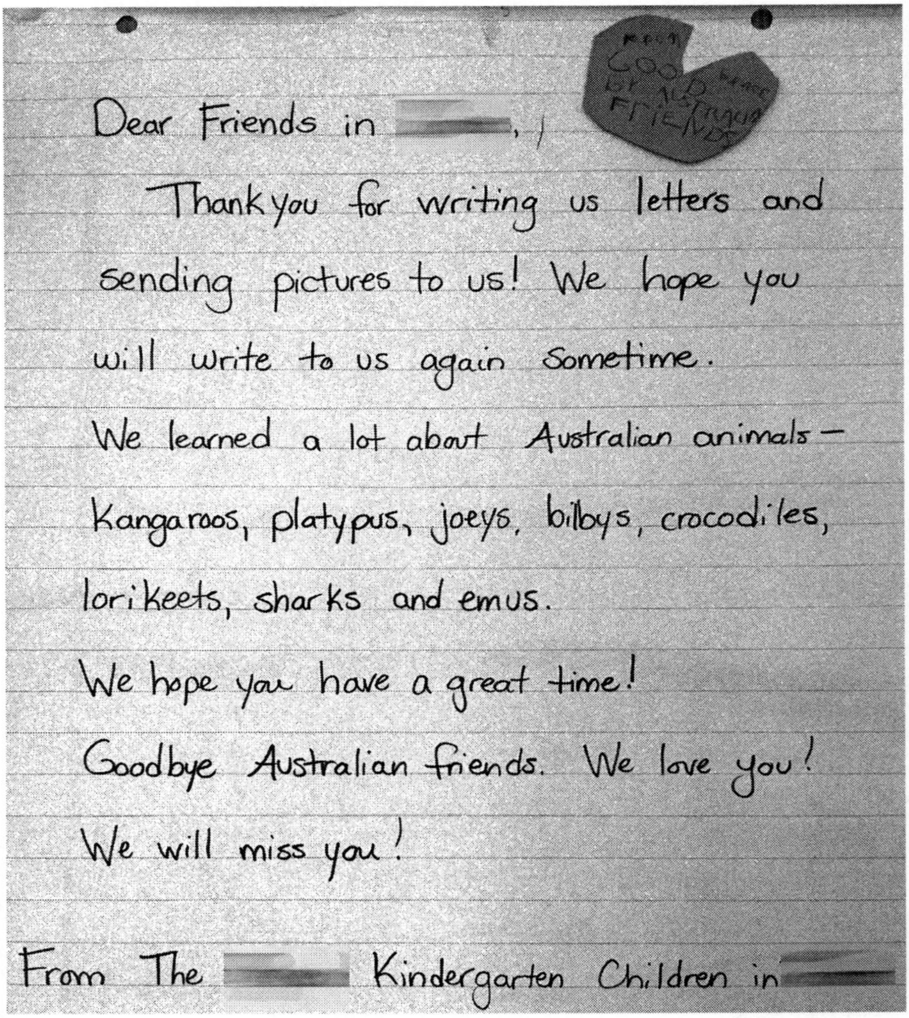

FIGURE 8.14 Farewell letter.

While multiple choices of expression were offered and taken up by the children, for some children this also gave them a voice. For example, one Australian child rarely spoke and did not participate in class activities. Her understanding of what was expected in terms of the postcard creation was not clear to the teacher. But after seeing the Canadian postcards, listening to class discussions and watching other children make postcards, she began working one on one with a researcher. A multimodal approach not only offered children choices of expression, but also gave more hesitant children a voice that would not have otherwise been heard (Sorin, 2014).

Conclusion

This project provided deeper insight into how young children make meaning of their lived experiences through different modalities such as drawing, painting, storytelling, song and photography (Binder & Kotsopoulos, 2011; Jewitt & Kress, 2003; Sorin; 2014; Wolfe & Flewitt, 2010). The use of online blogs offered an immediate, authentic and engaging way for the children to share their ideas to a wider audience (Lee, 2011; Nolan, 2003). A virtual community of learners was started (Nolan & Weiss, 2002) through sharing individual and class creations.

The researchers recognised the challenges with not only the time-zone differences but also the difficulty of synchronising the school year. More time would have benefitted the ongoing relationships the children were making with each other even further. As well, it would have built efficacy in working with the online blogs for the teachers in the room. Extending the timeline to create other opportunities for the children to use multimodal texts (Kress, 2003) with the blogs, such as oral components and videos, could allow children to share their stories more directly. This in turn could strengthen the agentic and emergent qualities of such learning approaches, building not only the capacities of the children but also of their teachers.

Multimodal meaning-making through digital postcards provided opportunities for children to make sense of their local and global worlds. This project demonstrated the importance of affording children the time and tools to explore not only their lived experiences but also those of others.

Acknowledgements

The authors would like to thank the following: Dr. Roger Wilkinson and Dr. Philemon Chigeza for their contribution as research team members in Cairns. Research assistants: in Toronto, Kyla Landon and Matthew Malbon; and in Cairns, Tamara Brooks, Miriam Torzillo and Ute Haring. The Faculty of Community Services (SRC travel grant), the School of Early Childhood Studies, Ryerson University and James Cook University for funding support. The EDGE Lab at Ryerson for technical and research support. This research was supported, in part, by a grant from the Canadian Social Sciences and Humanities Research Council (SSHRC).

References

Arya, P. & Feathers, K. M. (2012). Reconsidering children's readings: insights into the reading process. *Reading Psychology, 33*(4), 301–22.

Bamford, A. (2003). *The Visual Literacy White Paper*. Stockley, Uxbridge: Adobe System Inc.

Barone, T. & Eisner, E. W. (2012). *Arts Based Research*. Thousand Oaks, CA: Sage.

Berkes, M. (2011). *Over in Australia*. Nevada City, CA: Dawn.

Binder, M. (2011). Contextual worlds of child art: experiencing multiple literacies through images. *Contemporary Issues in Early Childhood, 12*(4), 367–84.

Binder, M. & Kotsopoulos, S. (2011). Multimodal literacy narratives: weaving the threads of young children's identity through the arts. *Journal of Research in Childhood Education, 25*(4), 339–63.

Boulay, M. C. & Lynch, K. A. (2012). Fostering environmental stewardship through creative expression: incorporating art into service-learning. *Interdisciplinary Humanities, 29*(3), 102–14.

Britsch, S. (2013). Visual language and science understanding: a brief tutorial for teachers. *Australian Journal of Language & Literacy, 36*(1), 17–27.

Buckingham, D. (2006). Defining digital literacy: what do young people need to know about digital media? *The Nordic Journal of Digital Literacy, 1*(4), 263–76.

Burnett, C. (2009). Research into literacy and technology in primary classrooms: an exploration of understandings generated by recent studies. *Journal of Research in Reading, 32*(1), 22–37.

Creswell, J. W. (2008). *Educational research*. Upper Saddle River, NJ: Pearson.

Davison, S. E. (2013). Yes, kindergartners can blog, and so can their teachers! *Learning & Leading with Technology, 40*(6), 26–28.

Duhn, I. (2012). Making "place" for ecological sustainability in early childhood education. *Environmental Education Research, 18*(1), 19–29.

Fesakis, G., Sofroniou, C. & Mavroudi, E. (2011). Using the internet for communicative learning activities in kindergarten: the case of the "Shapes planet". *Early Childhood Education Journal, 38*(5), 385–92.

Flewitt, R. (2013). Multimodal perspectives on early childhood literacies. In: J. Larson & J. Marsh (Eds), *The Sage Handbook of Early Childhood Literacy* (2nd ed.) (pp. 295–309). London: Sage Publications.

Gollmick, E. (composer) & Dunkley, A. W. (lyricist) (1918). "Over in Australia". Hobart, Australia: Mercury. Retrieved 2 August 2012 from http://nla.gov.au/nla.mus-an24537339

González, N., Moll, I. & Amanti, C. (Eds.). (2005). *Funds of Knowledge: Theorizing Practices Households, Communities and Classrooms*. Rahway, NJ: Lawrence Erlbaum.

Hacking, E., Barratt, R. & Scott, W. (2007) Engaging children: research issues around participation and environmental learning. *Environmental Education Research, 13*(4), 529–44.

Hopperstad, M. H. (2010). Studying meaning in children's drawings. *Journal of Early Childhood Literacy, 10*(4), 430–52.

Jenkins, H. (2006). *Convergence Culture: Where Old and New Media Collide*. New York: New York University Press.

Jewitt, C. & Kress, G. (2003). *Multimodal Literacy*. New York: Peter Lang.

Keats, E. J. (1999). *Over in the Meadow*. New York: Penguin Readers Group.

Kind, S. (2010). Art encounters: movements in the arts and early childhood education. In: V. Pacini-Ketchabaw (Ed.), *Flows, Rhythms, and Intensities of Early Childhood Education Curriculum* (pp. 113–31). New York: Peter Lang.

Knight, L. (2008). Communication and transformation through collaboration: rethinking drawing activities in early childhood. *Contemporary Issues in Early Childhood Journal, 9*(4), 307–16.

Krenz, A. (2004). The secret of children's pictures. In: D. Mitchell (Ed.), *Waldorf Journal Project #18*, (pp. 33–36). Chatham, NY: Waldorf Publications. Retrieved 2 June 2013 from http://www.waldorflibrary.org/images/stories/articles/WJP18_krenzdrawings.pdf

Kress, G. (1997). *Before Writing: Rethinking the Paths to Literacy*. London: Routledge.

Kress, G. (2003). *Literacy in the New Media Age*. London: Routledge.

Kress, G. & Selander, S. (2012). Multimodal design, learning and cultures of recognition. *Internet and Higher Education, 15*(4), 265–68.

Leavy, P. (2011). *Essentials of Transdisciplinary Research: Using Problem-centered Methodologies*. Walnut Creek, CA: Left Coast Press.

Lee, L. (2011). Blogging: promoting learner autonomy and intercultural competence through study abroad. *Language Learning & Technology, 15*(3), 87–109.

Louv, R. (2008). *The Nature Principle*. Chapel Hill, NC: Algonquin Books.

MacNaughton, G. & Hughes, P. (2009). *Doing Action Research in Early Childhood Studies – A Step by Step Guide*. Maidenhead: Open University Press.

McPake, J., Plowman, L. & Stephen, C. (2013). Pre-school children creating and communicating with digital technologies in the home. *British Journal of Educational Technology, 44*(3), 421–31.

Moore, R. A. & Seeger, V. (2009). Dear sincerely: exploring literate identities with young children and preservice teachers through letter writing. *Literacy Research and Instruction, 48*(2), 185–205.

Nelms, E. L. (2002). The effects of a teacher-created web page on parent communication: an action research study. *Action Research Exchange, 1*(2).

Noddings, N. (2011). Care ethics in education. In: J. A. Kentel (Ed.), *Educating the Young: The Ethics of Care* (pp. 7–19). Bern: Peter Lang.

Nolan, J. (2003). Blogs. In: K. Christensen & D. Levinson (Eds), *Encyclopedia of Community: From the Village to the Virtual World* (pp. 96–97). Thousand Oaks, CA: Sage.

Nolan, J. & McBride, M. (2014). Beyond gamification: reconceptualizing game-based learning in early childhood environments. *Information, Communication & Society, 17*(5), 594–608.

Nolan, J. & Weiss, J. (2002). Learning cyberspace: an educational view of virtual community. In: A. Renninger & W. Shumar (Eds), *Building Virtual Communities: Learning and Change in Cyberspace* (pp. 293–320). Cambridge: Cambridge University Press.

Nolan, J., Raynes-Goldie, K. & McBride, M. (2011). The stranger danger: exploring surveillance, autonomy, and privacy in children's use of social media. *Canadian Children Journal, 36*(2), 24–32.

Powell, G. & McCauley, A. W. (2012). Blogging as a way to promote family-professional partnerships. *Young Exceptional Children, 15*(2), 20–31.

Rose, G. (2007). *Visual Methodologies: An Introduction to the Interpretation of Visual Materials* (2nd ed.). London: Sage.

Shandomo, H. M. (2009). Getting to know you: cross-cultural pen pals expand children's world view. *Childhood Education, 85*(3), 154–59.

Shearer, K. M. (2010). Blogging and internet filters in schools. *Community & Junior College Libraries, 16*(4), 259–63.

Shuker, M.-J. & Terreni, L. (2013). Self-authored e-books: expanding young children's literacy experiences and skills. *Australasian Journal of Early Childhood, 38*(3), 17–24.

Sorin, R. (2014). Sharing postcards about where we live – early childhood environmental understanding. *International Journal of Early Childhood Learning, 20*(3), 35–49.

Soto, L. D. (2005). Children make the best theorists. In: L. D. Soto & B. B. Swadener (Eds), *Power and Voice in Research with Children* (pp. 9–19). New York: Peter Lang.

Theron, L., Mitchell, C., Smith, A. & Stuart, J. (Eds) (2011). *Picturing Research: Drawing as Visual Methodology*. Rotterdam: Sense Publishers.

Tobolka, D. (2006). Connecting teachers and parents through the internet. *Tech Directions, 66*(5), 24–26.

Vangsnes, V., Gram Økland, N. & Krumsvik, R. (2012). Computer games in pre-school settings: didactical challenges when commercial educational computer games are implemented in kindergartens. *Computers & Education, 58*(4), 1138–48.

Vasquez, V. M. & Felderman, C. B. (2013). *Technology and Critical Literacy in Early Childhood*. New York: Routledge.

Wolfe, S. & Flewitt, R. (2010). New technologies, new multimodal literacy practices and young children's metacognitive development. *Cambridge Journal of Education, 40*(4), 387–99.

WordPress (version 4.0). (computer software). Retrieved 3 April 2011 from http://wordpress.org.

Wright, S. (2010). *Understanding Creativity in Early Childhood*. London: Sage.

Zawilinski, L. (2009). HOT blogging: a framework for blogging to promote higher order thinking. *The Reading Teacher, 62*(8), 650–61.

9

AVAILABILITY AND USE OF PERSONAL COMPUTERS IN GERMAN KINDERGARTENS – PRECONDITIONS AND INFLUENCES

Martina Endepohls-Ulpe, Claudia Quaiser-Pohl and Christine Deckers

Abstract

This chapter is based on an overview of the developmental preconditions of preschoolers and the current state of the pedagogical discussion on the benefits and detrimental effects of computers on young children. It analyses the results of a questionnaire study with 493 headmasters and teachers of kindergartens from two German federal states (North-Rhine Westphalia and Rhineland-Palatinate), showing that the most important factor with respect to the extent and the way digital media are used seemed to be the teachers' commitment and their interest in this topic. Thus, to enhance the quality of technology education in the field of digital media, an improvement of teacher education and advanced training is essential.

Introduction

During the last decade, even very young children have had more and more contact with digital media in general and computers in particular in their everyday lives. However, in the German preschool education digital technology has officially been widely neglected. Participating in the German debate about computers in kindergarten there are still some authors who demand that computers should be kept out of the preschool classroom. They argue that computers not only do not improve children's development, but also make them "fat, stupid and aggressive" (Spitzer, 2009). Even German media educators do not see any urgent need to equip kindergarten classrooms with computers (Aufenanger, 2009). Hence, it is not surprising that practitioners are alienated by and not sure how to deal with new technologies in the preschool classroom.

The lack of theoretically well-grounded concepts for media education, in general, may be partly due to the fact that there are still a lot of reservations among scientists from different disciplines, as well as among practitioners in preschool education, about the idea of three- to six-year-old preschoolers using and profiting from the use of digital technology.

This chapter will present a study on preschool educators' attitudes towards the use of computers and consequences for the ways computers are used in German kindergartens. As the basis for an interpretation and discussion of the data, a short overview of the cognitive, communicative and socioemotional stage of development and the developmental needs for the learning of children aged between three and six years is provided first. The main pros and cons of the current psychological and pedagogical discussion about the early use of digital media and the current state of the debate are then depicted. Additionally, the curricular framework for German daycare institutions is analysed with respect to recommendations or guidelines for kindergarten teachers on how to deal with information technology in the preschool classroom.

Developmental preconditions of preschool children with respect to the use of digital media

Charlton (2007) postulates that children should have acquired three main competencies to be able to cope with and understand the content of digital media: 1) communicative, 2) cognitive and 3) emotional competence. For him, communicative competence is the ability to interact symbolically; cognitive competence means the ability to understand the meanings of content; and emotional competence is the ability to choose topics of interest and hold off threatening topics. Henninger (1994) emphasises the part of play as an important component of early learning and development. As a guarantee of healthy growth and development, preschool children have to get play opportunities of high quality.

According to Piaget's theory of cognitive development (Piaget, 1969), children are active and intrinsically motivated learners who develop their intelligence by acting upon the environment, interpreting and handling the environment by their existing cognitive schemata and by developing new cognitive structures when confronted with new environmental features. In the first two years, the stage of sensomotoric development, this acting upon the environment is an active, bodily handling of things. Children use their eyes, ears and hands to discover the world and to solve problems. At the end of this stage, they acquire the ability to mentally represent things. This new ability characterises the preoperational stage and also offers the possibility to mentally manipulate these representations (Sodian, 2008). What children are still lacking at this stage, according to Piaget's findings, are mental operations like the classification and conservation of mass or quantity. These abilities, as well as the ability to conduct simple logical operations, develop in the concrete operational stage, which starts at the age of seven. However, there is plenty of evidence that Piaget underestimated the abilities of young children and that they are capable of various symbolic manipulations not predicted in the Piagetian theory (for an overview, see Lipinski et al., 1986).

Understanding children's communicative competence is also important. From age one to two years, children already have the ability to symbolise. Young children continue to enlarge their vocabulary up to around 10,000 words until they are six years old. When they are three or four, children are able to adopt various grammatical rules. Their speech comprehension is always better than their ability to produce language. Preschoolers are skilled conversational partners who are able to keep up a dialogue (for an overview, see Berk, 2011).

Preschool children show increasing self-related emotions like pride, shame or guilt, depending on the kind of feedback on success or failure they get from their social environment. They are able to apply various strategies of emotional self-regulation, which is the ability to bring one's emotional state to a comfortable or at least acceptable level. It includes strategies like avoiding or withdrawing from unpleasant stimuli, restraining impulses or distraction.

Simultaneously with developing the ability of symbolic interaction, preschool children begin with pretend-play activities, which later pass on to sociodramatic role-play with peers. These types of play dominate the preschool age together with exploration and the construction of games. Henninger (1994) postulates that in favour of the best possible conditions for their development and learning, children need play opportunities that are active, child-selected and directed, experience- and process-oriented, which facilitate imagination and creativity as well as assimilative learning, which bear low risks and are enjoyable.

Debates about the use of computers in early childhood education and requirements for play and learning

The debate on the questions of whether or not preschool children should use computers and computers should be integrated in preschool classrooms is polarised between two positions: 1) computers are detrimental to health and learning, and 2) computers can make a key contribution to children's social and intellectual development (Plowman & Stephen, 2003, p. 151). Plowman and Stephen classify the first position as a response to fears about new technologies similar to the first concerns and research about the impact of television on children. They criticise the kind of "effect research" resulting from such positions as depicting children as passive and denying any agency of the children, who actually are active users of technology. The authors also complain about the lack of social and cultural dimensions in such a research framework.

Summarising the discussion on possible detrimental effects of young children using the computer, Plowman and Stephen (2003, p. 151) state that "there does not appear currently to be any clear evidence on the deleterious effects of exposure to ICT". Hence, using computers does not seem to be dangerous, at least when adequate preconditions are given. Rather, a focus is needed on what children can learn from digital technology. Plowman, Stevenson, Stephen and McPake (2012, p. 35 ff.) answer the question "What do children learn with ICT?" in a multimethod study with respect to the home environment. They conclude that:

1. Children acquire operational skills in the form of an understanding of the functions of several computer-related items, e.g. mouse, touch screen, game controllers, as well as the ability to operate them. They also develop concepts of technological interactivity, i.e. that taking a certain action can produce a specific response.
2. Children extend their knowledge and understanding of the world – this includes learning in areas like maths, language, knowledge about living things, people and places, all topics included in software websites and talking books.
3. Children's disposition to learn can be enhanced by gains of self-esteem and confidence as a consequence of success and independence, persistence and patience in the face of difficulties.
4. Children learn about the role of technology in everyday life and for social and cultural purposes, for example communication, employment, studying and entertainment.

Referring to a concept of "literacy development" that is not restricted to just acquiring the ability to read and write but to the way in which children generally develop inner control over meaning-making systems, Wolfe and Flewitt (2010) show that children acquire literacy both with new and traditional literacy-related technologies, and this happens due to what they call a "collaborative multimodal dialogue" (p. 393) with siblings and adults, a dialogue that encompasses action, spoken language and artefacts.

One general and frequently adduced argument for the necessity to foster and guide young children's access to ICT is that digital technologies play a big part in Western cultures with respect to communication and the transfer of information. Digital artefacts can be found in many areas of everyday life (Downes et al., 2001; McPake, Plowman & Stephen, 2013; Wolfe & Flewitt, 2010). Children get in contact with digital technology at home and through their peers. Digital devices have become ubiquitous cultural tools that are necessary to participate in society and culture. Children must learn to express themselves and make sense of their world with digital media, artefacts and tools just as they do with traditional media. Hence, it is an indispensable duty at all stages of the educational system to teach children how to use them successfully.

From the point of view that all children should have the same chances to become capable members of a society in which "knowledge and communication are highly prized commodities" (Wolfe & Flewitt, 2010, p. 397), all children should also learn to become "literate" regarding new media. As the chances to get access to the internet and computers are limited for many children in their early years, practitioners have to be provided with the curriculum guidance and training they need to understand how the children might achieve this most effectively (Wolfe & Flewitt, 2010).

This argument leads to the question of the preconditions that must be given to guarantee a joyful, fruitful and furthering interaction of young children with digital technologies. The first condition is that digital resources are child-oriented, which means that they are open-ended and promote communication, interaction, discovery and problem-solving (Downes et al., 2001). Second, "adult mediation" (Nir-Gal & Klein, 2004) or guided interaction by adults (McPake, Plowman & Stephen, 2013; Stephen & Plowman, 2008), be they parents or kindergarten teachers, seems absolutely essential to make the use of computers for young children efficient and to prevent them from frustrating experiences. Leaving the children alone without any guidance or only with some sort of reactive supervision limits the children's possible experiences with ICT, especially when children use the computer as complete novices (Plowman & Stephen, 2005). In contrast to this, adult-mediated computer activity seems to improve children's cognitive development (Nir-Gal & Klein, 2004).

Curriculum standards for technology education in German preschools

It is only since the year 2004 that there has been a common framework of the federal states of Germany for early education in daycare (Gemeinsamer Rahmen der Länder für die frühe Bildung in Kindertageseinrichtungen, Beschluss der Jugendministerkonferenz vom 13./14.05.2004/ Beschluss der Kultusministerkonferenz vom 03./04.06). Up to that date, early education in kindergartens in Germany had mostly had the character of care, at best of fostering development without any binding contents of learning. The new framework recommends a holistic approach, playful and explorative learning and the consideration of individual differences. Technology as an area of education is explicitly mentioned, appearing as "(information-) technology", which may include the use of computers, but they are not specifically listed.

Since a special characteristic of the German educational system is educational federalism (which means that the school system is under control of the federal states), each state has formulated its own curriculum for early childhood education. Even though the curricula of the states should be based on the guidelines cited above, they differ essentially in specification and mention different areas of learning.

For Rhineland-Palatinate, one of the two states in this study, computers are explicitly mentioned as one type of media in the recommendations for daycare education, and it is generally recommended that children should learn to handle media and to develop a critical attitude concerning the use of media. There is no explicit recommendation if and how computers should be established in the classroom (Ministerium für Bildung, Frauen und Jugend des Landes Rheinland-Pfalz, Referat Kindertagesstätten, 2004).

In North-Rhine Westphalia, the second of the two states, the "Principles for fostering the education of children from 0 to 10 years" (Ministerium für Schule und Weiterbildung & Ministerium für Familie, Kinder, Jugend, Kultur und Sport, 2010) mention computers in the education section "media". Here, computers are repeatedly and explicitly referred to in the guidelines, e.g. that children should learn about the connection of new (internet, computer) and old (typewriter, cassette tape) media, that there should be facilities for pretend and role play also with media topics (computer) and in the section "materials/settings as thought-provoking impulses", the use of computers as well as offering computer courses for children is recommended, as is the supply of age-appropriate games and software. However, there are only very vague and general statements about what and how children should learn with respect to the use of media, and recommendations on how teachers should guide the use of computers and software are missing.

Focus of study

This chapter reports the results from a questionnaire that focused on attitudes of German kindergarten educators and nursery nurses, as well as the motivations of heads of kindergartens and providers of kindergartens. The questionnaire was conducted in 2010. The study was part of the Ph.D. thesis of one of the authors (Deckers, 2012).

Participants

The study was conducted as an online study where 495 people completed the survey (response rate of 53 per cent). Most of the 88.03 per cent (n=434) of the participants were women and 11.97 per cent (n=59) were men, which reflects the situation that kindergarten staff are mainly female. The age range was 19 to 71 years. The majority of participants were heads of kindergarten (92.64 per cent, n=390); only 5.94 per cent (n=25) were educators/nursery nurses or others.

With regard to the federal state, about three-quarters (75.05 per cent, n=370) of the participants came from North-Rhine Westphalia and only 24.95 per cent (n=123) belonged to Rhineland-Palatinate, which approximately reflects the different sizes of the two federal states, with North-Rhine Westphalia having more than four times more inhabitants than Rhineland-Palatinate (Statistische Ämter des Bundes und der Länder [Statistical offices of the state and the federal states], 2014).

Size and type of kindergartens

The size of the kindergartens also differed from only one room to more than 10 rooms. Most of the kindergartens (52.02 per cent, n=219) had five to 10 rooms, another 35.15 per cent (n=148) of the institutions had even more than 10 rooms, while only almost 13 per cent of them had four rooms or less. With regard to the size, the amount of groups within the kindergartens also differed. The amount of children cared for in one kindergarten differed from 15 to 301 (M=65.01, SD=29.2).

With regard to the age of the children going to the kindergartens, most of them (n=198) were open for children from age two to six. However, some offered places (n=77) for children from one to two years and some (n=11) for children from four to six exclusively.

Most of the kindergartens (36.58 per cent, n=154) mentioned a "situation–orientated approach" as their pedagogical concept, another third of the kindergartens called their concept "open" (11.88 per cent, n=50) or "half-open" (19.48 per cent, N=82), and only a minority (less than 7 per cent) mentioned a specific pedagogy like Montessori, Waldorf or Reggio.

Results

Attitudes towards computers in kindergarten

There were some interesting findings on the attitudes of the participants towards computers in kindergarten. The majority of the participants (79.31 per cent) thought that children should be able to handle computers already in kindergarten; most of them (59.84 per cent) that the first approach towards the computer should start already at preschool age (4–6 year olds); another 26.17 per cent that it should happen in kindergarten; only 13.59 per cent that this should happen later (in primary school or at the transition to primary school or only from the age of 10 on). Asked about the group of children for which using computers was particularly necessary, the clear majority (90.06 per cent) said "for all children", only 3.45 per cent mentioned "children with special needs" and migrant children (2.23 per cent). However, most of the participants (65.52 per cent) thought that computers should have a subordinate role in kindergarten, and only 21.30 per cent had the opinion that computers should have a "normal" role. Not less than 11.65 per cent were sure that computers should play no role at all in kindergarten.

Asked about the constraints for the use of computers in a kindergarten, the majority (69.17 per cent) mentioned constraints of time and of the content/aim of computer use. Another 10.34 per cent thought that there should be no constraints; another 1.62 per cent agreed with a permanent use. The following factors were mentioned as predominantly influencing the amount of time the children spend with a computer activity: age (by 39.76 per cent of the participants) and the purpose for which the computer is used (i.e. gaming, surfing the internet, learning, by 30.02 per cent).

The majority of respondents (60.85 per cent) saw the use of computers in a kindergarten as not critical and the participants mainly (67.75 per cent) perceived working at the computer with children as a personal enrichment. With regard to specific domains for which using computers in a kindergarten are particularly beneficial, the eye–hand coordination was mentioned in the first place (by 23.9 per cent), followed by "the ability to concentrate" (19.5 per cent), language (17.0 per cent) and math (16.3 per cent). Another 8.7 per cent of the participants mentioned later life work here, as well as social behaviour (8.2 per cent) and creativity (6.3 per cent).

External and internal support for the use of computers

Another crucial question was, under what circumstances computers were used in the kindergarten. The first aspect was the availability of computers in kindergartens: although in most of the kindergartens that participated in the study (62.47 per cent) computers were available for the children, this was not the case in more than one-third (37.53 per cent) of the kindergartens. When asked about the reasons for not using the computer with children, 25.23 per cent of the participants mentioned a low financial budget and a lack of sponsors; while another 18.35 per cent mentioned the educational focus and program of the institution, which was not compatible with the use of computers by children. A lack of space/rooms (9.49 per cent), staff (8.23 per cent) and time (6.33 per cent), as well as a lack of knowledge/competence (7.59 per cent), were other reasons mentioned by the respondents.

Other questions focused on the training/education of the staff in the computer domain, i.e. the offers of additional training courses for the kindergarten staff and how they were financially supported. When the providers of kindergartens were asked whether they offered such additional training courses, the majority (63.89 per cent) answered "no". If such courses were offered, in the majority of the cases (50.51 per cent), they had been financially supported by the provider, and in 26.11 per cent of the cases they had not. In another 22.72 per cent of cases, they had been partly financed by the provider.

Computer knowledge and competence of the kindergarten staff

Most of the respondents estimated their knowledge and competence in this domain as fairly good (50.12 per cent), as good (35.39 per cent) or as very good (2.61 per cent); only about 13 per cent estimated it as bad. In addition, there was a discrepancy between the staff's motivation and wishes to participate in special training courses on computer education in kindergarten and in real life. The majority expressed that they were interested (58.43 per cent) or very interested (16.15 per cent), but also the majority (78.86 per cent) had not participated in such a training yet. Most of the participants had gained their computer competence through personal commitment.

The participants of the study were also asked who was responsible for media education in their institution. The number of persons responsible for this domain differed from 1 to 10 (mean=3.15, SD=1.58). Asked about the people responsible for media education (open question), educators/nursery nurses, heads of the kindergarten, group leaders, specific media representatives, particularly trained people, language therapists or people interested in computers were mentioned.

In most of the kindergartens (58.94 per cent), no pedagogical concept for the work on the computer with children existed. Only 16.35 per cent of the kindergartens had a clearly established pedagogical concept, and 24.71 per cent of the participants admitted that their institutions had one, but that it had not been written down yet.

Availability and locations of the computers

The number of computers available in kindergartens is another crucial aspect influencing its use. In the participating kindergartens, 2.07 (SD=1.28) computers on average were available for the children. But in most of the kindergartens (42.97 per cent), it was only one and only about 13 per cent of the kindergartens had four or more computers. In those kindergartens that had computers, they were financed either by the provider (22.43 per cent) or by the parents (19.77 per cent), by themselves (17.49 per cent) or by the sponsoring club of the kindergarten (7.22 per cent).

Where the computers are located in a kindergarten is also important for their use. In our inquiry, the location, however, differed extremely in the institutions. The computers were mainly located in a secondary room (33.08 per cent) or in the group room (28.52 per cent); another 14.45 per cent of the kindergartens had a mobile computer station; in 11.03 per cent of the institutions the computer was located in the bureau, the hall or the corridor (5.7 per cent); and in only 7.22 per cent of the kindergartens, the computer had a room of its own.

In most of the kindergartens, computers were available for all children (56.72 per cent). In almost one-third (29.66 per cent), however, computers were only available for preschool children (age 4–6). The availability of the computer for the children in most of the kindergartens (38.40 per cent) was controlled by a time set; only in 16.73 per cent of the kindergartens was it permanently available for the children or exclusively used for special projects (15.97 per cent). In 6.84 per cent of the kindergartens, the computer was only available on a fixed weekday.

The children were allowed to use computers only when accompanied by a staff member (25.1 per cent). Asked about the purpose for letting the children use a computer, the computer was mainly (52.09 per cent) seen as a learning aid; however, more unusually, computers were also seen as toys (16.73 per cent) or tools (12.55 per cent).

The ways of using the computers with the children also differed. Some institutions (35.36 per cent) only used application software and some kindergartens (6.08 per cent) only standard software, but the majority used both (55.89 per cent). Although almost all kindergartens had access to the internet (98.46 per cent), the majority (61.22 per cent) did not use it when working at the computer with the children. Asked about the aims for working with the computer in the institutions, most of the participants answered that they used it "as a research instrument", 26.47 per cent "as a dictionary or encyclopedia". Playing or organising things was only mentioned by less than 1 per cent of the respondents.

Conclusion

Looking at preschool children's cognitive, communicative and emotional competences, it can be stated that young children are able to handle a computer and – provided that input devices and software are child-oriented and that there is a guided interaction or instruction by competent adults – children can profit from the usage of computers due to having playful and furthering experiences using digital resources. Considering the importance of acquiring technological competences in a culture where digital artefacts are found in many areas of everyday life and play an important role with respect to communication and information transfer, it becomes clear that fostering literacy development also means fostering and guiding children's digital technologies competences. Children's chances of access to digital technology at home are not equal and parents differ in their skills to teach their children how to deal with digital devices effectively (Wolfe & Flewitt, 2010). Thus, already preschool education should try to provide all children with ICT competences.

But even though it seems pedagogically necessary to use computers already for preschool education, the appropriate preconditions for this do not seem to exist in German kindergartens. First, there are not enough computers, partly due to financial reasons, partly due to a lack of a pedagogical media concept. Second, educators do not seem to be well prepared to handle computers in kindergartens and not enough training in this domain seems to be offered, although the kindergarten staff is motivated to participate. Third, the educational values underlying the German preschool pedagogy (e.g. the situation-oriented approach, the focus on education via the senses) as well as the individual attitudes of the educators seem to keep them from offering computer-based activities to children and to provide a sensitive media education already in kindergarten. The German preschool pedagogy in this field still seems to be influenced by the educators' own way of using a computer (e.g. as a learning tool or as a dictionary), which does not meet the needs of children at this age and is not compatible with the opportunities computers can offer preschool education.

Altogether the results of the reported study in the preschool area are in line with the results of the International Computer and Information Literacy Study 2013 (Bos, Eickelmann & Gerick, 2014), where German students of the eighth grade only showed a moderate level of ICT competences. The authors of the study state a lack of modern technological equipment in German classrooms and a lack of competent and effective instruction. Likewise, computers appear to be a kind of redundant or optional accessory in German kindergartens, and fostering ICT competencies seems to be an arbitrary activity depending on the educators' personal attitudes and skills.

To change this unsatisfactory situation, the curriculum standards for technology and media education in the preschool area should be formulated in a more concrete and binding way first. The teaching of ICT competences, the handling of digital devices, computers and internet should be a compulsory part of the preschool curriculum. Second, education in the field of digital media likewise should be a compulsory part of teacher education and an advanced training also for kindergarten teachers. As Plowman and Stephen (2005) demonstrate it is not enough to just let children "play" with the computer. Children need guidance in the form of active assistance. Educators have to learn how to do this and they have to be competent users themselves. Third, digital tools and media should be part of the kindergarten equipment – like dolls, books, pencils or blocks.

References

Aufenanger, S. (2009). *Bildungs klick*. Retrieved 29 September 2014 from http://bildungsklick.de/a/65336/computer-im-kindergarten-wir-muessen-draussen-bleiben/ access

Berk, L. (2011). *Entwicklungspsychologie* [Developmental psychology]. München: Pearson.

Bos, W., Eickelmann, B. & Gerick, J. (2014). *ICLS 2013 auf einen Blick. Presseinformationen zur Studie und zu zentralen Ergebnissen* [International computer and infomation literacy study at a glance. Press information on the study and on central results.] Münster: Waxmann.

Charlton, M. (2007). Das Kind und sein Startkapital: Medienhandeln aus der Perspektive der Entwicklungspsychologie [The child and his/her cognitive seed capital. Acting with media from the perspective of developmental psychology]. In: H. Theunert (Hrsg.), *Medienkinder von Geburt an: Medienaneignung in den ersten sechs Lebensjahren* [Media children right from birth: acquisition of media in the first 6 years], (pp. 24–40). München: Kopaed.

Deckers, C. (2012). *Computereinsatz im Kindergarten – eine empirische Studie anhand der Bundesländer Rheinland-Pfalz und Nordrhein-Westphalen*. [The use of computers in kindergarten – an empirical study based on the federal states Rhineland Palatinate and North-Rhine-Westphalia]. Unpublished dissertation, University of Siegen, Germany.

Downes, T., Arthur, L. & Beecher, B. (2001). Effective learning environments for young children using digital resources: an Australian perspective. *Information Technology in Childhood Education Annual, 13*, 139–53.

Gemeinsamer Rahmen der Länder für die frühe Bildung in Kindertageseinrichtungen (2009), Beschluss der Jugendministerkonferenz vom 13./14.05.2004 and Beschluss der Kultusministerkonferenz vom

03./04.06. Retrieved 3 September 2014 from http://www.kmk.org/fileadmin/veroeffentlichungen_beschluesse/2004/2004_06_04-Fruehe-Bildung-Kitas.pdf

Henninger, M. L. (1994). Computers and preschool children's play: are they compatible? *Journal of Computing in Childhood Education, 5*(3/4), 231–39.

Lipinski, J. M., Nida, R. E., Shade, D. D. & Watson, J. A. (1986). The effects of microcomputers on young children: an examination of free–play choices, sex differences, and social interactions. *Journal of Educational Computing Research, 2,* 147–68.

McPake, J., Plowman, L. & Stephen, C. (2013). Pre-school children creating and communicating with digital technologies in the home. *British Journal of Educational Technology, 44,* 421–31.

Ministerium für Bildung, Frauen und Jugend des Landes Rheinland-Pfalz, Referat Kindertagesstätten (2004). *Bildungs- und Erziehungsempfehlungen für Kindertagesstätten in Rheinland-Pfalz*. Mainz.

Ministerium für Schule und Weiterbildung des Landes Nordrhein-Westfalen & Ministerium für Familie, Kinder, Jugend, Kultur und Sport des Landes Nordrhein-Westfalen. (2010). *Mehr Chancen durch Bildung von Anfang an – Entwurf – Grundsätze zur Bildungsförderung für Kinder von 0 bis 10 Jahren in Kindertageseinrichtungen und Schulen im Primarbereich in Nordrhein-Westfalen*. Düsseldorf.

Piaget, J. (1969). *Das Erwachen der Intelligenz beim Kinde* [The awakening of the child's intelligence]. München: dtv/Klett-Cotta.

Nir-Gal, O. & Klein, P. S. (2004). Computers for cognitive development in early childhood – the teacher's role in the computer learning environment. *Information Technology in Childhood Education Annual,* 97–119.

Plowman, L. & Stephen, C. (2003). A "benign addition?" Research on ICT and pre-school children. *Journal of Computer Assisted Learning, 19,* 149–64.

Plowman, L. & Stephen C. (2005). Children, play and computers in pre-school education. *British Journal of Educational Technology 36*(2) 145–58.

Plowman, L., Stevenson, O., Stephen, C. & McPake, J. (2012). Preschool children's learning with technology at home. *Computers & Education, 59,* 30–37.

Sodian, B. (2008). Entwicklung des Denkens [Development of thinking]. In: R. Oerter & L. Montada (Hrsg.), *Entwicklungspsychologie* [Developmental psychology], (pp. 436–79). Weinheim, Basel: Beltz-PVU

Spitzer, M. (2009). *Bildungs klick*. Retrieved 29 September 2014 from http://bildungsklick.de/a/65336/computer-im-kindergarten-wir-muessen-draussen-bleiben/

Statistische Ämter des Bundes und der Länder [Statistical Offices of the State and the Federal States]. (2014). *Gebiet und Fläche / Fläche und Bevölkerung (Stand 31.12.2013) [Territory and area/area and population (updated 31.12.14)]*. Retrieved 2 November 2014 from http://www.statistik-portal.de/statistik-portal/de_jb01_jahrtab1.asp/

Stephen C. & Plowman L. (2008). Enhancing learning with ICT in preschool. *Early Child Development and Care 178*(6), 637–54.

Wolfe, S. and Flewitt, R. S. (2010). New technologies, new multimodal literacy practices and young children's metacognitive development. *Cambridge Journal of Education 40*(4), 387–99.

10

iPLAY, iLEARN, iGROW

Tablet technologies, curriculum, pedagogies and learning in the twenty-first century

Nicola Yelland

Abstract

In this chapter I present some findings from the second year of an iPad project that explored the potential of the tablets for learning and meaning-making in the early years. The findings from the kindergarten (four-year-olds) and preparatory class (five- and six-year-olds) are presented and discussed. It is evident that playful explorations with iPads can provide contents for learning and investigations that are rich in engagement and interest. The children in this study were highly motivated to learn with the iPad apps, and the teachers extended their pedagogical repertoire by incorporating their use in their early childhood programs.

Introduction

Most of the research to date about young children and new technologies has been done in settings with computers and, to a lesser extent, with other devices, such as whiteboards and digital cameras. Research about the use of tablet technologies in education is relatively new. Touch technology devices emerged from 2007 with the iPhone, then the iPad was released in 2010. Since then Android tablets (e.g. Samsung, Galaxy, Asus and more recently the (Microsoft) Surface Pro) have come onto the market. These devices and their associated applications (apps) enabled more mobility with new technologies, and even created a new phenomenon called "the pass back effect" (Chiong & Shuler, 2010), defined as being when a parent or adult passes their own mobile device to a child, usually for entertainment, for short (15-minute) sessions.

Of the studies found that involved young children and mobile technologies, most are related to the *use* of iPods, iTouch and iPads and have been conducted in the US, with only a few in Australia. While many of these describe practitioner-based "pockets of innovation" (e.g. Clayton-Brown, 2012; Department of Education and Early Childhood Development [DEECD], 2010; Mullholland, 2011) they tend to be professional commentaries or usability studies on the impact of the devices in school, or in relation to how they have changed the lives of contemporary young children (e.g. Gliksman, 2011; Worthen, 2012). There are very few empirical investigations about the impact of touch technologies for teaching and learning, either in preschool or in school contexts. Rather, they advocate "tips" for successful use of iPads (e.g. DEECD, 2011) based on observations and implementations by teachers or consultants.

The majority of studies conducted since 2008 have been commissioned reports in the US, which were preliminary investigations of the potential of the technology in formal learning environments. For example, in the US, the Joan Ganz Cooney Centre at the Sesame Workshop sponsored investigations into the classification of apps (Shuler, 2012), conducted studies of young children's learning with apps (Chiong & Shuler, 2010) and initiated a blueprint for teaching young children in the digital age (Barron et al., 2011). Also in the US, the Department of Education funded a study of young children, iPads and their apps as part of their Ready to Learn program (Cohen, 2011). These studies have mainly considered classifying apps so that a more comprehensive consideration of their learning potential could be realised.

In Australia, education departments such as those in Victoria (DEECD, 2010) and New South Wales (Department for Education and Communities [DEC], 2012) have been involved in iPad "trials" and have described implementations in which children in the compulsory years of schooling have been using iPads as part of their daily activities. As yet, the results of systematic empirical studies with iPads form a very small pool of research. It is apparent that early childhood teachers regard the technology as useful (Olney, Herrington & Verenikina, 2008) because they enable young children to easily engage with digital content, but there still seems to be a general reluctance to dismiss new technologies as not being an integral part of early childhood curricula and pedagogical repertoires.

Also in Australia, Lynch and Redpath (2012) examined the emerging patterns of use of iPads in a preparatory class for literacy. They found a mismatch between policy and curriculum contexts and what the teachers really wanted to use the tablets for. They identified tension points that existed between the teachers' preference for print-based literacies and the new digital literacies, as well as between standards-based curriculum and more emancipatory agendas. There is the potential for transformation but essentially, thus far, the use of tablets reinforces traditional pedagogies and practices in schools.

The apps

When a new technology bursts onto the scene it will only be purchased and used if customers can identify their perceived needs to have one. With the iPad, the quality of the apps are fundamental to its success. iTunes has become the main repository for purchasing apps for tablet users, while Microsoft now has its own store and Google Play supports Android apps. A study by Shuler (2009) found that of *all* the 100 top-selling apps in iTunes, which at the time were only available for use on the iPhone and iPod, 47 per cent were classified as being appropriate for preschool and elementary (primary) aged children. Watlington (2011) studied the free apps that were designated as being designed for young children in iTunes (108 apps). She applied the criteria from the 1998 Haughland Developmental Scale (Haughland, 1999) that were based on the principles of Developmentally Appropriate Practice (DAP) and concluded that only 48 per cent of the apps could be regarded as being "developmentally appropriate".

Goodwin & Highfield (2012) conducted a systematic analysis of the "top 10 education Apps" (n=240) in iTunes on four different occasions over a period of six months in 2011. They classified the apps on the basis of their pedagogical design features in three categories:

instructional, manipulable and *constructive*. They considered instructional apps as primarily being drill and practice activities that had no opportunity for deviation from the design and required a "right" answer. Goodwin and Highfield (2012) contended that such apps have minimal cognitive investment on the part of the learner. Manipulable apps allowed for guided discovery and experimentation, but they both were limited to the design context. Constructive apps were more open-ended and allowed users to create their own content or digital artefact. Not surprisingly, 75 per cent of the apps were classified as being instructive, 23 per cent were manipulable, while only 2 per cent were constructive. This makes it difficult for the majority of apps to be used in preschool settings as the predominant form of pedagogy is based on play with minimal direction or instruction. Further, as Goodwin and Highfield (2012) suggested, the classification of content as being "Educational" is somewhat misleading in many instances, since many of the apps are simply reinforcing basic skills or concepts via repetition. However, it has to be noted that this seems very attractive to both parents and young children in *pass-back* contexts while travelling in cars and on planes or when the family is out shopping.

The classification of apps and a consideration of their content has led to recommendations regarding their appropriateness based on whether they are "developmentally appropriate" or not. Cohen (2011) in fact suggested:

> Children as young as two years old access, play and learn with touch screen devices. Children's initial reactions are characterised by fascination and shaped by their developmental level, prior experience with technology, and the design of the App interface and gameplay ... iPad access and use are relative to the design of the App interface, game experience and the fit between the App content and the child's developmental level. (p. 2)

Cohen (2011) classified apps into three groups: *gaming* apps, *creating* apps and *eBooks*. His study was based on observations and interviews with 60 children. The children were observed in classrooms and in a research facility and included a mix of novice and experienced users of tablet technology. Cohen (2011) concluded that children in the study preferred gaming apps, which he said "afforded ready access and provided interactive games that are easy to learn and compelling to master" (p. 3). But Cohen also suggested that creating apps, in particular, had

> High appeal ... based on children's interest in making things in a no-fail environment with endless possibilities and outcomes. Additionally, the child's experience is characterised by learning by doing, building on their existing skills and being motivated by their own interests. (p. 2)

Cohen contended that there were *three* different types of learning evident during app play. These included:

- *Tacit* learning: of the game and how it works
- *Mastery* of explicit learning tasks (e.g. counting, matching)
- Learning how to *transfer* the use of skills and content learned to *new* games or *levels* of play.

Thus, we have a lot of information about apps and their categorisation into various groupings. We also know that young children love to play with them for various amounts of time, depending on their needs and interests and the content and structure of the app. There are some more detailed observations that have also been made in various reports:

- Young children *enjoy* playing with iPads (Cohen, 2011; DEC, 2012; DEECD, 2010, 2011).
- Young children *explore* and *learn* in ways that are *natural* to them when using a touch device (Cohen, 2011; DEC 2012; DEECD, 2010).
- *Some learning gains* related to *specific content and skills* (reading and vocabulary) have been reported in studies with specific apps (PBS Kids, 2010).
- The majority of apps are classified as being *"drill and practice"* and characterised by limited choice and specifically controlled outcomes (Goodwin & Highfield, 2011; Shuler, 2012).
- *Open-ended apps* align more successfully with early childhood programs and their approach to learning (Cohen, 2011).
- There is *no* research that suggests ways in which teachers and parents might extend learning using apps as a catalyst for language and extension explorations.
- There is *no* research that considers the modality of learning with touch technologies and how this is different to traditional learning.

Yet, it is apparent that we still need more information and details about:

- the ways in which the new range of tablet technologies can help children to learn via productive play, to explore and investigate, and facilitate sharing of their ideas and discoveries (*communication*)
- the features of apps and other uses of tablet technologies that promote learning in young children
- the ways teachers can be encouraged and supported to incorporate tablets in their pedagogical repertoire to encourage twenty-first century learning.

In this chapter, I explore these issues with reference to a two-year study of the implementation and use of iPads in two particular educational contexts: one in the non-compulsory preschool years (four-year-olds in kindergarten) and one in the first year of compulsory schooling (five- and six-year-olds in prepatory).

Research design

This study sought to gather information about the ways in which tablet technologies might be supportive of learning in the two different educational contexts. A goal of the project was to explore the ways in which pedagogical actions influenced learning and how the children responded to the tablets as catalysts for their explorations and learning. We[1] were also interested in exploring the ways in which the tablets afforded opportunities for multimodal learning (linguistic, visual, spatial, oral and aural) in early childhood settings.

The research involved a total of 207 children over a period of two years (63 four-year-olds in preschool and 144 in the first year of school). As teachers and researchers, we wanted to observe and interact with the children, caregivers and teachers, so we adopted a participant observation methodology. Participant observation can be defined as a method in which "the researcher is taking part, to some degree, in the activities of the people being observed" (Deacon et al. 1999, p. 251). The aim of participant observation is to gain access to everyday practices, which are difficult to describe or reproduce in group discussion or interview (Mikos, cited in Struppert, 2011). Through participation in the context, the researcher can achieve a better understanding of the practice, roles and cultural patterns of the participants (Mikos cited in Struppert, 2011). In the second year of the project four pre-service teachers became part of the research team as a part of their undergraduate research unit in the four-year program.

We observed and interacted with the children in each group over a period of six weeks, during the course of a school term, for the duration of the morning session that extended from arrival at school to the lunch break, over the two-year period.

In the kindergarten, the tablets were introduced and then incorporated into the programme as an additional activity available for the children. After the observation period, each week, we left two tablets in the kindergarten setting (one for each group). In the preparatory class, the teachers indicated that they thought the most effective use would be to focus on particular children who would benefit from targeted teaching and learning experiences in small group contexts. The preparatory class also had access to a set of 10 school tablets and an additional 10 in the second year.

The contexts

Four-year-olds (kindergarten group): The kindergarten was located in a suburban region approximately 15 km from the centre of a large Australian metropolitan city. There were two four-year-old groups, each with their own room. There was a large outdoor area that facilitated the fluid movement of the children from indoor to outdoor activity. The teachers were both experienced early childhood educators and each one was supported by a teacher aide. The kindergarten had a play-based programme in which the children were able to select an activity from a range of materials that were available, both inside and out in the playground. Inside, this included painting materials, a carpet and book area, a puppet theatre and a large range of craft materials and plastic items. Outside there was a sand pit, water play, space to run and various forms of climbing frames. The tablets were available on a table inside, since the children were used to selecting an activity and completing it on a table. Additionally, in the second year, each pre-service teacher also occasionally asked the children if they wanted to participate in a tablet-based activity.

Five- and six-year-olds (preparatory class): In Victoria, the Australian state in which this study was located, the first year of compulsory schooling is the preparatory class. The three groups of preparatory children were team taught by three qualified teachers and supported by a full-time educational assistant. The children had a "home area" for administrative purposes but were mainly taught in the large group and moved to smaller needs-based groups to work with one of the teachers, the aide and, in some cases, a parent helper. The school was located in a multicultural, low socioeconomic income area, and for more than half of the group English was not their first language.

Findings

In the introduction I indicated that there was minimal information in the form of empirical data regarding the ways in which the new range of tablet technologies can help children to learn via productive play, explore and investigate and facilitate sharing of their ideas and discoveries (communication).The next two sections of this chapter will elucidate each of these as focal points for organising the data and then discuss the findings in terms of how useful the apps were and how the teachers were encouraged to use them as part of their programs.

Four-year-olds (kindergarten)

It was very important for the researchers and teachers that the iPad should enhance the interest, needs and learning in the play-based program. In this way we sought to encourage playing and exploring with both closed and open-ended apps. The three examples that follow occurred in the context of very different apps, the first being very open-ended and the second with one that only had one purpose.

We used an app called *MadPad*, which enables a montage, in the form of a matrix, of pictures and sounds to be created and replayed on the iPad. The learning story that follows is an amalgam of two learning experiences that occurred on the same day in the kindergarten with six children (four years of age). One of the things that we found to be useful when introducing a new idea to young children was to show them an example, so that they were able to either use it as a model to produce their own version or innovate on it because they could see some relevance to their experiences and interests. In this instance, *MadPad* enables users to view and play existing examples. In one, a series of 12 photos and sounds of a car are arranged in a 4 x 3 matrix, and in others there are various scenes and sounds from daily lives as well as others using a range of musical instruments. The idea is that the clips are "short and snappy" and can be played individually, or in a sequence created by the child. In this way they can innovate on the sounds and this makes it more fun as well as increasing the creative potential of the experiences.

The two MadPad sets that were created engaged the children in thinking about the sounds in their environment. They realised that they could make their own sounds (clicking fingers, clapping, moving their tongue to make clicking noises) and that they could also use the various objects in the centre (e.g. sieves, cups, saucepans, pieces of equipment) to create sounds. With this app, the video can be taken by the teacher or the children. Some minimal planning is needed, since the area has to be relatively quiet for an effective recording to be achieved, and the children need to know how to make the sound, and how long they need to maintain it for the recording.

The observations by Jena (pre-service teacher) about the students in the process of creating their MadPad montage reveal their enthusiasm:

> Allan said, "What about this sound?" And began clicking his tongue. Brandon followed with, "What about this?" and clapped his hands. We were walking around the playground searching for sounds we could hear. Allan said, "I know!" and ran to the swings. He stood on the swing and said, "Look at this sound!" (a loud squeaking sound came from the swing). Brandon ran to a large circular decoration that was in the garden. He began tapping on the decoration with his hands. He said, "We can use this sound!" We then went to the sand pit to find new sounds. Allan picked up two pots and said, "Look at this one!" and began banging the two pots together. Brandon continued to explore sounds by tapping on different objects that he could find (tapping a helmet, a bucket, a wooden plank and a metal box).

TABLE 10.1 A kindergarten learning story (Carr, 2001).

Learning outcomes	Examples	A learning story
Children have a strong sense of identity	• Feel safe, secure and supported • Develop their emerging autonomy, inter-dependence, resilience and sense of agency • Develop knowledgeable and confident self-identities • Learn to interact in relation to others with care, empathy and respect	The children (5 boys) showed an interest in the sounds and pictures from *MadPad* sets stored on the iPad. After demonstrating the features to them we talked about what sounds we could make with our bodies. Allan said, "What about this sound?" and made a clicking noise with his tongue. "What about clapping?" asked Brendan as he did the motion.
Children are connected with and contribute to their world	• Sense of belonging to group • Respect diversity • Recognise fairness • Socially responsible • Show respect	We then walked around thinking about other sounds we could make with objects around us. Allan stood on the swing and said, "Look at this sound!" He picked up two pots in the sandpit and began banging them together, "We can use this sound!" Later, when entering the sounds the boys made sure everyone had a turn.
Children have a strong sense of wellbeing	• Strong social and emotional wellbeing • Increasing responsibility for own wellbeing	Working collaboratively the boys were able to find an array of sounds to use for the *MadPad* collection and we recorded the video of them making the sounds in two sets. They were able to recognise what sounds would work and which ones were too soft – since in the playground noise levels tend to be elevated.
Children are confident and involved learners	• Develop dispositions for learning • Skills of learning – exploring and investigating • Transfer across context • Resource own learning in variety of contexts	The group was able to take turns and listen to each other and share their sound discoveries. They waited while some technical difficulties around recording sound levels were fixed and then played back the sounds for each other to listen to.
Children are effective communicators	• Interact with others • Engage with range of texts and make meaning • Express ideas in range of media • Use symbols to express ideas • Use ICT for learning	The *MadPad* sets contained the sounds that the boys made outside in the play areas. They waited while this process took place and shared their final products with their peers, explaining how they made them as they played the sets of pictures and sounds.

This app was open-ended so the children were able to create their own sets by taking photos and linking them to sounds around them. They were confident in their approach to the task and sustained their interest over a lengthy time span that involved some technical difficulties. Creating the "local" sets enabled them to feel connected to their environment using new materials and reflecting on the various sounds and images that are connected in our daily lives.

FIGURE 10.1 Outdoor sounds (*MadPad*).

The experience could be extended in a variety of ways to include children providing statements about themselves and what they enjoy, by telling stories, and for musical experiences with instruments and songs. Being able to combine the modalities of oral, aural and images represented a good opportunity to make and reflect on the sounds in our environment and the sounds that we listen to in a variety of formats. They can form the basis for different learning activities – some of which we extended in the preparatory class findings later in the report.

In the second example of using technology for play, we took photos of the children so that they could use them in an app called *Jigsaw Puzzle Maker*. The children had shown an interest in puzzles and Nicky (the teacher) had said that it would be great if we could extend this to their iPad use.

Jess (pre-service teacher) observed that when playing with the jigsaw maker, Abby (kindergarten student) was able to take a photo of herself, and then together they inserted it into the app. Jess noted that it was "a great app for the children" and that it would be useful to always have different images of the children available to use when they wanted to make a jigsaw. It was valuable as it personalised the puzzles and extended their play with three-dimensional jigsaws. Further, it meant that they had a much wider range of puzzles available to them and that they could continually have to think about new ones rather than build a puzzle they might know from memory after playing it each day at the centre. Jess wrote that Abby was very competent in putting the jigsaw together, starting with corners and edges and working into the middle, while explaining that she was looking (at one point) for a puzzle piece with pink on it as it would join the other puzzle piece with pink on it, creating her sweater in the photo.

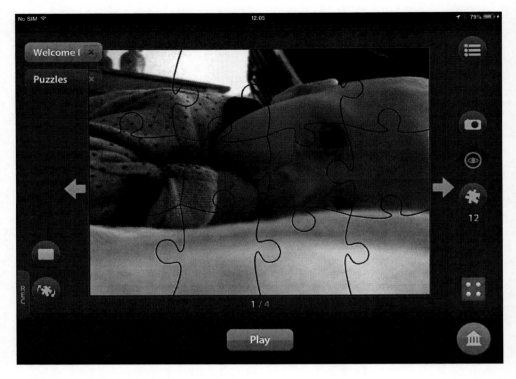

FIGURE 10.2 *Jigsaw Puzzle Maker.*

The kindergarten children also used the tablet in their investigations about hermit crabs, since they had two in the kindergarten. An overview of the potential of exploring this topic is provided in Figure 10.3 in the form of a curriculum web.

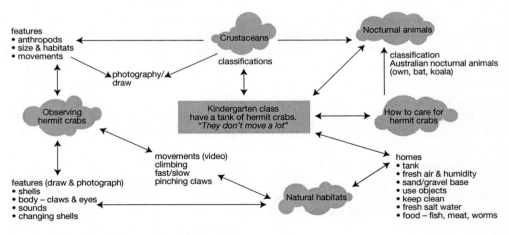

FIGURE 10.3 Curriculum web – hermit crabs.

The children were fascinated by the crabs, and in particular their lack of movement while they watched them. This led Nicky (the teacher) to help them to search for more information about the crabs using the tablet, and the discovery that they were nocturnal animals. Photos could be taken on the tablet and saved for discussions, and some of the children brought items to add to the crab environment, such as additional shells. Charlotte brought in a new shell for the crab when she discovered that they liked to move into larger ones as they grew (Figure 10.4). Here, the tablet was used to extend their experience by enabling the children to search out more information easily and also to keep a record of their observations. They drew pictures of the crabs, and moved like crabs in some of their play sessions. Again, the tablet provided a context for multimodal learning as they found videos of the crabs on YouTube and this enabled them to actually see the crabs move, which was not possible in their viewing of the crabs in the daytime.

In these examples, and indeed in all the learning activities that we participated in with the four-year-old children, they always wanted to share what they had done with their teacher and the other children in the group. Both teachers noted that this was a new dimension to learning in the preschool context that the iPads facilitated in the centre.

Summary

The various apps that we used with the children were selected on the basis that they would encourage play, exploration and investigations, and enable the children to share their ideas about what they had learned in this new learning with technology scenario. The range of apps available is overwhelmingly limited in scope, and the apps only enable activity that the designers had visualised. Yet we were able to find ways to incorporate them into play-based contexts with positive results. This was evident with the *Jigsaw Puzzle Maker*, for example, which enabled personalised jigsaw making, as well as with an open-ended app like *MadPad*. The teachers had not used an iPad prior to the commencement of the research and had specific ideas about how they might be used. For example, they did not want the children to be sitting playing games (apps) all day when they could be engaged in play-based learning inside and outside. In this way we worked with them to choose the apps to introduce to the children gradually. There were teachable moments as we all learned with the children how to use the features of the app, and we explored many alternative ways to extend the use of

EYLF Learning Outcome 3 – Children have a strong sense of wellbeing. This is evident when they take increasing responsibility for their own health and physical wellbeing.

In a previous session Charlotte asked if we should have a shell in the hermit crab house for Spike or Sprinkles to relocate into once their shell gets too small. She shared that she could bring in some shells – and she did. They were perfect and Charlotte chose one she thought they might like and placed it inside their house. We will now wait and watch to see if either of them make it their new home.

FIGURE 10.4 Charlotte brings a new shell for the hermit crab.

each app since we wanted the experience to be rich in learning. The teachers indicated that they had been pleasantly surprised by the quality of the learning experiences and how they were able to use the iPads easily. They noted however that teachers would need to have an iPad of their own in order to fully realise the potential of their use on a continuing basis.

Five and six year olds (preparatory class)

The primary school teachers in this study were a cohesive and well-organised team with a range of teaching experience from two to 17 years of being in the profession. They planned collaboratively for literacy and numeracy blocks that occurred in the morning session each day of the week. The children were allocated to groups based on an initial diagnostic test, but the groups were fluid and the children could change groups if and when required.

We worked with the teachers to identify the skills that they felt were their priority for the time period that we were to be there, and we sought out apps that were suitable to use in small-group contexts (two to six children). We worked with the children in the classroom at a table, in order to use the tablets for focused teaching and learning activity time. Some of the investigations also extended to the playground area.

In the examples that follow we highlight the ways in which various apps were used to:

- *support number* recognition and sequencing of numbers to ten for two groups of six children
- *extend* opportunities to *explore numbers* by applying them in various contexts.

For one activity in the second year of the study, the teachers identified 11 children who, after six months of being in preparatory class, were unable to recognise, draw or sequence the numerals to 10. These were foundational conceptual knowledge for the first year of compulsory schooling in the National Curriculum for Mathematics (Australian Curriculum and Assessment Reporting Authority, 2012).

We selected number-based apps that we felt would enable the children to increase their number knowledge and worked with them for an hour a week, over six weeks.

The apps used were:

- *Bugs and Numbers* (numeral recognition, sequencing, counting)
- *Bugs and Buttons* (using numbers in games)
- *Meet the Insects* (1:1 correspondence, matching how many)
- *Tally Tots* (recognising numerals, sequencing, counting to 20)
- *Intro to Math* by Montessorium (tracing and recognising numerals to 10)
- *Bull's Eye Math* (recognising numerals and filling in missing numerals).

In the first week we started using *Bugs and Numbers* with each group. *Bugs and Numbers* contains six games:

- Circus identification – recognition of (matching) numerals. In this game the children are given a number/numeral (and hear the number name). They then have to find (by tapping) all the numerals that pass by them that are pegged on two parallel lines. The game gets faster the more answers you answer accurately, so you are encouraged to move more quickly.

- Arcade – recognition of left and right. The players have to follow the oral instructions to press either right or left in order to navigate a bug/ant forwards through obstacles. A score is provided in the upper left corner. A final score is provided when the ant crashes into an obstacle.
- Junk yard – the player moves items to uncover hidden ladybugs. The number of bugs starts with three and increases as the successful numbers are uncovered. A tally of the score is provided in the left-hand corner.
- Diner – tap and count. Bugs appear on a turntable and as the player touches them, the number is spoken and a white numeral appears on the screen. The player then matches that number to a choice of two numerals on the left and as the game goes on the choice of numerals is extended to three.
- Gallery – colour by numbers. Pictures of bees, ladybird and snail are provided – you have to match numerals and colours and complete the drawings.
- Matching shapes – this starts with numerals in which the player has to drag the matching ones together as they are told the names of the numerals. The game then progresses to shapes, then real world (fruit) items, followed by robots in two parts, to animals (caricatures of bees, bugs etc.) that have to be matched and assembled.

Our observation notes indicate the sequence of events that occurred and our interactions with the children as we questioned and scaffolded their learning as they played the games. In the first session the children played some of the games with assistance, since they needed some help with recognising the numerals, counting how many in order to select the correct numeral. They were able to play with the matching game and the Arcade game without assistance. Their enjoyment was shown on their faces and they were very engaged with the graphics and sounds of this well-produced game. At the end of the 30-minute session all the children, except two, were able to count to 10, recognise randomly chosen numerals and point to a numeral that came before or after another one.

In weeks two to six the children consolidated their understanding about the numbers from 0 to 10 in various activities using the other five apps. In each of the sessions the pre-service teacher (Dean) scaffolded and questioned the children about what they were doing so that he could consider what level of concept attainment they had achieved. Dean's observations indicated that he thought a structured approach, in preference to letting the children choose their own games, was more appropriate. He was able to support the children more effectively in this way, catering for individual needs:

> A considered plan to integrate iPad use in the math program would map the progression of focus skills across multiple apps, so that there was a progression path from one app to another in building on those skills.
>
> (Dean Reflections, 18 June)

In the final session each child was questioned to ascertain their level of understanding and ability to use numerals to 10, their sequence and their capacity to reproduce each numeral. All of the children except two demonstrated that they could now do these things. The two (boys) who could not complete the tasks were identified by their teacher as having specific learning difficulties that spanned all curriculum areas. Nonetheless, they could say the numbers in sequence when prompted and were able to trace over the numerals while the app advised them of its number name.

In this way, it was apparent that the dedicated short and focused activity sessions, incorporating the use of the tablet, had a positive impact on the conceptual understandings and skill levels of nine of the 11 children in the group. They had not mastered these understanding in the previous six months of schooling when the content was taught with traditional materials. Focused small-group work, which is a common pedagogical technique in preparatory classes, with a variety of materials might have achieved this sooner. We believe that, ideally, the use of multimodal experiences that incorporate iPads with manipulative materials, games and writing could have the potential to achieve this earlier on in the school year for these children.

Extension numeracy activities

While the group of 11 children had experienced difficulty with recognising and using the numbers from 0 to 10, others in the class had "mastered" them and moved on to larger numbers from 11 to 20. The national curriculum (Australian Curriculum and Assessment Reporting Authority [ACARA], 2012) suggests that they should be able to count to 20, recognise the numerals, connect the number names to quantities, compare and order collections, subitise small collections and represent addition stories.

We wanted to provide learning contexts in which the children could apply the number knowledge that they had acquired in the first six months of school. We did this in various ways including using *MadPad*, by writing number stories in electronic number books, writing books in different genres (e.g. *Comic Life*) and by using numbers to create data that was represented in graphs.

While the children had demonstrated the capacity to understand numbers to 10 as required by the foundational stage in the National Curriculum (ACARA, 2010), we were keen to enable them to use and apply their number knowledge in a variety of ways. One way included creating data sets and recording the results as graphs. We took photographs of 14 children in one group and embarked on a data collection to find out various things about them (e.g. what was their favourite farm animal and were they left or right handed?). We live in a data-drenched society (Steen, 1999) and becoming fluent with numbers to represent ideas and phenomena is a very important practical manifestation of being numerate. Amy (pre-service teacher) described the process in her notes:

> I modelled a bar graph for them by drawing the vertical and horizontal axes and placing pictures at the bottom. I then asked K (the child) if she would like to draw the lines on a new page. This strategy worked effectively as she performed this with ease. I then showed K and A (another child) where the pictures of the animals were, and in turn they navigated and moved the pictures to the correct positions. They then interviewed the children to ask which was their favourite animal … A held the iPad and showed the children their options while K talked to the children. After each one they would sit on the floor to place the photo above the corresponding animal. They took turns and navigated the iPads successfully without any direction needed.
>
> (Amy Reflections, June)

When they had finished interviewing the children they created the graph on the iPad (Figure 10.5). Amy asked the pair which animal had the most amount of people and therefore was the favourite animal. They immediately knew it was the pig and, when asked,

FIGURE 10.5 Our favourite farm animals.

one of the children said it was because it had the tallest line. A boy then told Amy that six people liked pigs the best. After this both children accurately counted the number who chose the other animals (horses, dogs, cows, ducks and sheep).

> This activity was so valuable for the children's learning. It saw them gain an understanding of graphs and the purpose for them, something which they had not been exposed to before. The social and linguistic aspects of this lesson were evident from the start. K and A (children) worked collaboratively and their confidence grew with each person they interviewed.
>
> (Amy Reflections, June)

The children were going to a farm on the following Friday. Being able to use this as a basis for the activity was an enjoyable experience for the children as indicated by their comments and enthusiasm. It linked the two tasks together and it made the activity purposeful for their learning.

Summary

In thinking about the use of new technologies in educational contexts, Puentendra (2011) created the SAMR framework that enables teachers to reflect on the ways in which they want to use them in their programme. The framework can act as a pedagogical prompt to assist teachers in planning learning scenarios that incorporate the use of new technologies. It has the following elements:

- *Substitution* – in which the technology acts as a substitute for traditional teaching materials and thus there is no fundamental change to the learning context, apart from the fact it is digital.
- *Augmentation* – the technology being used changes the learning context with some functional improvements being made.
- *Modification* – where the technology allows for some significant task redesign.
- *Redefinition* – in which the use of technologies allows for the design of new learning experiences that were previously not possible.

Puentendra (2011) described the first two contexts as *enhancing* learning, while the second two have the potential to *transform* learning. At first it might appear that all learning experiences should be designed to be at the level of modification and redefinition, but it is apparent that depending on the type of learning experiences that a teacher is planning, each one has potential relevance as a pedagogical approach. For example, when introducing a concept, a teacher may decide to show a video to her class on a tablet (augmentation). Yet, she might also diverge in a completely different direction and create a "flipped learning" scenario where the children use technology at home and then come to school ready to contribute in a different way (modification or redefinition). On balance we would hope that the new technologies would result in the transformation of learning contexts, but there will also be times when they enhance traditional pedagogical approaches.

In the context of this project, in the preparatory class, we explored the possibilities of using the tablet with the teachers in ways that they believed would support their curriculum and pedagogical work. In thinking about this in the context of the SAMR model (Puentendra, 2011) the activities on the tablet were used as a *direct substitute* for traditional activities that had not enabled the children to come to understand the concept in the first instance, then as *augmentation* for activities that were usually presented in two or three dimensions. Finally the app made possible *modifying* those activities offered with manipulatives, taking them into a new modality. The experiences encouraged us to rethink the ways in which the children could explore number via the context and modality.

However, it was also apparent that it was difficult for the teachers to incorporate the use of tablets without specific and directed additional adult involvement. This came in the form of the pre-service teachers as well as the Educational Assistant (EA) they were allocated for the morning sessions. Yet the EAs were often not confident in their use of tablets. They were able to build the use of the tablets into their programming, but at this stage the implementation required having a pre-service teacher working with them to ensure there could be focused teaching. This was despite the fact that the children became fluent with the technology very easily and quickly. Thus, while the tablet had the potential to transform learning and teaching, the implementation was problematic from a practical perspective.

This was even more evident for the extension activities, which used more open-ended apps. These apps were more complex to understand and use, until you had the opportunity to practice working with them. While the pre-service teachers had time to do this and were able to withdraw the children from the numeracy rotations, these enriched learning contexts were more of an "add on" to existing practice, rather than transforming the whole range of experiences in the classroom. Nevertheless, both in terms of supporting and extending the children's numeracy learning, the tablet-based activities more than achieved the learning and engagement goals set.

Conclusion

I have maintained (e.g. Yelland, 2007, 2010, 2011) that we should not be mapping new technologies onto heritage, or traditional, curriculum but rather should be reconceptualising curriculum, pedagogies and assessment. There seems to be a lack of willingness by schooling systems to move away from traditional approaches towards promoting twenty-first-century learning with new technologies. Some schools have initiated projects that incorporate exciting and original uses of new technologies – they act as pockets of innovation. However, there seems to be a reluctance to generate systemic change that incorporates new technologies as an essential resource in schools and to abandon old ways of doing things, on the basis that they have worked in the past. Research to date, including the project described here, and the work of Lynch and Redpath (2012) illustrate that transformation is possible. However, in order for it to be applied more broadly across schooling contexts, not only does there need to be policy support, but also a recognition that the nature of teaching and the role of schools in society today have fundamentally shifted away from the industrial model (Yelland, 2007) to a knowledge economy where citizens of the twenty-first century require different skills (Partnerships for the 21st Century, 2008; Trilling & Fadel, 2009) to be productive in this new era.

Note

1   Research team members were Caja Gilbert (VU, Research Officer), teachers, pre-service teachers, Amy Henderson, Jena Najman, Jessica Mitchell and Dean Hammence.

References

Australian Curriculum and Assessment Reporting Authority. (ACARA) (2012). *Australian Curriculum – Mathematics*. Retrieved 2 April 2014 from http://www.australiancurriculum.edu.au/Mathematics/Curriculum/F-10

Barron, B., Cayton-Hodges, G., Bofferding, L., Copple, C., Darling-Hammond, L. & Levine, M. H. (2011). *Take a Giant Step: A Blueprint for Teaching Young Children in the Digital Age*. New York: The Joan Ganz Cooney Center at Sesame Workshop.

Carr, M. (2001). *Assessment in Early Childhood Settings: Learning Stories*. London: Sage.

Chiong, C. & Shuler, C. (2010). *Learning: Is There an App for That? Investigations of Young Children's Usage and Learning with Mobile Devices and Apps*. New York: The Joan Ganz Cooney Center at Sesame Workshop.

Clayton-Brown, K. (2012). iPads make learning a delight for pupils. *The Southland Times*. Retrieved from http://www.stuff.co.nz/southland-times/news/6418994/iPads-make-learning-a-delight-for-pupils

Cohen, M. (2011). *Young Children, Apps and iPad*. New York. Retrieved from http://mcgrc.com/publications/publications/

Deacon, D., Pickering, M., Golding, P. & Murdock, G. (1999). *Research Communications: A Practical Guide to Methods in Media and Cultural Analysis*. New York: Oxford University Press.

Department for Education and Communities (DEC) (2012). *Use of Tablet Technology in the Classroom*. Sydney, NSW. Retrieved from http://clic.det.nsw.edu.au/clic/tablets.htm

Department of Education and Early Childhood Development (DEECD) (2010). *iPads for Learning*. Retrieved 15 June 2012 from http://www.education.vic.gov.au/school/teachers/support/Pages/ipads.aspx

Department of Education and Early Childhood Development (DEECD) (2011). *21 Steps to 1 to 1 Success*. Retrieved 15 June 2012 from www.education.vic.gov.au/school/teachers/support/Pages/ipads.aspx

Gliksman, S. (2011). Assessing the impact of iPads on education one year later. *Edutechdebate*. Retrieved 15 July 2013 from https://edutechdebate.org/tablet-computers-in-education/assessing-the-impact-of-ipads-on-education-one-year-later/

Goodwin, K. & Highfield, K. (2012). iTouch and iLearn: an examination of "educational" Apps. Paper presented at the Early Education and Technology for Children conference.

Haughland, S. W. (1999). What role should technology play in young children's learning? *Young Children, November,* 26–31.

Lynch, J. & Redpath, T. (2012). "Smart" technologies in early years literacy education: a meta-narrative of paradigmatic tensions in iPad use in an Australian preparatory classroom. *Journal of Early Childhood literacy, 14*(2), 147–74.

Mullholland, J. (2011). iPads in the classroom. *Government Technology*. Retrieved 13 July 2013 from http://www.govtech.com/education/iPads-in-the-classroom.html

Olney, I., Herrington, J. & Verenikina, I. (2008). iPods in early childhood: mobile technologies and story telling. In: Hello! Where are you in the landscape of educational technology? Paper presented at the ASCILITE. Retrieved from http://www.ascilite.org.au/conferences/melbourne08/procs/olney.pdf

Partnerships for the 21st Century. (2008). *21st Century Skills, Education & Competitiveness: A Resource and Policy Guide*. Washington, DC: The Partnership for 21st Century Skills.

Puentendra, R. (Producer) (2011) SAMR and TPRK in action. Retrieved 2 April 2013 from http://www.hippasus.com/rrpweblog/archives/2011/10/28/SAMR_TPCK_In_Action.pdf

PBS Kids (2010). *There's an App for That*. PBS Kids. Retrieved 15 July 2013 from pbskids.org/read/files/cooney_learning_apps.pdf

Shuler, C. (2009). *iLearn: A Content Analysis of the iTunes App Store's Education Section*. New York: The Joan Ganz Cooney Center at Sesame Workshop.

Shuler, C. (2012). *iLearn II: An Analysis of the Education Category of Apples App Store*. New York: The Joan Ganz Cooney Center at the Sesame Workshop.

Steen, L. A. (1999). Numeracy: the new literacy for a data drenched society. *Educational Leadership, 57*(2), 8–13.

Struppert, A. (2011). *Developing Intercultural Awareness and Sensitivity through Digital Game Play*. East Ryde: Macquarie University,

Trilling, B., & Fadel, C. (2009). *21st Century Skills: Learning for Life in Our Times*. San Francisco: Jossey-Bass.

Watlington, D. (2011). Using iPod Touch and iPad Educational Apps in the Classroom. Paper presented at the Proceedings of Society for Information Technology & Teacher Education International Conference.

Worthen, B. (2012). What happens when toddlers zone out with iPad. *The Wall Street Journal*. Retrieved 15 July 2013 from http://online.wsj.com/article/SB10001424052702304363104577391813961853988.html

Yelland, N. J. (2007). *Shift to the Future: Rethinking Learning with New Technologies in Education*. New York: Routledge.

Yelland, N. J. (2010). New technologies, playful experiences, and multimodal learning. In: I. R. Berson & M. J. Berson (Eds), *High Tech Tots: Childhood in a Digital World* (pp. 5–22). Charlotte, NC: Information Age.

Yelland, N. J. (2011). Reconceptualising play and learning in the lives of children. *Australasian Journal of Early Childhood, 36*(2) 4–12.

11

THE TABLET COMPUTER AS A MEDIATIONAL MEANS IN A PRESCHOOL ART ACTIVITY

Malin Nilsen, Mona Lundin, Cecilia Wallerstedt and Niklas Pramling

Abstract

In this chapter we will study what happens when a new technology in the form of a tablet computer enters into a well-established early childhood education practice: an art activity. Sociocultural theory is used to analyse the evolving activities and the participants' projects. In the studied activity, one child (four-year-old Vera) is to use a biology app to locate a bug that will serve as a template for her art-making activity where she tries to construct a butterfly. The results show that the hardware and software of the technology delimit her project, and that she and the teacher have difficulties establishing intersubjectivity due to them being engaged in partly different projects. The technology is used in accordance with an established tradition rather than engendering a new kind of art activity.

Introduction

In this chapter we will focus on one kind of technology, the tablet computer, recently introduced in many Swedish preschools. We will investigate how this technology is used and whether it transforms a familiar activity, that is, an art activity where children (and teachers) are to make material objects (in Swedish: *pysselaktivitet*). There are well-established discourses on the arts in Swedish early childhood education, as Saar (2005) points out. According to one of these discourses, art is a useful *tool* for learning: "Aesthetics is seen as an engine generating energy, activity and knowledge" (Saar, 2005, p. 22, our translation). While both art and technology may be seen as learning tools, how to understand their relationship is contested. According to one view, new technologies can "engage all the senses, connect across time and space, as well as adapt to the experiences, interests, and abilities of the user" (Bruce, 2007, p. 1357), properties that have traditionally been associated with the arts. On the one hand, if telling "the stories of Art and Technology", it can appear that technology is only a technique, a limited tool that plays a subordinated role in relation to the artistic content. On the other hand, art is "the body of stuff which can be stored, organized, searched, and displayed, but is ultimately irrelevant to the lives of young people today, who find their excitement in new technologies, which are dynamic, individualized, and more alive" (Bruce, 2007, p. 1357). These conflicting notions of technology and art emphasise the importance of research on how individuals and groups engage with art and technologies, particularly paying attention to the learners' perspectives on objects and activities.

Peterson (2014) discusses technology in education and finds several examples of how new technologies are introduced along with hyped expectations: they will bring the world to the classroom and widen the universe for the children (cf. when the radio was new, Cuban, 1986), and computer games, for example, should have an inbuilt force to fundamentally change the way we learn. Peterson (2014) concludes that the role of technology is always a question of what we *do* with it and, consequently, that it is of great importance that research investigates technologies in use in educational practices. As she points out, it is important to take a critical stance and be mindful of technological determinism.

This chapter is based on empirical data from a larger study of children's activities with tablet computers in a Swedish preschool (Nilsen, 2014). The aim of the larger study was to examine what kind of activities evolved when children and teachers in a Swedish preschool used tablet computers, how they participated in these activities and what kind of learning was made possible. The results showed that mainly two types of activities evolved: 1) activities that were initiated by the children and allowed for them to exert agency and to explore, and 2) activities that were planned by the teachers beforehand and were more strictly organised. An important finding was that children and teachers, in both types of activities, had difficulties in coordinating their perspectives.

Research on children and tablet computers

Although tablet computers have become increasingly common in educational settings in the last few years, empirical research is still scarce. This is especially noticeable when it comes to research on tablet use in preschool, since most studies have been carried out in primary and secondary school, or higher education. However, when it comes to research regarding children's use of tablet computers in institutional settings, it is possible to differentiate between strands of studies.

1. There are several studies that are concerned with implementation issues and what happens when tablets and apps are introduced in educational environments (Culén & Gasparini, 2011; Jahnke & Kumar, 2014).
2. The most extensive category focuses on children's language development, early literacy and narrative skills supported by tablets and specific apps. Some of these studies were carried out in preschool settings (Kucirkova, Messer, Sheehy & Panadero, 2014; Sandvik, Smørdal & Østerud, 2012), but most were made in primary school (Falloon, 2013; Lynch & Redpath, 2014), secondary school (Hutchinson Beschorner & Schmidt-Crawford, 2012) and special education (Flewitt, Messer & Kucirkova, 2014).
3. Due to the properties of the touch-screen technology there is an emerging strand of research that is concerned with multimodality in connection with tablet use (Davidsen & Christiansen, 2014; Kjällander & Moinian, 2014).
4. There are a few studies that can be categorised as connected to play and/or creativity (Fleer, 2014; Verenikina & Kervin, 2011). This is a very diverse strand of research and includes, among other subjects, children's art activities, animation and playing.

Many of these studies emphasise the teacher as important when it comes to supporting and scaffolding children in their interaction with novel technologies. Falloon (2014) emphasises that teachers should keep a close eye on children's interaction with tablets and be ruthlessly critical about the kind of apps they introduce to children. Furthermore, he argues that tablet computers have an incomparable potential as a tool for learning based on their "unique interface, simplicity, intuitive design, portability, connectivity, speed, range of apps and relative affordability" (p. 334), a potential that needs to be realised by teachers. The aim of this chapter is to make such a contribution. More specifically, we ask the following research questions: (i) what role does the technology play in an art activity where a tablet computer is used, and (ii) what challenges do the participants (child and teacher) face in such an activity and how do they respond to these?

A sociocultural perspective on communication and learning

In order to examine a technology-mediated activity, in this case in the form of a preschool art activity with tablet computers, we adopt a sociocultural perspective on learning and communication. This perspective conceptualises learning as a socioculturally informed process. Importantly, human forms of knowledge, such as reasoning, problem solving and voluntary perception, remembering and attention, are explained in terms of the law of socio-genesis (Vygotsky, 1998). Through participation in social practices and communicating with others, the individual comes in contact with, is introduced to and starts taking over cultural tools and practices (Luria, 1976). Being skilled means being able to participate by using cultural tools in relevant and flexible ways (Wertsch, 1998). Cultural tools mediate the individual's engagement with the world, that is, such tools re-present phenomena in distinct ways (Pramling, 2006). As Säljö (1997) argues, "cultural development, i.e., learning at the level of collectives, is largely a matter of transforming ideas and concepts into material artifacts" (p. 6). On a more local level, educational practices fundamentally build on representing the world in distinct ways (e.g. in terms of stories, mathematics, scientific vocabulary) and in making representational artefacts (predominantly texts). One such practice in early childhood education is art activities, where children make material objects of various kinds. Transforming – or transducing (Kress, 2003), that is, going from one mode of representation into another – is central to art activities (Wallerstedt & Pramling, 2012). Some examples would be to verbalise poetically what in some sense lies outside (established) language (e.g. felt sensations) or to put music (an auditory form of representation) to a dance (a bodily and visual form of expression). Different forms of representation mediate the world differently (Wertsch, 2007). Much knowledge is re-presentational, that is, it is a means for us to make sense of something.

Rather than independent exploration or discovery through maturation, according to this perspective it is thus through engaging in mutual activities that the child learns. By implication, other, more experienced peers as well as caregivers, parents and other adults become important to the child's learning. Of particular importance is whether participants, a more experienced peer, a teacher or another participant, on the one hand, and the child, on the other, manage to coordinate their respective perspectives. This is necessary in order to constitute a mutual activity. Theoretically, this is conceptualised in terms of establishing temporarily sufficient intersubjectivity (Rommetveit, 1974). Hence, intersubjectivity is achieved through a process in which perspective setting and perspective taking on the parts of the participants' communicating are coordinated and "state of affairs are brought into joint focus of attention, made sense of, and talked about from a position temporarily adopted by both participants" (Rommetveit, 1992, p. 23). If communicative partners do not manage to coordinate perspectives, they will in effect talk past each other and engage in distinct, uncoordinated activities.

Teachers and more experienced peers tend to point out to a learner important phenomena and features to attend to. This is typically done by using deictic references (Ivarsson, 2003), that is, pointing with one's fingers and/or words (e.g. using words such as *that*, *there* and *this*). Language (cf. gesturing) is an important cultural tool for directing someone's attention (Tomasello, 1999). However, contingent on what cultural tools they have appropriated, their perception is mediated in different ways (Wertsch, 2007). It therefore becomes crucial for participants to establish intersubjectivity, particularly in instructional or educational activities. This feature of learning is referred to in terms of agency (Kozulin, 1998). The distribution of agency among participants tends to be uneven. However, typically in educational settings, it would be expected that teachers initially carry agentive power, with learners increasingly coming to take over the agency of an activity. Furthermore, if teachers and children are uncoordinated in perspectives, the teacher's project and the child's project may be divergent (Bendroth Karlsson, 2011). From a sociocultural perspective, the participants' actions are understood as situated, which means that they orientate towards each other's actions but they also respond (explicitly or implicitly) to the sociocultural context they engage in. This responsiveness is theorised in terms of double dialogicality (Kullenberg, 2014; Linell, 2009).

Empirical study

The empirical data consist of video observations of 33 children (one to five years old) and their five teachers engaged in activities with tablet computers in a Swedish city. Interviews as well as informal conversations with the teachers also took place during the four-month long period of generating data.

When the study was initiated the preschool had taken part in a one-year local development project in which the two classrooms had been provided with four tablets, that is, eight tablets in total. Initially, the teachers who participated in the study expressed an ambition that the tablets would be part of and used as a learning tool in everyday preschool activities.

For the purpose of this chapter, one specific activity, lasting for 10 minutes, was selected for analysis. It was chosen since it is an example of an activity where the preschool teachers had planned to use the tablets in an *art project*. In a Swedish preschool context an art activity is often related to crafts, that is creating objects out of different kinds of material. Previous analyses of teacher-planned activities with tablet computers in this specific setting have focused on what from the teachers' perspective are seen as mathematics and literacy activities (Nilsen, 2014).

Analysis

Taking a sociocultural perspective (Vygotsky, 1998), where communication is seen as the mechanism of learning, an analytical approach that is responsive to unfolding interaction and communication is necessary. Arguing that human knowing is contingent on cultural tools (intellectual as well as physical artefacts) present or appropriated, how children and teachers (when present) take part in and contribute to establishing and maintaining activities needs to be analysed. From these theoretical premises, the unit of analysis in this study is tool–mediated activities (Säljö, 2009). In order to clarify a participant's perspective, typically a minimum of three consecutive utterances are analysed (Wells, 1999). This allows us to analytically attend to how an action is initiated, responded to by others, and the response to the response (i.e., continuing with the activity and thus implying that some coordination is established or objecting to and clarifying a discrepancy in understanding among participants). The video data was transcribed verbatim (and with non–verbal action marked out). The analysis is conducted and compared closely to transcribed excerpts from the videos, along with some illustrative pictures from the app used in the activity.

Findings: An art activity with the tablet

In this specific activity the teacher and the children use a children's biology app called *My First Bug App*.[1] The children are expected to first choose a photograph of a bug from the app, and then make their own bug out of the craft supplies available on the table. The biology app contains a collection of photographs and some text–based factual information about 37 different kinds of bugs and insects. The bugs are categorised according to how many legs they have: no legs, one foot, six legs, eight legs and many legs.[2]

When the observation starts the preschool teacher is sitting at a table with four–year–old Vera on her left side. On the table are many different types of arts and craft supplies (see Figure 11.1).

The findings will be presented as themes emerging from the activity. These are presented in chronological order to make visible the development of the activity.

A biology app as a mediational means in an art activity

In the following sequence the preschool teacher has just initiated the activity by opening the main menu of the app. She is holding the tablet, which she has put in a clear plastic bag to protect it from glue stains. Before the exchange in the example that follows the teacher has asked Vera what bug she wants to make, but Vera has not answered. In the following extract below the teacher again encourages Vera to make a decision about what bug she wants to choose.

FIGURE 11.1 Vera at craft table.

Extract 11.1 Choosing a bug from the app

7	Teacher:	What did you want to choose Vera? [Softly. Looks at the screen.]
8	Vera:	I wanted one like *that*. [Quietly. Points at a photo of a butterfly in the main menu.]
9	Teacher:	Did you want a butterfly? [Points at the same photo.]
10	Vera:	M–hm. [Nods.]
11	Teacher:	M–hm. Let's see if we can find one then.
12	Teacher:	How many legs do you think a butterfly has? Does it *have* any legs? [Looks at Vera.]
13	Vera:	[5 sec] Yes. [Nods slowly.]
14	Teacher:	Do you think so? [Chooses the category with eight-legged bugs. Starts to flip through photographs in the app by swiping her finger over the pictures.]
15	Teacher:	Let's see here if we can find a butterfly here somewhere … there maybe … [Keeps flipping through photographs.]
16	Teacher:	We probably ended up in the wrong place here … Here we've got spiders … Spiders … [As if talking to herself.]

When the teacher asks Vera to choose a bug from the app (turn 7) she clearly shows by looking directly at the tablet that Vera is to choose a bug that is represented in the app. In this manner the teacher introduces a premise for the activity, that is, the bugs Vera is to choose among need to be represented within the app. Thus, the teacher mediates the activity as an activity in which the tablet and the specific app are to be used. Vera orients to this mediation of the activity by selecting a picture of a butterfly (turn 8) in the main menu of the app. Once the activity is established, the teacher can continue with her instruction about finding a butterfly in the app (turn 11). The possibility of using a web browser or doing an image search on the internet, which could allow for a much more diversified variety of photographs of bugs, is not brought up in the activity. Thus, the activity is mediated by the teacher, who has control over the tablet and thereby restricts Vera's agency on the development of the activity.

The teacher continues, asking Vera "How many legs do you think a butterfly has?" (turn 12). Such a question is also a response to the app, that is, as we have already mentioned, bugs are categorised according to the number of legs they have (from no legs to many). This inherent logic of categorisation makes it more or less impossible for the teacher to browse through photos to find (turn 11) a butterfly for Vera. Instead the teacher accommodates to the logic of categorisation and acts to involve Vera in this categorisation work (turn 12). The teacher quickly reformulates this question, "Does it *have* any legs?" (turn 12), which is a response to the distinction in the app between the category "No leg" and the other categories. However, to be able to answer such a question presumes that Vera has some prior knowledge and experience of looking at butterflies in this specific manner. In what follows it is quite difficult to decide whether or not the teacher knows the conventional categorisation herself. Vera in turn comes up with a very tentative "yes" (turn 13), which indicates that the answer is not obvious to her, marking a gap in the interaction. The teacher addresses this gap by following up on Vera's stance that butterflies have legs by checking if she still thinks so (turn 14). As the teacher receives no response from Vera, she selects the category "eight-legged" and starts to look through the pictures to find a butterfly for Vera (turn 15). She takes Vera's suggestion seriously, that butterflies have legs, and starts to work her way through the other categories in the app.

The teacher talks in the past tense when she asks the question "What did you want to choose Vera?" (turn 7). Vera is indirectly encouraged to select a bug that is represented in the app and she points at a photo of a butterfly (turn 8). Her choice indicates that she is becoming attuned to the institutional premises of the activity. The teacher initiates the art activity as such and gives feedback on Vera's choice and responses, but notably the teacher is also in physical control of the tablet throughout the activity. Consequently, Vera's possibilities of agency in the activity are clearly defined.

As the activity evolves, it may seem limiting to use an app structured on the logic or categorisation of the number of legs of bugs. The teacher's actions can be understood within this tradition and not only in response to the child's concrete actions. In theoretical terms, the teacher can be seen to orient herself according to a double dialogicality (Linell, 2009). In this situation at least four valued areas of knowledge are integrated: art, nature, mathematics and technology use. But as a close reading of the transcript shows, combining these interests and areas is difficult, and in this case they come to lead the participants in partially different directions.

In the next sequence the teacher makes more attempts to include Vera in the search for a butterfly photo when five-year-old Greta comes up to the table and gets involved in the activity (see Figure 11.2):

Extract 11.2 Looking for a butterfly

21	Teacher:	Which one do you want here? You have to flip through here yourself, see which one you want to have ... You can see here ...
22	Teacher:	[Still holding the tablet but moves it a little bit closer to Vera.]
23	Greta:	[Comes up to the table.] What?
24	Teacher:	*You* flip through it ... [To Vera.]
25	Teacher:	[Does a flipping motion with her hand above the tablet.]
26	Teacher:	She is looking for a butterfly. She wants a butterfly. [To Greta.]
27	Teacher:	Let's see if we can find a butterfly. [To Vera.]
28	Vera:	[Starts to flip through photos on the screen.]
29	Greta:	Stink bug. [Points at the screen]
30	Teacher:	Yes exactly! Did you see that? [Smiles.] Yes and what's that then? [Looks at the screen.] A grasshopper, that was ...
31	Greta:	Butterfly!
32	Vera:	There! [Points to the screen and looks at the teacher.]
33	Teacher:	Oh, look at that! That was a beautiful one. Do you want to choose that one?
34	Greta:	But maybe there is ...
35	Greta:	[Starts flipping through photos on the tablet.]
36	Teacher:	But Greta ... Greta ...
37	Greta:	Oops!
38	Teacher:	Now you'll have to go back. [To Greta.]
39	Greta:	[Flips through the photos again to make it right.]
40	Teacher:	It was ... it was actually Vera who wanted to choose.

The teacher invites Vera to be more involved in the activity by moving the tablet closer to her and instructing her to flip through the pictures herself (turns 21 and 22). As Vera does not respond to the call for more involvement in the activity, the teacher reformulates the instruction by first explaining to Vera, "You flip through it" (turn 24) and then by showing her the flipping motion (turn 25). This is followed by a more direct instruction from the teacher encouraging first and foremost Vera to get started with the activity.

The teacher's use of "we" is thus taken by Greta to include her as well, as seen in her starting to contribute to the activity (turn 29). Vera also responds to the teacher's instruction through starting to flip through pictures in the app in search of a butterfly (turn 28). Whilst Vera flips through photos, Greta sees a stink bug (turn 29) and the teacher latches onto Greta's naming of the bug, identifying a grasshopper (turn 30). In this way, the teacher also legitimises Greta's participation in the activity. In a collaborative endeavour, Vera and Greta find a photo of a butterfly in the app, Greta by naming it and Vera by pointing at it (turns 31 and 32). This sequence ends with the teacher in some sense voicing Vera's intention in this part of the activity, "it was actually Vera who wanted to choose" (turn 40).

This sequence shows how the matter of agency is redistributed over the course of the activity, in terms of who has control over the touch screen (cf. Ljung-Djärf, 2008). Greta actively involves herself in the activity by temporarily taking the responsibility for flipping through the pictures. As the following examples will show, the teacher is oriented toward the norms of art activities in general, that is, an activity that is carried out individually (i.e., does not involve distributed agency) and consists in individual creations. Hence, as the activity develops, the task is constituted by the teacher as a single-child activity.

FIGURE 11.2 Vera and Greta.

Transforming a digital representation into a material object

As the activity continues, Vera finally makes a choice of a butterfly: a Pearl-Bordered Fritillary (*Boloria euphrosyne*) (see Figure 11.3).

FIGURE 11.3   Vera's butterfly.

The teacher puts the tablet on the table in front of Vera and encourages her to begin her art project. This marks a shift in the activity where the app and the logic and categorisation in the app become more in the background and the art project is foregrounded. In the following, it becomes evident that Vera and the teacher are not coordinated in their perspectives, which leads to a gap in their communication:

Extract 11.3 Communicative gap

52	Teacher:	And what will you need to make a butterfly, do you think? If you look at the table here … What do you think you'll need?
53	Vera:	[Looks at the material on the table.]
54	Teacher:	[Adjusts the plastic bag that is covering the tablet.] If you see what it looks like, the butterfly, what do you think you'll need to *make* a butterfly, Vera?
55	Vera:	[Looks at the photo on the screen for five seconds, then looks at the material on the table again.]
56	Vera:	Ings. [Very quiet, almost inaudible.]
57	Teacher:	What did you want? [The teacher tucks a strand of hair behind Vera's ear.]
58	Vera:	To have ings.
59	Teacher:	[Looks at the material on the table.]
60	Teacher:	Was it *rings* that you said?
61	Vera:	No, *ings*. [Much louder.]
62	Teacher:	Now I don't know. You'll have to show me what you want to have. Show me what you want.
63	Vera:	Ings.
64	Teacher:	There are things here that you can choose.
65	Teacher:	[Looks at the material at the table.]
66	Teacher:	Look here you have some paper and here you have an egg carton if you need cut it to make a butterfly or if you need some other things … Some toilet rolls, coffee filters and here you have some coloured stuff and glitter and things like that.

This part of the activity starts off as the teacher asks Vera what she will need to make a butterfly (turn 52), referring to the different materials on the table in front of them. Vera initially responds to the teacher's question by looking at the material but makes no verbal response to the instruction (turn 53). The teacher directs their attention to the picture in the app again for Vera to see what it looks like (turn 54), as a starting point for her to make a butterfly (turn 54). Evidently, the teacher shows some difficulty hearing Vera's suggestion and asks the same question again (turn 57) and gets the same answer: "To have ings" (turn 58). It becomes evident that there is a gap in their communication, which the teacher tries to bridge by matching what Vera might have suggested to the material represented on the table (turn 59), leading to her guessing rings (turn 60). Vera clearly shows by raising her voice that the teacher's guess is not correct and repeats her initial suggestion (turn 61). This response makes evident that there is still a gap in their communication, that is, they are not coordinated in perspectives (see Figure 11.4).

FIGURE 11.4 Communication gap.

The teacher again addresses the communicative gap, first by taking on the responsibility for the appearance of this gap: "Now I don't know" (turn 62) and then by asking Vera "to show me what you want" (turn 62). However, the teacher's perspective on what she expects Vera to show continues to be about the materials Vera will need to make a butterfly (turn 62), and not what Vera orients towards, that is, the specific parts she will need to make a butterfly. The teacher uses a deictic reference, 'here', as well as looking at the materials to direct Vera's focus of attention (turn 66). However, what Vera means by "ings" is not solved at this point.

This shows that the challenges the participants face are related to the situation here and now, as visible in their struggle to reach agreement on what "ings" refers to (whether "ings" means rings or wings), but there is also a challenge with wider applications. The role of the teacher in early childhood arts education is often expected to be "the supplier of material" (Bendroth Karlsson, 2011). Thus, the teacher's focus on the material on the table and on how to make the object can be seen as a response to established preschool norms and culture (cf. Kullenberg, 2014, on double dialogicality). The child, in turn, meets a partly new kind of activity where the technology – the tablet computer and the particular software – are integral parts. This poses a challenge for her and the teacher in achieving intersubjectivity.

The activity continues with Vera picking up a small white paper-spun ball from a bowl and rolling it between the palms of her hands. Vera responds by placing the paper ball onto the photo on the screen to show the teacher that the ball would form the middle part of the body of the butterfly. In the following sequence the teacher follows up on Vera's plans and asks Vera to figure out how she can go about making the wings.

Extract 11.4 How to make wings

81	Teacher:	What is this? [Points at the wings of the butterfly.]
82	Vera:	They're ings.
83	Teacher:	Wings yes. How can you make the wings? How can you create them?
84	Vera:	You could make them with those. [Points at a roll of pink curling ribbon.]
85	Teacher:	Was it this one you were pointing at? [Picks up the ribbon.]
86	Vera:	[Nods and smiles faintly.]
87	Vera:	You could do like that, up and down. [Moves her index finger along the edge of the wings of the butterfly, on the screen.]

The teacher asks Vera, by using the picture in the app and by pointing to the wings of the butterfly specifically, "What is this?" (turn 81). Vera's answer is "ings" (turn 82), which the teacher rephrases as wings and evaluates positively (turn 83). In other words, the teacher initiates a point of departure for the activity that is the same as Vera has tried to establish through a number of turns previously in the activity. Once they have established that what they see are wings the teacher goes on to ask Vera how she can make or create them (turn 83). Vera responds hesitantly to the teacher's question on how to make the wings. In her response she suggests a specific material to use (turn 84). The teacher picks up on this suggestion and wants Vera to develop her ideas about using a ribbon (turn 85). In developing her idea, Vera uses the picture in the app to refer deictically how "You could do like that, up and down" (turn 87).

Again, this shows that an activity can be seen as a response to existing preschool culture; that the child creates something of her own is highly valued by teachers (Änggård, 2005).

Extract 11.5 Measuring the ribbon

105	Vera:	[Takes the piece of ribbon and puts it on the screen to measure if it is the right length. When she touches the screen with her hand the photo "flips around" and the backside becomes visible.]
106	Vera:	It turned around. [Almost inaudible.]
107	Teacher:	What did you say?
108	Vera:	It turned around. [Quietly. Looks at the ribbon which she is holding in her hands.]
109	Teacher:	[Helps Vera to flip the photo back again.]

What Vera orients to is examining if the piece of ribbon she has cut out is the appropriate size for making the edge of the butterfly wing. She does this by carefully placing the ribbon over the photograph of the wings in the app, shaping it along the outline of the wing (turn 105). However, when Vera puts the ribbon over the photograph in the app her hand touches the screen, which makes the photograph flip over (turn 105). Vera makes no attempt to undo this. Instead she reports to the teacher what has happened, "It turned around" (turn 106), "it" referring to the photograph in the app. She does this with a lowered voice and the teacher consequently does not hear what Vera is saying (turn 107). Vera repeats what she has already said but without making eye contact with the teacher and talking in a very low voice (turn 108). Although Vera does not explicitly ask for help, the manner in which she verbally reports on her trouble and her uncertainty towards the task is responded to by the teacher as a request for help. The teacher responds by helping Vera to flip the photograph back by pressing the screen once with her index finger. The fact that the teacher again takes control of the tablet could be considered not only as supporting Vera in her project but also as limiting her agency in it. Vera makes no further effort to measure the ribbon and instead goes on making the rest of the wing.

This example shows that the specific role the technology has in this activity, that is, working as a digital two-dimensional model of something to be transformed into a physical object, has clear limitations. First, it was problematic in providing the specific bug that the child wanted (a butterfly), due to the software. Second, it was difficult for Vera to keep the image visible due to the hardware; when she accidently touches the screen the picture disappears. The use of this expensive technology in an activity with glue and paint forces the teacher to protect the screen with a plastic bag. Again, the issue of the teacher's consideration of the purpose for using the technology in the activity can be raised.

The child's aesthetic values and preferences

In the next part of the activity, Vera has decided to use a shimmering gold ribbon to form the inside of the wings of the butterfly. After cutting off a piece of the ribbon she is determined to glue the pink curling ribbon onto the organza ribbon as a border. Vera asks the teacher if she is allowed to bring the butterfly home when it is finished. The teacher promises her that she can bring it home when the glue has dried. Vera expresses that her parents will think that it is pretty since it is what she calls "silvery". However she soon realises that the glue is making the ribbon change colour.

Extract 11.6 Material difficulties

165	Vera:	[Brushes white glue on the ribbon until it is completely covered on one side. She then holds it up and looks at it.]
166	Vera:	Now there's white on it. [To the teacher. Looks upset.]
167	Teacher:	Mm, but it doesn't matter because it's going to dry in a while and then it won't be white anymore. Then it will just be pretty.
168	Teacher:	Have you got anything that you will be gluing onto that?
169	Vera:	But there is glue there … [Almost crying.]
170	Teacher:	[Turns the ribbon around to the other side.]
171	Teacher:	That's what you have to do, turn it around. You can glue on that side now. Like that.
172	Vera:	But there is glue on it …
173	Vera:	[Starts to cry.]
174	Teacher:	Yes, but it doesn't matter because then it's going to dry and it won't show then. It doesn't matter. It so sheer and thin, that fabric … You know it's bound to seep through.

In this part of the activity Vera is quite engaged. It seems that her earlier ambition (making a butterfly that is as similar as possible to a photo in the app) has shifted to an interest in making something pretty that she can bring home and show to her parents. Vera also appears to invest more emotionally in the activity towards the end. Studies of children's art-making in preschool have shown how strong children's wish to make beautiful things is (oriented towards a norm within art and arts education). From an adult perspective, informed by the modernistic idea of originality, the child's authentic creation is most valued. However, children often prefer to use templates and copy older children's creations in striving for "perfection" (Änggård, 2005). The teacher tries to mitigate Vera's disappointment (turn 167) by pointing out that the colour of the glue is a temporary matter and that it will correct itself eventually. Furthermore, the teacher tries to direct Vera's attention to the next step in the process, which is gluing the wing to another part of the body of the butterfly (turn 168). However, Vera is still upset (turn 169). Again the teacher tries to redirect Vera's attention away from the fact that the ribbon has changed colour (turns 170 and 171). However, the activity ends with Vera starting to cry after once again stating that there is glue on the ribbon (turn 172). Vera's repetitions of the material difficulties (turns 166, 169 and 172) show that she has a hard time letting go of her "failure" in making a pretty butterfly, which seems to be the goal for her project in this activity. The teacher's support seems to be less important at this point. As a response to Vera's tears, the teacher partly changes strategy and attempts to make Vera accept the logical and inevitable fact that the glue will permeate the thin ribbon due to the properties of the fabric (turn 174).

This last part of the activity shows how engaged Vera becomes in making a beautiful butterfly as something to later on be exhibited and admired and evaluated by others, primarily her parents. In contrast, the teacher makes efforts to leave the here-and-now of the problem with the wings to talk about how the finished product will be as soon as the glue has dried. In this way she tries to make Vera continue her gluing work. However, the teacher is not able to have Vera ignore such material difficulties (how the butterfly looks) in order to orientate to how the butterfly will look later.

Discussion

The aim of this chapter has been to contribute with empirically grounded research on the use of tablet computers in early childhood education. From a sociocultural perspective it is important to analyse how cultural tools mediate the activities with technology that the children and teachers participate in. We also wanted to explore the challenges that the participants faced in the art activity and how they responded to these.

When it comes to the role of the technology it is important to make a distinction between the hardware (the tablet computer) and the software (the app). The reason for this is that hardware and software offer different kinds of opportunities and limitations, contingent on their design and properties. The software is utilised as a source for inspiration regarding which bug to choose in the beginning of the observation. It thus serves a function similar to what a book or a collection of photographs could have filled.

The results also show that the app is used as a measuring tool. Hence, Vera places the ribbon on the screen in order to estimate how much ribbon she will need. However, due to properties of the touch screen of the tablet computer and the design of the app as responsive to touch, this particular kind of manoeuvre is impossible. Since the hardware has to be protected, the teacher has put it into a transparent plastic bag, which restricts the children from seeing and using the touch screen. As the activity goes on, the photograph in the app serves as a digital, two-dimensional model that is to be transformed into a material artefact. Thus the software both supports and limits Vera in her art project. The teacher also restricts Vera's agency on several occasions during the activity, mainly by taking control of the technology in the beginning of the activity.

We also found that the teacher and the children had some difficulties in establishing common ground in the activity. Hence, Vera and the teacher had problems in establishing temporarily sufficient intersubjectivity (Rommetveit, 1974) due to them being focused on different features of the environment and thus carrying out partly different projects (cf. Bendroth Karlsson, 2011). The teacher's actions were interpreted as oriented not only to the here-and-now but also to traditional ideals of art activities in preschool more generally (cf. Kullenberg, 2014; Linell, 2009, on double dialogicality). It is thus critical for the more experienced (i.e., the teacher) to relate these different projects to be able to contribute to the child's learning process. The technology as such does not readily transform educational practice.

Notes

1   Swedish: *Min första småkrypsapp*. In Swedish *småkryp* serves as a colloquial umbrella term for many different kinds of bugs, insects, spiders, snails, slugs and worms, much like the informal meaning of the English word *bug*.
2   The app can also be used as a "bug-spotting journal" where the child can upload her own photographs of bugs and also make notes about where and when the bug was seen.

References

Änggård, E. (2005). *Bildskapande. En del av förskolebarns kamratkulturer* [Art making: a part of children's peer cultures]. Linköping: Linköping University.

Bendroth Karlsson, M. (2011). Pictures of spring: aesthetic learning and pedagogical dilemmas in visual arts. In: N. Pramling & I. Pramling Samuelsson (Eds), *Educational Encounters: Nordic Studies in Early Childhood Didactics* (pp. 85–104). Dordrecht: Springer.

Bruce, C. B. (2007). Interlude: technology and arts education. In: L. Bresler (Ed.), *International Handbook of Research in Arts Education, Part 2* (pp. 1355–61). Dordrecht: Springer.

Cuban, L. (1986). *Teachers and Machines: The Classroom Use of Technology since 1920*. New York: Teachers College Press.

Culén, A. & Gasparini, A. (2011). iPad: a new classroom technology? A report from two pilot studies. In: C. Billnness, A. Hemera, V. Meteljan, M. Banek Zorica, H. Stancic & S. Seljan (Eds), *Information Sciences and E-society* (pp. 199–208). Zagreb: Department of Information Sciences, University of Zagreb.

Davidsen, J. & Christiansen, E. (2014). Mind the hand: a study on children's embodied and multimodal collaborative learning around touchscreens. *Designs for Learning*, 7(1), 34–52.

Falloon, G. W. (2013). Young students using iPads: app design and content influences on their learning pathways. *Computers and Education*, 68, 505–21.

Falloon, G. W. (2014). What's going on behind the screens? Researching young students' learning pathways using iPads. *Journal of Computer Assisted Learning* 30(4), 318–36.

Fleer, M. (2014). The demands and motives afforded through digital play in early childhood activity settings. *Learning, Culture and Social Interaction*, 3(3), 202–209.

Flewitt, R., Messer, D. & Kucirkova, N. (2014). Touching the virtual, touching the real: iPads and enabling literacy for students experiencing disability. *Australian Journal of Language and Literacy* 37(2), 107–16.

Hutchinson A., Beschorner, B. & Schmidt-Crawford, D. (2012). Exploring the use of the iPad for literacy learning. *The Reading Teacher* 66(1), 15–23.

Ivarsson, J. (2003). Kids in Zen: computer supported learning environments and illusory intersubjectivity. *Education, Communication & Information*, 3(3), 383–402.

Jahnke, I. & Kumar, S. (2014). Digital didactical designs: teachers' integration of iPads for learning-centered processes. *Journal of Digital Learning in Teacher Education, 30*(3), 81–88.

Kjällander, S. & Moinian, F. (2014). Digital tablets and applications in preschool: preschooler's creative transformation of didactic design. *Designs for Learning, 7*(1), 10–33.

Kozulin, A. (1998). *Psychological Tools: A Sociocultural Approach to Education.* Cambridge, MA: Harvard University Press.

Kress, G. (2003). *Literacy in the New Media Age.* London: Routledge.

Kucirkova, N., Messer, D., Sheehy, K. & Panadero, C. F. (2014). Children's engagement with educational iPad apps: insights from a Spanish classroom. *Computers & Education 71*, 175–84.

Kullenberg, T. (2014). *Signing and Singing: Children in Teaching Dialogues.* Gothenburg: Art Monitor.

Linell, P. (2009). *Rethinking Language, Mind and World Dialogically: Interactional and Contextual Theories of Human Sense-making.* Charlotte, NC: Information Age.

Ljung-Djärf, A. (2008). The owner, the participant and the spectator: positions and positioning in peer activity around the computer in pre-school. *Early Years, 28*(1), 61–72.

Luria, A. R. (1976). *Cognitive Development: Its Cultural and Social Foundations* (M. Lopez-Morillas & L. Solotaroff, Trans.). Cambridge, MA: Harvard University Press.

Lynch, J. & Redpath, T. (2014). 'Smart' technologies in early years literacy education: a meta-narrative of paradigmatic tensions in iPad use in an Australian preparatory classroom. *Journal of Early Childhood Literacy, 14*(2), 147–74.

Nilsen, M. (2014). *Barns aktiviteter med datorplattor i förskolan* [Children's activities with tablet computers in preschool] (Licentiate thesis, National research school in didactics in multicultural preschool, 3) Gothenburg: University of Gothenburg.

Peterson, L. (2014). Vikten av ett kritiskt granskande förhållningssätt. In: A. Lantz-Andersson & R. Säljö (Eds), *Lärande i den uppkopplade skolan* [Learning in the Internet-connected school] (pp. 197–231). Malmö: Gleerups.

Pramling, N. (2006). *Minding Metaphors: Using Figurative Language in Learning to Represent* (Göteborg Studies in Educational Sciences, 238). Gothenburg: Acta Universitatis Gothoburgensis.

Rommetveit, R. (1974). *On Message Structure: A Framework for the Study of Language and Communication.* London: Wiley.

Rommetveit, R. (1992). Outlines of a dialogically based social–cognitive approach to human cognition and communication. In: A. Wold (Ed.), *The Dialogical Alternative: Towards a Theory of Language and Mind,* (pp. 19–45). Oslo: Scandinavian Press.

Saar, T. (2005). *Konstens metoder och skolans träningslogik* [Methods of art and the training logic of school]. Karlstad: Karlstad University Studies.

Säljö, R. (1997). *Learning and Discourse: A Sociocultural Perspective* (The Sixteenth Vernon-Wall Lecture). Leicester: The Education Section of the British Psychological Society.

Säljö, R. (2009). Learning, theories of learning, and units of analysis in research. *Educational Psychologist, 44*(3), 202–08.

Sandvik, M., Smørdal, O. & Østerud, S. (2012). Exploring iPads in practitioners' repertoires for language learning and literacy practices in kindergarten. *Nordic Journal of Digital Literacy, 7*(3), 204–21.

Tomasello, M. (1999). *The Cultural Origins of Human Cognition.* Cambridge, MA: Harvard University Press.

Verenikina I. & Kervin L. (2011). iPads, digital play and preschoolers. *He Kupu, 2*(5), 4–19.

Vygotsky, L. S. (1998). *The Collected Works of L. S. Vygotsky, Volume 5: Child Psychology* (R. W. Rieber, Ed.; M. J. Hall, Trans.). New York: Plenum.

Wallerstedt, C. & Pramling, N. (2012). Conceptualising early childhood arts education: the cultivation of synesthetic transduction skills. *International Journal of Early Childhood, 44*(2), 127–39.

Wells, G. (1999). *Dialogic Inquiry: Towards a Sociocultural Practice and Theory of Education.* New York: Cambridge University Press.

Wertsch, J. V. (1998). *Mind as Action.* New York: Oxford University Press.

Wertsch, J. V. (2007). Mediation. In: H. Daniels, M. Cole & J. V. Wertsch (Eds), *The Cambridge Companion to Vygotsky* (pp. 178–92). New York: Cambridge University Press.

12

BEGINNING THE CONVERSATIONS ABOUT YOUNG CHILDREN'S ENGAGEMENT WITH TECHNOLOGY IN CONTEMPORARY TIMES

Karen McLean and Susan Edwards

Abstract

This chapter explores the potential of iPads in playgroups for engaging families in young children's learning. It takes a sociocultural view of children's learning in the playgroup context where iPads were introduced in ways that encouraged interactions between children, parents and playgroup facilitators. In this chapter we refer to findings from our research with parents about their perspectives of children's early learning experiences with digital technologies, including iPads in supported playgroups. We conclude with some recommendations to inform further conversations with families about children's engagement with technology in contemporary times.

Introduction

The pervasiveness of digital technologies in society has led to unprecedented debate around the influence of these technologies on young children's lives (McLean, 2013). These debates have largely focused on outcomes associated with children's engagement with digital technologies, which position this engagement as either beneficial or detrimental to learning and development. Burnett and Merchant (2013) put forward that technological growth and expansion in society has led to increasingly sophisticated technologies in the home. This subsequent immersion from birth of young children in these technologies (McPake, Plowman & Stephen, 2013) has contributed to what has been described as technologized childhoods (Burnett & Merchant, 2013) and has been an impetus for research into how technologies, media and popular culture influences children's lives (Hedges, 2011). The research in this area has provided important insights into a range of practices children engage in with new technologies in the home and in formal education early childhood contexts (Marsh, 2006, 2011; Wohlwend, 2013) and more recently into uni-directional patterns in meaning-making which occur across these contexts from school to home (McTavish, 2013). The contention that children in contemporary society have technologized childhoods has challenged traditional notions of play. This is because through a sociocultural lens children's play is influenced by social and cultural contexts and the different forms of play that children engage in serve different purposes within these contexts (Wood, 2009). Hence, as digital technologies are inherent in these contexts, it follows that young children's engagement with technologies in their play will take on different forms and serve different purposes. This suggests that to enable parents to make informed decisions about how children engage with digital technologies in the home and community contexts (Edgar & Edgar, 2008) there are important conversations that need to occur in partnership with parents around digital technologies and children's play (Plowman & McPake, 2013).

This chapter provides insights into parent perspectives of young children's early experiences of touch-screen technologies in supported playgroups. iPads as a form of touch-screen digital technology were of particular interest to us because of the prevalence of touch-screen technology in the home reported in other studies (see for example Auld, Snyder & Henderson, 2012) and young children's subsequent access to these from an early age (Yelland & Gilbert, 2012). We contend that conversations with families about children's play with touch-screen technologies are important for fostering parental awareness of children's learning through play with technologies in the home (Plowman & McPake, 2013), and in particular that touch-screen technologies have a place in early childhood education beyond a tool to support skill development (Yelland & Gilbert, 2012). The chapter begins with an overview of the research that has been happening in this area and provides an outline of the sociocultural theoretical perspective informing this chapter. We describe findings from our interviews with parents about their perspectives of children's early learning experiences with digital technologies, including iPads in the playgroup, and conclude with recommendations for fostering parental awareness of children's learning through play with digital technologies as a contemporary form of play.

Young children's experiences with digital technologies prior to school

Concerns fuelled through the media about negative impacts of digital technologies in early childhood have contributed to parental anxiety about children's use of digital technologies prior to school. For example, the Kaiser Family Foundation study (Rideout, Foehr & Roberts, 2010) raised concerns about increased media use and possible connections to children disengaging from learning at school. Other reports have also cited "the negative effects of mass media" (Alper, 2011, p. 176) and hidden costs associated with health conditions including reduced vision and weight gain. These concerns are highlighted in the Tech Tonic report (Alliance for Childhood, 2004) where the influence of digital technologies in the lives of children is blamed for obesity and difficulties with relationships with others. However, counter arguments to these claims suggest that technologies are not to blame for these issues and that parents and educators need to actively engage in making ethically informed choices about young children's engagement with media and technologies (Edgar & Edgar, 2008). These arguments suggest that parents have a role to play in ensuring the quality of their children's technological engagements in the early years. In our research we have been considering the role of supported playgroups in enabling parents to learn about their children's play with iPads through encouraging quality interactions and conversations as children play with touch-screen technologies in the playgroup setting.

The home learning environment in early childhood (Sylva, Melhuish, Sammons, Siraj-Blatchford & Taggart, 2004) has been linked to children's later educational outcomes

(Schweinhart & Weikart, 1997). Given recent advances in technologies and increased uptake in the family home, the concept of home learning environment now also has implications for the quality of children's early experiences with digital technologies (Marsh et al., 2005). Research has shown that children have access to a diverse range of technologies in the home (Marsh et al., 2005; McPake, Plowman & Stephen, 2013). A sociocultural view of children's play and learning also recognises that children's use of technologies is strongly influenced by the social and cultural context (Edwards, 2011). This is an important concept given that digital technologies including touch-screen technologies are widely accessible in home environments.

Supported playgroups are potential sites for engaging parents in conversations about children's play experiences with iPads. This is because supported playgroups have the advantage of being led by a playgroup coordinator who plans and implements play-based activities with an educational focus in the playgroup. These activities usually vary depending on the interests and needs of the group and hence enable the social and cultural influences of the playgroup community, such as the use of touch-screen technologies in the home, to be implemented into the playgroup setting. In our work we have been particularly interested in the social and cultural context of supported playgroups as sites for engaging parents in partnership with early childhood professionals to explore the potential of iPads for children's learning through play.

Plowman and McPake (2013) identify four areas of learning at home with digital technologies that have relevance to the playgroup context. These are 1) operational learning focusing on learning to use the technologies in functional ways; 2) extending knowledge of the world through internet applications and use; 3) positive dispositions to learning through learning from mistakes and maintaining concentration; and 4) technologies in everyday life through observing modelled use by adults (p. 30). These areas of learning were of interest to us because it would seem that if parents could recognise benefits similar to those described by Plowman and McPake (2013) for children's learning through play with iPads in playgroups, then it may increase the likelihood of parents using this knowledge to inform decisions made about children's use of these technologies in the home. In particular, we were interested in finding out about parent perspectives of the value they attached to children's play with touch-screen technologies in supported playgroups.

Research into the use of touch-screen technologies in early childhood is an emerging field (Fleer, 2013). Of the available studies, there is a developing focus on the idea that children's use of technologies is characterised by playful activity (O'Mara & Laidlaw, 2011) as a basis for learning. Yelland (2011) describes this form of learning with technologies as "playful explorations" (p. 6). These studies were of interest to us because they have the potential to inform conversations with families and early childhood professionals about children's play with iPads. In one study Yelland and Gilbert (2012) reported on ways that children's learning can be fostered through their explorations of educational apps using tablet technologies, and the findings indicated that more work needed to be done to support parents and early childhood professionals to develop an awareness of the affordances of touch-screen technologies for young children's learning. Yelland and Gilbert (2012) describe tablet technologies in early childhood as a "viable learning context" (p. 17) and recommend that the focus of their use in early childhood extend beyond skill and concept development. Other work in this area has produced similar arguments. For example, the Cohen Group (2011) indicate that touch-screen tablet technologies are accessible to young children and are particularly useful for fostering operational learning and skills such as mathematics or literacy skills or those that could be applied to another app (i.e. skills for levels of mastery). They reported that parents' awareness of the educational content of different apps was limited and further suggested that raising awareness of the affordances of different apps would alleviate some of the anxieties parents had about iPads in early childhood. Given the pervasiveness of tablet technologies in young children's lives our attention was focused on parents' perspectives of the potential of iPads through the use of this form of touch-screen tablet technology in supported playgroups.

Theoretical perspective

Sociocultural theory is a commonly used theoretical perspective to understand young children's learning with technologies through play in the early years. Sociocultural theory has been used to explain how young children learn to use technologies through social interactions with others, peer to peer guidance and direct modelling from more expert others (Plowman et al., 2010). Research increasingly proposes sociocultural perspectives on young children's learning to use technologies through play, including the concept of contemporary play (Edwards, 2014), the idea of playful explorations (Yelland, 2011) and the notion of dialectical relations between technologies and children in social situations (Fleer, 2013). These ideas hold in common that children's learning to use technologies through play represents a newly emerging form of play for young children that is significant and relevant to the cultural context in which young children actually use technologies (see for example Goldstein, 2011).

What are supported playgroups?

The term "playgroups" is used to describe groups where parents and their children come together on a regular basis to engage in play-based activities. There are two main types of playgroups operating in Australia. These are community playgroups and supported playgroups. Community playgroups are generally parent-run groups that meet in homes or community spaces on a weekly basis to participate in shared play activities. These playgroups operate across all sectors of the community, typically for around two hours per week. The play activities that occur during community playgroup sessions may vary considerably depending on access to resources and parental knowledge about play. In contrast, a playgroup coordinator who has some knowledge of play-based learning activities through formal training runs a "supported playgroup". This person is usually employed by a community service agency to coordinate playgroups in communities that are considered to have vulnerable or marginalised families within them. As sites for engaging families in play-based learning activities there has been increased interest in co-locating supported playgroups in schools (McLean, Edwards, Colliver & Schaper, 2014). Our research has been carried out in playgroups of this type and we call this form of playgroup provision Supported Playgroups in Schools (SPinS).

Our research in SPinS

The findings referred to in this chapter form part of a broader study aimed at enhancing community connections through providing families with access to play-based learning activities and connections to services, resources and schools prior to beginning formal education. It involved the provision of five Supported Playgroups in Schools (SPinS) to families in areas identified through data from the *Australian Early Childhood Development Index* (AEDI), *Early Childhood Community Profile* (DEECD, 2011) and *Best Start Atlas* (DEECD, 2009). A playgroup coordinator was employed by the project group to oversee the implementation of the five SPinS and to work alongside pre-service teachers from a local university to facilitate play activities in each of the SPinS. The playgroup coordinator and the pre-service teachers worked collaboratively in the planning of these play activities using the Australian Early Years Learning Framework (DEEWR, 2009) and implemented this planning in two-hour weekly playgroup sessions. In this chapter we report on parent perspectives of the provision of iPads in SPinS. We were also interested in the connections parents made between children's play with iPads in the SPinS and their play with similar technologies in the home. In beginning these conversations we sought to gain insight into parent perspectives of how children played with iPads, what children can learn through play with iPads and whether or not parents valued the opportunity for children to use iPads in the SPinS.

The implementation of iPads in SPinS

As part of the implementation process two iPads were introduced at each SPinS. The pre-service teachers and playgroup coordinator incorporated the use of iPads into their planning for play-based activities at each SPinS. A range of apps were available on the iPads, including various *Thomas the Tank Engine* apps, *Frozen* apps, interactive stories such as *Sesame Street – The Monster at the End of this Book*, drawing apps, *Playschool Art Maker* and *Puppet Pals*. The planning for the use of the iPads in the SPinS aimed to embrace contemporary play perspectives described by Edwards (2014) and Yelland (2011) to foster positive interactions between parents, children and playgroup facilitators. Using a Vygotskian approach, the planning and implementation of the iPads involved modelled, shared and independent play activities with the iPads.

Focus group interviews

Parents were interviewed before and after the implementation of iPads in the SPinS. Of the 50 parents involved in the broader study 12 self-selected to participate in the initial focus group interviews and 17 self-selected to participate in focus group interviews at the end of the study. The focus group interviews lasted for approximately 20 minutes, were audio-recorded and transcribed by a professional transcript company. An inductive approach to analysis (Grbich, 2013) was used to identify the main themes from the interviews, which inform the following discussion.

Parent perspectives

Is there a place for iPads at playgroup?

Our findings from focus group interviews prior to the implementation of iPads in the SPinS indicated that parents were not opposed to iPads being integrated into the play-based activities at SPinS as long as the implementation was balanced alongside other play activities. The following response was typical of responses by many of the parents expressing their view that the introduction of iPads should not be the central focus of children's play:

> I know they need it [to use technologies] and it's [digital technologies] going to be a useful
> tool for them in life, but I think that those types of devices [iPads] are taking away from our
> social skills, so it's going to have to be a happy balance. (Tom, FG2)

However, as this parent also indicated there appeared to be some resignation, even by the most reluctant parents, that young children have wide access to touch-screen technologies in the home and community and hence the view that the use of devices such as iPads in playgroup provides a way for parents to "monitor their [children's] use and their time on using these devices and active time socialising" (Melanie, FG2).

The idea that children's use of technologies such as iPads needed to be monitored seemed to have consensus among parents who described a need for controlled, supervised or monitored use. For example, one parent indicated:

> I wouldn't necessarily let the children have an iPad that has got full internet connection
> and leave them to it. That would be just totally irresponsible ... It would have to be
> monitored for sure. It's just too dangerous with internet access and things like that these
> days. (Josie, FG2)

These types of responses seemed to be suggesting that parents to some extent saw SPinS as a place where children could safely play with iPads and explore the various apps.

Some parents also indicated that the opportunity for children to play with iPads in the SPinS setting would ensure that all children had access to iPads:

> I definitely think that with limited [controlled] use they [iPads] are a good idea, because
> some children might not have them at home, or parents can't provide for them. At least
> they are getting access to one and [will get to] know what one is. (Melanie, FG2)

This notion of all children having access to iPads seemed to be important, particularly in relation to skills for use in wider society:

> I think it [screen digital technologies] has its place. It's part of society. You can't say we are
> not having it ... it has a place in our lives now. I would not want to not use the technology.
> If it is there I will use it. (Tonya, FG3)

Although parents were open to the idea of having iPads available for children to play with in SPinS some parents expressed concerns about the possible negative effects of this use. These concerns were about opportunities to socialise their children through play with other children. Parents with these concerns did not want the introduction of iPads to detract from the fundamental purpose of playgroups to provide opportunities for socialisation. The response from this parent captured this perspective:

> I just think it [iPads] is a good thing for playgroups, but it is going to have to be limited,
> because I think playgroups are more about interaction of children, and ... the way of the
> world is we've got too much of these things like Xboxes ... where they [children] don't

socialise. All they do is sit and I think we need to start bringing the children back to going outside and playing on their bikes and all that sort of stuff. (Tom, FG2)

Parents seemed to recognise through observing children's play with technologies in other contexts that there could be some benefits associated with having iPads in SPinS. These benefits were in relation to learning skills, particularly mathematics skills such as counting and number recognition and literacy skills such as alphabet recognition and word recognition, or operational skills related to learning how to use particular apps. The following example shows how one parent described the early experiences of her toddler using a maths app outside of SPinS:

Well Sasha plays with a number game, she tries to get one, two, three, four in line and she pushes the wrong one it says *try again*. So she sits there and you hear *try again, try again*, till she gets it right. (Marsha, FG1)

The influence of popular culture on children's use of screen technologies was also noted as parents made reference to apps and internet games involving characters such as *Peppa Pig* and *Thomas the Tank Engine*, which they also attached an educational value to:

My children … just like to go on the *ABC* site and click on the videos for *Peppa Pig* and *Fireman Sam*, and they'll just sit there and they'll go through and they'll watch all those. … Warren actually plays the matching the cards game, like matching the different characters on the cards and sometimes making new games and stuff. (Mandy, FG2)

Prior to the implementation of iPads in SPinS parents drew largely from their own direct observations in informing their perspective of children's early experiences with touch-screen tablet technologies. When asked about how they thought children would play with iPads at playgroup parents' comments seem to mirror what they had observed in other contexts. Typical comments included "I think they would mainly do it by themselves, because that's the way they play with it" (Millie, FG1) and seemed to suggest that parents did not think about iPads being used in ways that could encourage social interactions, which may have contributed to their concerns about the use iPads in SPinS.

Having had three months to experience using iPads with their children in SPinS, the parents were again invited to share their perspectives in focus group interviews. The conversations that occurred in these final interviews both built on the themes that emerged in the initial interviews and produced some new themes. The opportunity to participate in these focus group interviews seemed to generate more interest than the initial interviews, suggesting that after having experienced iPads in SPinS parents valued the opportunity to engage in further conversation about the use of iPads in this setting.

During the implementation period not all families engaged with using the iPads in SPinS. However, whether or not their children had been using the iPads at playgroup parents were still willing to contribute to the conversations that were occurring as part of our data collection. Some parents made a conscious decision for their children not to use the iPads at playgroup because they had access to them in the home, but these parents could still identify benefits for other children playing with them at playgroup:

> I'm not totally against them [iPads] for kids that haven't got them at home or that haven't been exposed to them before, but no, my kids don't play with them here and I would be disappointed if they did sit and play with an iPad rather than playing with other kids and toys. (Raja, FG11)

Overwhelmingly across initial and final focus group interviews, parents valued the opportunity for children to play with iPads in the SPinS. However, this perspective was also viewed with a cautionary note for maintaining a balanced approach where children's play not iPads was the central focus. Overall, there was consensus that iPads should be in playgroups but as captured in this parent response "not for the whole time" (Annie, FG1).

Having experienced iPads in the playgroups further seemed to confirm for some parents the need for the supervision and responsible use that was identified in initial interviews. This was an area of vibrant discussion with parents sharing examples of iPads and smartphones being used in the home and community in ways that they believed did not support learning and development, such as using them as a babysitting tool. This perspective was captured in the following parent comment: "there's definitely a place for them [iPads] as an educational tool, but not being used as a babysitter" (Wanda, FG5). Responses such as this one prompted references to conversations that parents had engaged in with other parents since the introduction of iPads in the SPinS and suggested some critical reflection among families on their use. In one example, a parent described a story of a toddler playing with an iPad before bed each night until the toddler's parents suspected that it might be contributing to some interrupted sleep patterns and ceased the practice. Discussions such as this one seemed to generate further talk about what were good practices for iPads with young children and further reflection on practices with iPads that parents were observing in the SPinS.

Young children's early experiences with iPads in SPinS

The strongest emerging theme in the final focus group interviews seemed to be in contrast to parents' initial perspectives of how they thought children would use the iPads in SPinS. In the initial interviews parents indicated that children would most likely engage with iPads in the SPinS setting in solitary ways, which seemed to be a contributing factor to their concerns about children using iPads in SPinS. However, there was some change in this perspective after the implementation period, with parents describing children's play with the iPads in SPinS in ways that involved social interactions. Parents descriptions of children's interactions with iPads in SPinS included children playing with other children using the iPads, adults and children playing with iPads and/or apps on the iPads together and children teaching other children and other adults about apps and iPads.

Children playing with iPads with other children was noted across all five SPinS and represented a significant shift in perspective from the initial interviews prior to implementation. An example from one parent that was typical of comments across the playgroups referred to how the children at the playgroup were really enjoying having the iPads to play with, and this parent noted in particular how her daughter and another child were "interacting nicely together" (Erin, FG1) with the iPads. One parent even noted that although she had observed in the home that her child's use of tablet technologies was usually solitary, at playgroup her son had been playing with the iPads with other children and was also willing to wait for his turn if others were using the iPads. Comments such as these indicated that parents were thinking about the different interactions that were occurring as children used iPads in their play in SPinS.

Adults and children interacting with iPads together was described in terms of scaffolding children's experiences. This was often in the form of a parent or facilitator sitting beside a child and talking about the activity together. For some parents the purpose of these interactions was operational where they noted that having an adult nearby to assist with problems supported the children in their play:

> For the time that Susie plays with them [iPads] she likes the teacher [facilitator] to be there so that when she gets stuck the teacher can organise the next step. (Lottie, FG7)

In this example the parent seemed to value the modelled interactions provided by the facilitators for the support or scaffolding they provided to children during their play with iPads.

Parents also described children teaching other children at playgroup and siblings learning from each other in the home. One parent described how she encouraged a four-year-old sibling to play with the iPad with a younger sibling "because the two-year-old bashes [the screen]" (Mari, FG6). This parent described how the four-year-old showed the two-year-old how to swipe the screen and then how the seven-year-old sibling also "teaches them as well" (Mari, FG6). Another similar example included a grandmother who described how her one-year-old grandson showed her how to turn the iPad on and off: "He just got it and turned it on – swiped it" (Maureen, FG6). These types of comments indicated that parents had reflected on the different ways that children were playing with the iPads and the types of interactions that seemed to have benefits for children's socialisation.

In the final interviews parents' willingness to talk freely about the different apps that were available on the iPads, whether or not they thought these were beneficial for the children's learning and development, suggested a heightened awareness in this area. Rather than merely naming particular apps that the children explored in SPinS parents were eager to talk about the different purposes these apps served in children's play. For example, one parent talked about the *ABC Art Maker* app as being useful for creating stories, another parent described various drawing apps that her "creative two-year-old" (June, FG3) liked to play with, and yet another parent described *Letter School* as useful for learning about the alphabet and letter formation skills. Apps for children's mathematics learning were described mainly in relation to counting, number recognition and matching, and parents also described their familiarity with a range of apps for engaging in stories, songs and rhymes with their young children.

Overall these conversations seemed to suggest that parents did identify a role for iPads in the playgroup that was connected to fostering confidence with technology in all children in preparation for the world they will live in as adults. The comment of one parent seemed to summarise the collective thoughts of many parents about this important role of iPads in playgroups:

> They [children] need to be part of that [technological world], and be able to maybe use it [technology] appropriately … and I guess the earlier they start doing that the easier it is. (Lani, FG1)

Similar perspectives by other parents indicated that whether or not their children engaged with the iPads in SPinS they valued the affordances having iPads in SPinS provided for all families to have access to them and for children's early learning experiences.

Conclusion

From our research we found that parents described children's experiences with iPads in SPinS in similar ways to Plowman and McPake's (2013) descriptions of operational learning, positive dispositions to learning and technologies in everyday life (Plowman & McPake, 2013). Operational learning appeared in examples where parents observed the need for the facilitator to be nearby to scaffold the steps; positive dispositions were referred to in references to children interacting with others during playful explorations; and technologies in everyday life were described in relation to the modelled use of iPads by the facilitators. Each of these descriptions align with research regarding children's play with technologies from a sociocultural perspective, particularly regarding the role of social interactions, problem solving and working with expert peers to support learning through play. What is interesting from this study is that the implementation of iPads in the SPinS over the three-month period seems to have contributed to a heightening of parental awareness of children's play using iPads in the SPinS that aligns with sociocultural perspectives on using technologies in the early years (Edwards, 2014; Fleer, 2013; Yelland, 2011).

We identified some themes that could serve to inform further research. The first was in relation to the conscious decision of some parents *not* to allow their children to use iPads in SPinS. This is a particularly important consideration given research highlighting the influence of children's early childhood play experiences on positive outcomes in formal education (McPake, Plowman & Stephen, 2013).

References

Alliance for Childhood. (2004). Tech tonic: towards a new literacy of technology. Retrieved 2 July 2013 from http://www.allianceforchildhood.org/sites/allianceforchildhood.org/files/file/pdf/projects/computers/pdf_files/tech_tonic.pdf

Alper, M. (2011). Developmentally appropriate New Media Literacies: supporting cultural competencies and social skills in early childhood education. *Journal of Early Childhood Literacy, 13*, 175–97.

Auld, G., Snyder, I. & Henderson, M. (2012). Using mobile phones as placed resources for literacy learning in a remote Indigenous community in Australia. *Language and Education, 26*(4), 279–96.

Burnett, C. & Merchant, G. (2013). Learning, literacies and new technologies: the current context and future possibilities. In: J. Larson & J. Marsh (Eds), *The SAGE Handbook of Early Childhood Literacy* (2nd ed., pp. 575–87). London: SAGE Publications Ltd.

Cohen Group. (2011). *Young Children, Apps and iPad*. New York. Retrieved 10 November 2014 from http://mcgrc.com/publications/publications/

Department of Education and Early Childhood Development (DEECD) (2009). *Best Start Atlas: Children Aged 0–8 Years in Victoria*. Melbourne: DEECD. Retrieved 3 September 2014 from www.eduweb.vic.gov.au/edulibrary/public/beststart/bs_atlas2nd-ed.pdf

Department of Education and Early Childhood Development (DEECD) Victoria (2010). *Early Childhood Community Profile. Grampians Region*. Melbourne: DEECD. Retrieved 3 September 2014 from www.education.vic.gov.au/Documents/about/research/ecprofgrampiansreg.pdf

Department of Education, Employment and Workforce Relations (DEEWR) (2009). *Belonging, Being and Becoming. The Early Years Learning Framework for Australia*. Canberra: DEEWR.

Edgar, D. & Edgar, P. (2008). *The New Child. In Search of Smarter Grown Ups*. Melbourne, VIC: Wilkinson Publishing.

Edwards, S. (2011). Lessons from "a really useful engine": using Thomas the Tank Engine to examine the relationship between play as a leading activity, imagination and reality in children's contemporary play worlds. *Cambridge Journal of Education, 41*(2) 195–210.

Edwards, S. (2014). Towards contemporary play: sociocultural theory and the digital-consumerist context. *Journal of Early Childhood Research, 12,* 291–333.

Fleer, M. (2013). Digital positioning for inclusive practice in early childhood: the cultural practices surrounding digital tablets in family homes. *Computers in New Zealand Schools: Learning, Teaching, Technology, 25*(1–3), 56–76.

Grbich, C. (2013). *Qualitative Data Analysis: An Introduction* (2nd ed.). Thousand Oaks, CA: Sage.

Goldstein, J. (2011). Technology and play. In: A. D. Pellegrini (Ed.), *The Oxford Handbook of the Development of Play,* (pp. 322–41). Oxford: Oxford University Press.

Hedges, H. (2011). Rethinking SpongeBob and Ninja Turtles: popular culture as funds of knowledge for curriculum co-construction. *Australasian Journal of Early Childhood. 36*(1), 25–39.

Marsh, J. (2006). Emergent media literacy: digital animation in early childhood. *Language and Education, 20*(6), 493–506.

Marsh, J. (2011). Young children's literacy practices in a virtual world: establishing an online "interaction order". *Reading Research Quarterly, 46*(20), 101–18.

Marsh, J., Brooks, G., Hughes, J., Ritchie, L., Roberts, S. & Wright, K. (2005) *Digital Beginnings: Young Children's Use of Popular Culture, Media and New Technologies.* Sheffield: University of Sheffield.

McLean, K. (2013). Literacy and technology in the early years of education: looking to the familiar to inform educator practice. *Australasian Journal of Early Childhood, 38*(4), 30–41.

McLean, K., Edwards, S. Colliver, Y. & Schaper, C. (2014). Supported playgroups in schools: what matters for caregivers and their children? *Australian Journal of Early Childhood, 39*(4).

McPake, J., Plowman, L., & Stephen, C. (2013). Preschool children creating and communicating with digital technologies in the home. *British Journal of Educational Technology, 43*(3), 421–31.

McTavish, M. (2013). "I'll do it my own way!": a young child's appropriation and recontextualisation of school literacy practices in out-of-school spaces. In: J. Larson & J. Marsh (Eds), *The SAGE Handbook of Early Childhood Literacy* (2nd ed., pp. 319–44). London: SAGE Publications Ltd.

O'Mara, J. & Laidlaw, L. (2011). Living in the iworld: two literacy researchers reflect on the changing texts and literacy practices of childhood. *English Teaching: Practice & Critique, 10*(4), 149–59.

Plowman, L., Stephen, C. & McPake, J. (2010). *Growing Up with Technology: Young Children Learning in a Digital World.* London: Routledge.

Plowman, L. & McPake, J. (2013). Seven myths about young children and technology. *Childhood Education,* 27–33.

Rideout, V. J., Foehr, U. G. & Roberts, D. F. (2010). *Generation M2: Media in the Lives of 8–18 year olds. A Kaiser Family Foundation Study.* Menlo Park, CA: Henry J. Kaiser Family Foundation.

Schweinhart, L. & Weikart, D. (1997). The HighScope Perry Preschool Curriculum comparison study through age 23. *Early Childhood Research Quarterly, 12*(2), 117–43.

Sylva, K., Melhuish, E., Sammons, P., Siraj-Blatchford, I. & Taggart, B. (2004). *The Effective Provision of Preschool Education: Final Report.* London: Institute of Education, University of London.

Wohlwend, K.E. (2013). Play, literacies and the converging cultures of childhood. In: J. Larson & J. Marsh (Eds), *The SAGE Handbook of Early Childhood Literacy* (2nd ed., pp. 80–96). London: SAGE Publications Ltd.

Wood, E. (2009). Developing a pedagogy of play. In: A. Anning, J. Cullen & M. Fleer (Eds), *Early Childhood Education. Society and Culture* (pp. 27–39). London: Sage.

Yelland, N. (2011). Reconceptualising play and learning in the lives of young children. *Australasian Journal of Early Childhood, 36*(2), 4–12.

Yelland, N. & Gilbert, C. (2012). *iPlay, iLearn, iGrow.* Report. Melbourne: IBM.

INDEX